Health care in central Asia

European Observatory on Health Care Systems Series

Series Editors

Josep Figueras is Head of the Secretariat and Research Director of the European Observatory on Health Care Systems and Head of the European Centre for Health Policy, World Health Organization Regional Office for Europe.

Martin McKee is Research Director of the European Observatory on Health Care Systems and Professor of European Public Health at the London School of Hygiene & Tropical Medicine as well as a co-director of the School's European Centre on Health of Societies in Transition.

Elias Mossialos is Research Director of the European Observatory on Health Care Systems and Brian Abel-Smith Reader in Health Policy, Department of Social Policy, London School of Economics and Political Science and Co-Director of LSE Health and Social Care.

Richard B. Saltman is Research Director of the European Observatory on Health Care Systems and Professor of Health Policy and Management at the Rollins School of Public Health, Emory University in Atlanta, Georgia

The series

The volumes in this series focus on key issues for health policy-making in Europe. Each study explores the conceptual background, outcomes and lessons learned about the development of more equitable, more efficient and more effective health systems in Europe. With this focus, the series seeks to contribute to the evolution of a more evidence-based approach to policy formulation in the health sector.

These studies will be important to all those involved in formulating or evaluating national health care policies and, in particular, will be of use to health policy-makers and advisers, who are under increasing pressure to rationalize the structure and funding of their health systems. Academics and students in the field of health policy will also find this series valuable in seeking to understand better the complex choices that confront the health systems of Europe.

Current and forthcoming titles

Martin McKee and Judith Healy (eds): *Hospitals in a Changing Europe*
Martin McKee, Judith Healy and Jane Falkingham (eds): *Health Care in Central Asia*
Elias Mossialos, Anna Dixon, Josep Figueras and Joe Kutzin (eds): *Funding Health Care: Options for Europe*
Richard B. Saltman, Reinhard Busse and Elias Mossialos (eds): *Regulating Entrepreneurial Behaviour in European Health Care Systems*

The European Observatory on Health Care Systems is a unique project that builds on the commitment of all its partners to improving health care systems:

- World Health Organization Regional Office for Europe
- Government of Greece
- Government of Norway
- Government of Spain
- European Investment Bank
- Open Society Institute
- World Bank
- London School of Economics and Political Science
- London School of Hygiene & Tropical Medicine

The Observatory supports and promotes evidence-based health policy-making through comprehensive and rigorous analysis of the dynamics of health care systems in Europe.

European Observatory on Health Care Systems Series

Edited by Josep Figueras, Martin McKee, Elias Mossialos and Richard B. Saltman

Health care in central Asia

Edited by

Martin McKee, Judith Healy and Jane Falkingham

Open University Press

Buckingham · Philadelphia

Open University Press
Celtic Court
22 Ballmoor
Buckingham
MK18 1XW

email: enquiries@openup.co.uk
world wide web: www.openup.co.uk

and
325 Chestnut Street
Philadelphia, PA 19106, USA

First Published 2002

A catalogue record of this book is available from the British Library

ISBN   0 335 20926 2 (pb)   0 335 20927 0 (hb)

Library of Congress Cataloging-in-Publication Data
Health care in central Asia / edited by Martin McKee, Judith Healy, Jane Falkingham.
    p. cm. — (European Observatory on Health Care Systems series)
   Includes bibliographical references and index.
   ISBN 0-335-20927-0 (hb) — ISBN 0-335-20926-2 (pb)
   1. Medical care—Asia, Central.   2. Medical policy—Asia, Central.   3. Health care reform—Asia, Central.   4. Medicine—Asia, Central.   I. McKee, Martin.   II. Healy, Judith.   III. Falkingham, Jane.   IV. Series.

RA395.A783 H43 2002
362.1'0958—dc21

2001036105

Typeset by Graphicraft Limited, Hong Kong
Printed in Great Britain by Biddles Limited, Guildford and Kings Lynn

Contents

List of figures and tables

List of contributors

Shirin Akiner is Lecturer in Central Asian Studies at the School of Oriental and African Studies, University of London, United Kingdom.

Cheryl Cashin is a deputy director with ZdravReform, Abt Associates in Almaty, Kazakhstan.

Laurent Chenet is Lecturer in Public Health Demography at the London School of Hygiene & Tropical Medicine, United Kingdom.

Marian Craig is a Health Service Consultant and is currently studying at the London School of Hygiene & Tropical Medicine, United Kingdom.

Tim Ensor is Senior Research Fellow and Head of the International Programme at the Centre for Health Economics, University of York, United Kingdom.

Jane Falkingham is Reader in Social Policy and Population Studies at the London School of Economics and Political Science, United Kingdom.

Mark G. Field is Associate at the Davis Centre for Russian Studies and Adjunct Professor at the School of Public Health, Harvard University, Cambridge, MA, USA.

Gülin Gedik is Project Officer for CARNET Countries in the Health Sector unit at the WHO Regional Office for Europe in Copenhagen, Denmark.

Steve Hajioff is a Visiting Fellow at the European Centre on the Health of Societies in Transition at the London School of Hygiene & Tropical Medicine, United Kingdom.

Judith Healy is Senior Research Fellow of the European Observatory on Health Care Systems, and is an honorary Senior Lecturer in Public Health and Policy at the London School of Hygiene & Tropical Medicine, United Kingdom.

Farkhad A. Ilkhamov is Head of the main Curative Department at the Ministry of Health of Uzbekistan in Tashkent.

Elke Jakubowski is Research Officer at the European Observatory on Health Care Systems based at the WHO Regional Office for Europe in Copenhagen, Denmark.

Maksut Kulzhanov is Dean of the Kazakhstan School of Public Health in Almaty.

Joe Kutzin is Senior Resident Adviser for the WHO Regional Office for Europe at the Ministry of Health of Kyrgyzstan in Bishkek.

Jack Langenbrunner is Senior Economist with the World Bank, working on health financing in the central Asian republics, eastern Europe, the Russian Federation and the Middle East.

Antony Lewis is Senior Lecturer in Primary Care at the University of Exeter and a general practitioner in Exmouth, Devon, United Kingdom.

Ian MacArthur is International Policy Manager at the WHO collaborating centre for environmental health, working primarily with the WHO Regional Office for Europe on the assessment and reform of sanitary epidemiology services.

Chary Mamedkuliev is Head of the Health Management and Organization Department of the Ministry of Health of Turkmenistan in Ashgabat.

Martin McKee is Research Director of the European Observatory on Health Care Systems and Professor of European Public Health at the London School of Hygiene & Tropical Medicine in London, United Kingdom.

Zafer Oztek is in the Medical Faculty of the Department of Public Health at the Hacettepe University School of Medicine in Ankara, Turkey.

Richard Pomfret is Professor of the Department of Economics at the University of Adelaide, South Australia.

Rahmin Rahminov is an adviser to the Minister of Health of Tajikistan.

Acelle Sargaldakova is at the Department of Reform Coordination and Implementation, Ministry of Health of Kyrgyzstan in Bishkek.

Serdar Savas is a former Director, Programme Management at the WHO Regional Office for Europe and is currently Director of United Health Systems Ltd in Istanbul, Turkey.

Elena Shevkun is Technical Officer for the Health Sector unit at the WHO Regional Office for Europe in Copenhagen, Denmark.

Johannes Vang is in the Faculty of Health Sciences, Centre of Public Health Sciences at the University of Linköping, Sweden.

Series editors' introduction

European national policy-makers broadly agree on the core objectives that their health care systems should pursue. The list is strikingly straightforward: universal access for all citizens, effective care for better health outcomes, efficient use of resources, high-quality services and responsiveness to patient concerns. It is a formula that resonates across the political spectrum and which, in various, sometimes inventive configurations, has played a role in most recent European national election campaigns.

Yet this clear consensus can only be observed at the abstract policy level. Once decision-makers seek to translate their objectives into the nuts and bolts of health system organization, common principles rapidly devolve into divergent, occasionally contradictory, approaches. This is, of course, not a new phenomenon in the health sector. Different nations, with different histories, cultures and political experiences, have long since constructed quite different institutional arrangements for funding and delivering health care services.

The diversity of health system configurations that has developed in response to broadly common objectives leads quite naturally to questions about the advantages and disadvantages inherent in different arrangements, and which approach is 'better' or even 'best' given a particular context and set of policy priorities. These concerns have intensified over the last decade as policy-makers have sought to improve health system performance through what has become a European-wide wave of health system reforms. The search for comparative advantage has triggered – in health policy as in clinical medicine – increased attention to its knowledge base, and to the possibility of overcoming at least part of existing institutional divergence through more evidence-based health policy-making.

The volumes published in the European Observatory series are intended to provide precisely this kind of cross-national health policy analysis. Drawing on an extensive network of experts and policy-makers working in a variety of academic and administrative capacities, these studies seek to synthesize the available evidence on key health sector topics using a systematic methodology. Each volume explores the conceptual background, outcomes and lessons learned about the development of more equitable, more efficient and more effective health care systems in Europe. With this focus, the series seeks to contribute to the evolution of a more evidence-based approach to policy formulation in the health sector. While remaining sensitive to cultural, social and normative differences among countries, the studies explore a range of policy alternatives available for future decision-making. By examining closely both the advantages and disadvantages of different policy approaches, these volumes fulfil a central mandate of the Observatory: to serve as a bridge between pure academic research and the needs of policy-makers, and to stimulate the development of strategic responses suited to the real political world in which health sector reform must be implemented.

The European Observatory on Health Care Systems is a partnership that brings together three international agencies, three national governments, two research institutions and an international non-governmental organization. The partners are as follows: the World Health Organization Regional Office for Europe, which provides the Observatory secretariat; the governments of Greece, Norway and Spain; the European Investment Bank; the Open Society Institute; the World Bank; the London School of Hygiene & Tropical Medicine and the London School of Economics and Political Science.

In addition to the analytical and cross-national comparative studies published in this Open University Press series, the Observatory produces Health Care Systems in Transition Profiles (HiTs) for the countries of Europe, the Observatory Summer School and the *Euro Observer* newsletter. Further information about Observatory publications and activities can be found on its web site at www.observatory.dk.

Josep Figueras, Martin McKee, Elias Mossialos and Richard B. Saltman

Foreword

The central Asian republics are facing enormous challenges in embarking on health sector reform, owing to their changing economic circumstances combined with the process of constructing new systems of government.

The rising burden of disease in many of these countries is a matter of great concern, both to their own health policy-makers and to international agencies. Nevertheless, the health status of the populations in this region has been the subject of very little research. Also, little is known outside the region about the health care systems of these countries, or their experiences over the last decade in seeking to restructure and improve their health services. Despite these many difficulties, however, the central Asian republics remain optimistic and committed to meeting the challenges involved in producing better health care for their populations.

This volume fills some large gaps in our knowledge about health care in central Asia. It will thus be a valuable resource for policy-makers in the region and in the international agencies, and for others interested in these culturally diverse countries.

In producing this book, the European Observatory on Health Care Systems has drawn on the conceptual skills of academics and consultants, as well as the practical experience of policy-makers, in offering some insight into effective health policy-making in the central Asian republics.

Marc Danzon
WHO Regional Director for Europe

Acknowledgements

This volume is one in a series of books undertaken by the European Observatory on Health Care Systems. We are very grateful to our authors, who responded promptly in producing their chapters despite busy schedules that included ongoing work in the central Asian region.

The editors owe a debt of gratitude to Serdar Savas, former Director, Programme Management at the WHO Regional Office for Europe, who supported the idea of this book and helped to develop the original concept, drawing on his extensive experience of the central Asian republics. We also wish to acknowledge his leadership of a series of programmes in the region that provided valuable input to this study: the MANAS programme in Kyrgyzstan, the SOMONI programme in Tajikistan, the LUKMAN programme in Turkmenistan, the Kazakhstan School of Public Health, and CARNET, the Central Asian Republic Network on Health Care Reform.

We very much appreciate the constructive comments made by our reviewers, Michael Borowitz, Gülin Gedik, Denise Holmes, Gillian Holmes and Robin Thompson. Gillian Holmes also provided very valuable support at the inception of the project. We should also like to thank the Observatory's partners for their review of, and input to, successive versions of the manuscript.

Our special thanks go to Caroline White, who processed and formatted the chapters. We also thank all our colleagues in the Observatory. In particular, we are grateful to Suszy Lessof for her coordinating and managerial role, to Jeffrey Lazarus, Jenn Cain and Phyllis Dahl for managing the book production and delivery and to Jerome Rosen for his copy-editing. Myriam Andersen was, as always, very helpful with many administrative tasks.

Finally, we are grateful to the United Kingdom Department for International Development, which provided financial support for this project. The Department cannot, however, accept any responsibility for the views expressed.

Martin McKee, Judith Healy and Jane Falkingham

part one

Context

chapter one

Health care systems in the central Asian republics: an introduction

*Martin McKee, Judith Healy and
Jane Falkingham*

Introduction

At the crossroads between Europe and Asia, the countries of central Asia have been occupied over the last decade with the enormous challenges of establishing and stabilizing their states and societies and with claiming their place in the international community. Although the term 'central Asia' covers a wide region, we use it here to refer to the five countries of former Soviet central Asia: Kazakhstan, Kyrgyzstan, Tajikistan, Turkmenistan and Uzbekistan (Figure 1.1). These central Asian republics gained their unexpected independence in 1991, upon the dissolution of the Soviet Union. Since these dramatic events, these five republics have received more attention from the international community, especially given the political and economic significance of the region.

Because these health care systems are not well known outside their own countries, this book aims to describe and analyse them for a wider audience, both within and without the region. We do so for several reasons. First, policy-makers within central Asia face enormous challenges in bringing about health sector reform in an environment with extremely adverse macroeconomics and major internal economic and political changes. To assist them in reorganizing their health systems, these policy-makers need better information about their own and other health care systems (as do policy-makers in developed countries). Second, the countries in the region are interested in the experiences of other countries, so that they can learn about what works and why, and which initiatives might transfer successfully across borders. Finally, those working for international organizations need to share more information and analysis on how and why health care systems work in these countries and on the impact of the many changes underway.

This book has three parts. The first part (Chapters 1–6) sets out the context in which health care systems must function in the central Asian republics. These chapters explore the challenges that arise from the ancient and complex history of the region, the current very difficult economic situation, the rising burden of disease and the legacy of the past. The second part (Chapters 7–14) analyses health sector reforms in the different countries, such as efforts to find new sources of health sector revenue, the introduction of new payment systems, and the initiatives that are underway to improve both preventive and curative health services. The third part of the book (Chapter 15) contains brief descriptions of the health care systems in each country based on the Health Care Systems in Transition country profiles published by the European Observatory on Health Care Systems (www.observatory.dk).

Themes and chapters

Before the twentieth century, central Asia was inhabited mainly by the nomadic people of the steppes and deserts, and by settled people living in the oases and river valleys. For thousands of years, the region was a crossroad for the intermingling of populations, cultures and religions, with a long history of successive invasions by powerful neighbours, including Persians, Greeks, Arabs, Turks and Russians. Central Asia is perhaps best known in the West as the setting for the 'Silk Road' over which trade was conducted between Europe and China before the inception of the sea route to the east.

During the eighteenth century, the khanates of Bukhara, Kokand and Khiva retreated into isolation in the face of pressure from Russia and Britain, who waged a long, largely covert campaign, the 'Great Game' (Hopkirk 1990), to control this region and thus the land route to India. By the late nineteenth century, however, central Asia had been annexed by the Russian Empire. From 1918 on, Soviet rule brought fundamental social and economic changes. Large-scale movements of population, including the imposition of a ruling Russian elite and the forced migration of minorities (coupled with rapid urbanization and collectivization), transformed the region. The present-day borders were drawn in 1924, when Joseph Stalin divided the region into several nominally independent republics.

In Chapter 2, on the history and politics in central Asia, Akiner outlines the massive social engineering undertaken by the Soviet regime, which changed most aspects of life for people in the region. Although this involved political and cultural oppression, it also produced substantial benefits, such as the establishment of a comprehensive health care system. Throughout the Soviet era, the region continued to be isolated from the outside world, with all contacts tightly controlled – in part, because it was the location of many elements of the military–industrial complex. One result of this isolation was to cut these countries off from developments in medical research, education and clinical practice in the rest of the world. The removal of central control, following the collapse of the Soviet Union in 1991, allowed these countries, albeit very cautiously, to open up to outside ideas and contacts.

To the existing ethnic diversity of the peoples of the region was added huge numbers of Russian settlers in the nineteenth century, followed in the Stalinist period with the forced migration of minorities, such as Meshketian Turks, Volga Germans and Chechens. It so changed the ethnic mix that, by the 1990s, most of the population of Kazakhstan was non-Kazakh. Although the borders drawn in 1924 sought to create homogeneous entities, they nonetheless cut across ethnic groups (Sabol 1995). For example, present-day Uzbekistan contains two ethnically imbalanced neighbouring cities: Tashkent, which is largely populated by Uzbeks, and Samarkand, which is largely populated by Tajiks, and the two are divided by countryside that is largely populated by Kazakhs. Also, the division of the fertile and densely populated Fergana Valley between Uzbekistan, Kyrgyzstan and Tajikistan remains particularly problematic. Although much political effort has gone into developing national identities since independence (Atkin 1993), independence has exposed pre-existing ethnic, regional, religious and political tensions; in Tajikistan, this has led to outright civil war. The disintegration of the Soviet Union also led to further population movements, as many of the people relocated during the Soviet era returned to their places of origin.

Traditionally, nomadic or pastoral groups in central Asia were organized according to clan, tribal and regional affiliations, with a clearly defined hierarchy from the family upwards to the khan (the ruler). During the Soviet era, these links formed the basis of a parallel system of power, with the purges of the 1930s enabling some groups to eliminate others, thus achieving positions of power that they have largely retained throughout the political changes. These clan and regional ties have been extended to encompass other shared experiences. The pyramid form of societal organization largely remains, however, whereby loyalty extends upwards to a particular patron or leader and patronage extends downwards, which has important implications for political and social institutions and the growth of civil societies.

After independence the republics developed a formal policy of building more democratic societies. The central Asian states are typified by a governmental culture of strong presidential rule supported by family and clan ties. Reference is often made to ancient or mythical leaders such as Genghis Khan in Kazakhstan, Manas in Kyrgyzstan and Tamerlane in Uzbekistan. In most republics, the existing leadership has remained in power, albeit with some relabelling and changes in ideology. Most of the current generation of political leaders, except for the President of Kyrgyzstan, held high office during the Soviet era, but nevertheless are seen as the 'founding fathers' of independence. Opposition parties are either weak or, as in Turkmenistan and Uzbekistan, banned. In each republic there was a revival of Islamic beliefs during the period of *perestroika*. This revival has continued, although largely under political control, ostensibly, as in Uzbekistan, to prevent the emergence of fundamentalism.

New constitutions have been drafted and parliamentary and judiciary systems established in each country, but authority resides mainly with the presidents

(Dawisha and Parrott 1997). At the sub-national level, each republic is divided into *oblasts* (regions) and *rayons* (districts), called *velayats* and *etraps*, respectively, in Turkmenistan. Each level has its own elected administration. The president appoints the governor (*hakim*) in each *oblast*; this person wields considerable power and typically reinforces presidential authority. Any significant changes to the health care system, therefore, require the backing of the president and his nominees at the regional level.

The many visible manifestations of change in these countries since independence, however, range from the newly acquired freedom to travel to massive advertising campaigns by Western tobacco companies. The isolation imposed by the Soviet Union gave way to a situation in which visitors from western Europe are able to fly directly to most capital cities in central Asia.

Some other things have not changed. The earlier rivalry over the land route to India has given way to a new Great Game, in which a larger constellation of powers, including China, India, Pakistan, Turkey, the Russian Federation and the United States, vie with one another for political and commercial clout. This is mostly driven by the desire for access to the large reserves of natural resources, such as oil, gas and precious metals.

In Chapter 3, Pomfret outlines the role of central Asia as a producer of raw material in the Soviet Union division of labour. As the least developed parts of the Soviet Union (Akhtar 1993), the central Asian republic economies were based on the production of a few commodities, such as grain, gas and oil in Kazakhstan, agricultural produce in Kyrgyzstan and Tajikistan, cotton and natural gas in Turkmenistan, and cotton and gold in Uzbekistan. This lack of diversification had many adverse consequences, of which the best known is the serious environmental degradation around the Aral Sea. Moreover, the collapse of the interlocked Soviet production system brought down the economies of each of the republics. These countries experienced severe economic depression and rapid inflation, with negative economic growth until 1995, followed by gradual improvement, although production is still below pre-independence levels.

Kazakhstan and Kyrgyzstan, both facing serious balance of payments problems after independence, soon introduced austerity programmes. Uzbekistan, which is somewhat better endowed with natural resources than the other central Asian republics, has pursued a more gradual programme of stabilization. Tajikistan, beset by civil war for most of this period, was for several years unable to tackle its serious financial problems, and there has been little attempt to do so in Turkmenistan. In the first half of the 1990s, real public spending in these countries declined by about 50–70 per cent. In all five countries, real economic output, in 1999, remains lower than a decade earlier.

Since independence, poverty has increased dramatically in the five republics. In Chapter 4, Falkingham shows that over a third of the population of Kazakhstan and Turkmenistan are living below the poverty line, based on World Bank Living Standard Measurement Surveys, with an even higher proportion in the struggling economies of Kyrgyzstan and Tajikistan. Because of shrinking government health budgets, households now pay much more for health care services (previously virtually free), both in official charges and under-the-table payments. There is growing evidence that many poor people can no longer afford access to 'free' health care.

In Chapter 5, McKee and Chenet analyse patterns of health and disease in the region. While cautioning that the validity of much of the data is questionable, they note that life expectancy is similar to that of other countries of the former Soviet Union, but 10 years less than that in European Union (EU) countries. The region exhibits some of the worst features of both developed and developing countries, with high rates of heart disease and childhood infections. This pattern indicates the importance of strengthening health promotion and primary health care.

In Chapter 6, Field examines the legacy of the Soviet health care system that was implemented in all the republics. Although the central Asian countries share many similarities, some differences have emerged since independence, reflecting their differing political trajectories. Under the former Soviet system, the distribution of resources was based on norms set by the Semashko All Union Research Institute in Moscow, while the administration of health services was extremely hierarchical. The Ministry of Health in Moscow formulated policy and, within each republic, health ministries were responsible for implementing these policies, which they did through *oblast* health departments. Within the *oblast* there were further health administrations at the *rayon* level and at the city level. The Academy of Medical Sciences under the Ministry of Health in Moscow supervised the national-level research institutes in each country.

Most of the hierarchical health service delivery system set up in Soviet times (Petrov 1983; Khudaibergenov 1986) remains in place, although the infrastructure is deteriorating. Rural areas are served by health posts (*feldsher accousherski punkt*, FAPs) staffed by feldshers with basic medical training and by midwives. Rural polyclinics (*selskaya vrachebnaya ambulatorya*, SVAs) are generally staffed by four types of physicians (until recently, there were no general practitioners): adult therapist, paediatrician, obstetrician and stomatologist (dentist). Small rural hospitals (*selskaya uchaskovaya bolnitsia*, SUBs) with about 20–30 beds offer very limited treatment, although increasingly these are being closed. Each *rayon* has a central town hospital that offers basic care, as well as ambulatory polyclinics staffed by specialists, with different clinics for adults and children. The main city in the *oblast* has specialist hospitals, and specialized dispensaries for long-term conditions, such as tuberculosis and cancer. At the national level in a capital city, hospitals provide more advanced and specialist treatment, for conditions such as cardiovascular diseases and cancer. In addition, a sanitary epidemiological service (Sanepid or SES) concentrates on environmental surveillance and the control of communicable diseases.

The Soviet model of health care may have the advantage of universal access to at least a basic level of care, but it also has many drawbacks. For example, facilities suffer from years of under-investment, and many in rural areas lack even basic amenities, such as running water or sewerage (Feshbach 1989). The worsening economic situation in the 1980s and 1990s led to a slow deterioration in services, as equipment became antiquated or needed to be replaced, drug stocks dwindled and the fabric of buildings decayed. There is still very little modern equipment. In general, health facilities are funded according to rigid input budget line items, an approach that offers no room for innovation and encourages wasteful patterns of treatment. Primary health care remains poorly developed and health promotion activities are just beginning. Overall, medical staff are poorly prepared. Many doctors specialize during their under-graduate training and are not trained to undertake general practice, while nurses have limited skills and undertake only basic tasks. Furthermore, clinical management is often outdated, allowing admissions to hospitals for many conditions that would be treated in ambulatory care units elsewhere. Such treatment regimes require a large number of hospital beds (although supply often exceeds demand) and lead to low occupancy levels. Health care staff work under difficult conditions that are not conducive to offering high-quality care, while the public is very dissatisfied with the health services provided.

Overall, the health care system was wasteful, ineffective and, in the long term, unsustainable. The prolonged economic crisis after independence in 1991 made reform unavoidable. In response to various reform efforts, the health system inherited at the beginning of the 1990s has begun to change slowly, with the type and pace of change differing among countries.

In Chapter 7, Savas, Gedik and Craig examine the process of health care reform in the five central Asian republics. They argue that, because of a hierarchical administrative tradition (with the power of the central government vested mainly in the president), health reform had to proceed initially through a top-down process driven by specialist policy teams within the ministries of health. A major barrier to the implementation of reform in each country, however, has been the lack of policy analysis and management capacity.

In Chapter 8, Kutzin and Cashin show that real government spending on the health system has declined by a quarter to a third of its pre-independence level. They argue that pressure from international financial institutions to reduce public-sector borrowing and restore fiscal balance has kept these govern-ments from increasing health care spending. Since the options for increasing health revenue through insurance contributions and taxation are generally very limited, health services must do more with less. If resources are to be freed and shifted to other parts of the health system, reform strategies must concentrate on improving efficiency and reducing costs.

In reviewing the way that funds are allocated within central Asian health systems, Ensor and Langenbrunner (Chapter 9) conclude that new payment methods, introduced mainly by the insurance funds, so far are marginal in comparison with the traditional method of input funding. Kazakhstan, Kyrgyzstan and, to a lesser extent, Turkmenistan are testing new methods, but little change has occurred in Tajikistan and Uzbekistan. Given the limited capacity in the region and the institutional barriers to change, a simple reim-bursement system has the greatest chance of success. The way in which funds are allocated to regions remains a key weakness.

Although the health sector relies on its staff to produce effective and efficient health care services, health sector reform in these countries has been slow to address human resource issues (Healy, Chapter 10). Few steps have been taken to reduce the large health sector workforce; this is socially and politically very difficult, given the lack of alternative employment and the likely adverse effect on public morale. Most of the central Asian countries, however, now are investing more strategically in their human resources. First, education and training needs are being addressed through changes in the medical curriculum and through some retraining. Second, some countries have reduced their large number of physicians and have sought to broaden the professional skill mix. The widespread practice of informal payments to health workers remains a serious problem, because it distorts accountability to employers and impoverishes patients. One alternative is to raise salaries, but higher pay for all health care workers must be matched by increased productivity. To provide better quality care to patients, the skill mix, pay, conditions and training of staff need to be addressed.

In Chapter 11, Gedik, Oztek and Lewis describe the extensive primary health care system, where (theoretically) most people have access to services: a health post or physician clinic in rural areas and a polyclinic in urban areas. The problems faced by primary care services include inadequate funding, since primary care receives less than 10 per cent of the already small health budget. Furthermore, primary care is geared to clinical care rather than to disease prevention and health promotion. The quality of care is poor for a number of reasons: physicians were not trained as general physicians, they lack the necessary professional support (such as up-to-date treatment protocols) and also they are constrained by severe shortages of equipment and drugs. Most central Asian countries have begun retraining specialists as family physicians and have introduced general practice into undergraduate and postgraduate curricula. Under the present system, primary care remains funded and administered by the state, but some alternatives are being explored. Kazakhstan and Kyrgyzstan have introduced demonstration projects with capitation for family group practices, but earlier enthusiasm for fundholding (whereby primary practices hold a budget to buy specialist services on behalf of those enrolled) based on the British model has waned.

In Chapter 12, Vang and Hajioff note concern among health sector reformers in the central Asian republics about the dominant role of hospitals. While some quantitative change can be tracked, such as closures of hospital beds, it is much more difficult to assess whether the quality of hospital care has improved.

Public health services (Sanepid) in the region have been a major component of the Soviet health care system, concentrating on the traditional tasks of disease prevention and surveillance of sanitary standards, such as water and food safety. In Chapter 13, MacArthur and Shevkun argue that, to be prepared to respond to new population health needs, staff should be retrained and service structures reorganized. The Sanepid senior staff believe, however, that service reforms call for more funds and recognition, but only incremental change to their functions.

In looking to the future, Healy, Falkingham and McKee (Chapter 14) assess the achievements in managing the transition from a health care system based on the Soviet model. They conclude that, while much thought and considerable effort has been expended on health sector reform, progress in the central Asian republics has been very difficult, given the adverse economic climate. Much still needs to be done to develop and implement sustainable and fair systems of financing and appropriate means of health care delivery. The urgent problem of how to secure adequate finance for the health system as well as issues that relate to the efficiency of allocations and the use of technology have commanded most attention. Issues that relate to the quality and outcomes of health

Figure 1.1 Map of central Asia

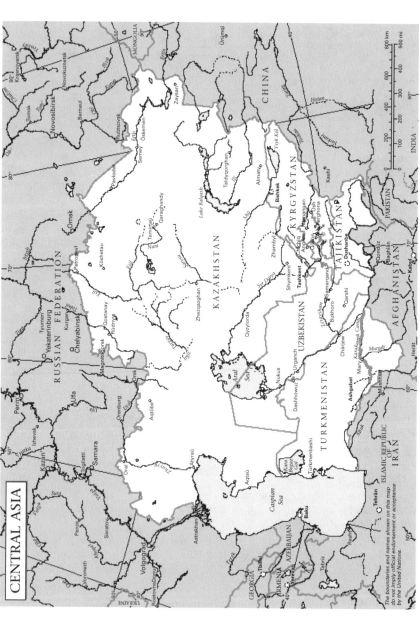

Source: Map No. 3763 Rev. 4 UNITED NATIONS, October 1998, Department of Public Information, Cartographic Section

services remain to be addressed in the next phase of health care reform. They end by reviewing the challenges that these countries still face.

References

Akhtar, M.R. (1993) Economic effects of Soviet rule on the Central Asian Muslim, *Journal of Economic Co-operation among Islamic Countries*, 14: 1–34.

Atkin, M. (1993) Tajik national identity, *Iranian Studies*, 26(1–2): 151–8.

Dawisha, K. and Parrott, B. (1997) *Conflict, Cleavage and Change in Central Asia and the Caucasus*. Cambridge: Cambridge University Press.

Feshbach, M. (1989) Demographic trends in the Soviet Union: serious implications for the Soviet military, *NATO Review*, 37(5): 11–15.

Hopkirk, P. (1990) *The Great Game: On Secret Service in High Asia*. London: John Murray.

Khudaibergenov, A. (1986) Middle-level workers in Uzbekistan, *World Health Forum*, 7: 237.

Petrov, P.P. (1983) Kazakhstan: reaching people in isolated places, *World Health Forum*, 4: 316–18.

Sabol, S. (1995) The creation of Soviet Central Asia: the 1924 national delimitation, *Central Asian Survey*, 14: 225–41.

chapter two

History and politics in central Asia: change and continuity

Shirin Akiner

Geography

The term 'central Asia' is often used loosely, not only to designate the former Soviet republics, but also to designate Mongolia, Xinjiang, Tibet and other adjacent territories. Here it is used only to refer to the territory of Kazakhstan, Kyrgyzstan, Tajikistan, Turkmenistan and Uzbekistan. The total area encompassed by these five former Soviet republics amounts to about 4 million square kilometres (km²) and is thus considerably larger than India (3.3 million km²). By area, the largest of these states is Kazakhstan (2.7 million km²), which dominates the northern tier. Turkmenistan and Uzbekistan (488,100 km² and 449,600 km², respectively) are situated in the southern belt, on the plains. The two smallest republics, Kyrgyzstan (198,500 km²) and Tajikistan (143,100 km²), occupy the mountains of the south-east. Uzbekistan is the most centrally located, sharing common borders with the other four republics.

Central Asia is landlocked in all directions. To the north it merges into the Siberian Plain, and to the west into the steppes in the centre of the Russian Federation; to the south lie Afghanistan and the Islamic Republic of Iran, and to the east China. There are high mountain ranges in the east and south-east, steppe lands in the northern belt, semi-desert and desert regions in the centre, and river valleys and oases in the south (including the Fergana Valley that stretches from the foothills of Kyrgyzstan and Tajikistan through southern Uzbekistan). The region is rich in hydrocarbons and minerals, but water and productive land are relatively scarce, especially in the south.

Population levels have always been low. At the beginning of the twentieth century, the population of the entire region numbered about 10 million people. Today, the combined populations of the five republics are about 55 million people. The highest concentrations of human settlement have traditionally been in the fertile valleys of the south, and the lowest concentrations have been in the desert regions of the centre and the barren mountains of the south-east. This remains the pattern today: population densities vary from 300 to 400 inhabitants per km^2 in the Fergana and Murgab valleys to about 5 inhabitants per km^2 in the desert regions. About 48 per cent of the total population of central Asia live in urban areas, but the majority of these people are immigrants (mostly Slav) from outside the region; about 77 per cent of the main indigenous nationalities live in rural areas.

Early history

The early history of central Asia is a long chronicle of invasion and subjugation by the peoples of neighbouring sedentary states such as the Achaemenians, Graeco-Bactrians and Sassanians, as well as by nomad hordes, such as the White Huns, Turks and Mongols. For nearly 2000 years, central Asia was also the pivot of a vast network of transcontinental trade routes, the Silk Roads of antiquity. These contacts resulted in a ceaseless influx of new ideas and created a rich centre of cross-cultural fertilization. Zoroastrianism, Buddhism, Nestorian Christianity and many other religions and cults co-existed here, as did a profusion of languages and scripts. There was a constant process of ethnic intermingling, as the local population absorbed each new wave of immigrants. Eventually, in most parts of central Asia, the Turkic element came to predominate.

Islam was introduced into central Asia by Arab invaders in the late seventh century A.D. It spread quite rapidly in the cities of the oasis belt, but took centuries longer to reach the more distant peoples of the steppe and the desert. Even after conversion, the latter retained many pre-Islamic practices. Central Asians, especially in the south, were extraordinarily receptive to the cultural and intellectual impact of Islam; the region produced a pleiad of outstanding scholars, among them al-Bukhari, al-Khwarezmi, al-Farabi, Ibn Sina (Avicenna) and al-Biruni. With the introduction of Muslim architectural forms, the cities of central Asia took on an Islamic aspect. Arabic script replaced the writing systems that had been used previously, and the local languages adopted a large body of Arabic words.

Traditionally, the chief cultural division in central Asia was between the nomads of the steppe and desert, and the sedentary peoples of the oases and river valleys. Within these two broad divisions of nomads and settled peoples there were further subdivisions, based on clan, tribal and regional affiliations. Among both nomads and settled peoples, the primary sociopolitical structure was pyramidal. At every level, from the nuclear family unit upward, there was a clearly defined hierarchy of power, with its concomitant implications of allegiance and responsibility. At the apex of the whole complex was the Khan, who wielded supreme authority.

Central Asia has never been a unified political and economic entity. The closest approach to political unity in the pre-modern period was in the thirteenth century, when most of the region was incorporated into the Mongol

Empire. Even then, it was divided between two of Genghis Khan's sons. By the eighteenth century, the main regional powers were the Kazakh Hordes in the north (known respectively as the Great, the Little and the Middle Hordes), the Khanates of Bukhara, Khiva and Kokand in the centre, and the Turkmen tribes in the south-west. By this time, the development of maritime links between Europe and Asia had caused the balance of trade to shift from land to sea routes. It marked the demise of the Silk Roads. The trade that remained was mostly of a short-haul nature, thus largely isolating the region from external influences. This, in addition to endemic political instability, led to economic decline. Intellectual and artistic vitality was also reduced to a pale reflection of earlier glories.

Russian rule

In the eighteenth century, Russia (a sporadic trading partner of central Asia since the mid-sixteenth century) began to extend its power beyond the Ural Mountains. Within a century, the Kazakh lands were firmly under Russian control and the rule of the Kazakh khans had been abolished. In the second half of the nineteenth century, Russian troops moved southward, to capture Tashkent in 1865 and Samarkand in 1868; the Emirate of Bukhara became a Russian protectorate that same year, followed by Khiva in 1873. In 1876, the Khanate of Kokand was fully integrated into the Tsarist Empire. The subjugation of central Asia was completed by the conquest of Turkmen lands in 1886.

Thereafter, Russian efforts were largely directed towards creating a stable administrative framework, expanding economic ties with the European part of the empire (particularly through the increased cultivation and export of cotton to Russia), and generally establishing the institutions that would make life both profitable and bearable for the expatriate community. The construction of the Transcaspian railroad, which ran from the Caspian port of Krasnovodsk (modern Turkmenbashy) to the Fergana Valley, via Samarkand and Tashkent, was carried out between 1885 and 1899; the Orenburg–Tashkent line was completed in 1906, thus strengthening the links with Russia.

In the south (mostly the area that is now Uzbekistan), Russian rule was, in general, less intrusive than that of other colonial regimes in Asia (Skrine and Ross 1899). There was little interference in native institutions. The main changes were in the economic sphere (the production of cotton, for example, was geared to the needs of the Russian textile industry). The influx of Russians was concentrated in the cities. In the north, however, in the Kazakh steppes, the Russian presence was more dominant and, by the middle of the nineteenth century, the Kazakh aristocracy was largely Russified. Yet at the end of the century, relations between Russians and Kazakhs deteriorated rapidly under the pressure of a huge influx of Slav settlers. The majority of these were farmers who appropriated large tracts of pasture land, traditionally the grazing grounds of the Kazakh nomads. This was one of the main causes of a major revolt against Russian rule in 1916. The uprising was put down with great brutality.

Soviet era

Soviet rule was established in central Asia in 1918–20. In 1920, the protectorates of Bukhara and Khiva were transformed into nominally independent People's Soviet Republics; these were dissolved 4 years later and their lands incorporated into the Soviet Union. The external frontiers of the Soviet Union were sealed, thereby severing traditional trade and cultural links with neighbouring peoples. Thereafter, Soviet central Asia developed predominantly in isolation from adjacent countries and from the Muslim world as a whole.

In 1924, the region was subjected to an internal territorial division, known as the National Delimitation, which resulted in the creation of the present-day central Asian republics. The boundaries between the new republics were not drawn in arbitrary fashion, but for the most part closely followed existing ethnolinguistic groupings. Within its own terms of reference, the National Delimitation was successful, since without any movements of population, between about 80 and 95 per cent of the Uzbeks, Kazakhs, Kyrgyz, Turkmen and Karakalpaks were included within their own eponymous administrative unit (republic or province) (Akiner 1986; Capisani 2000). The outstanding exception was the Tajiks. They lost Samarkand and Bukhara, their main urban centres and the historic heart of their culture, to Uzbekistan. Only 63 per cent of the Tajiks were actually included within the territory of Tajikistan at the time of the National Delimitation. This has been a source of resentment ever since.

The creation of the new republics was the first step in a truly massive feat of social engineering. The goal was to raise the socioeconomic level of the region to the same standard as that of other parts of the Soviet Union and, in so doing, to bring about full political, economic and social integration. It was a colossal undertaking, one that could only have been conceived and executed under a totalitarian regime. Every public and many private areas of human activity were affected, ranging from education to entertainment, language to dress, and patterns of employment to patterns of marriage. The built environment was likewise transformed, particularly in the capitals of the republics, where the jumble of narrow streets and crumbling mud–brick structures of the older world were swept away to make room for broad avenues, high-rise concrete apartment blocks and government offices. Foreign travellers who visited central Asia in the early 1930s gave vivid accounts of the physical transformation that was then taking place, particularly in Tashkent. Selected historical monuments were preserved as museum exhibits, but otherwise the onslaught on the relics of the past was relentless (Goldman 1934).

Social transformations

The first priority for the Soviet regime in central Asia was mass education. This was as important for political reasons as it was for economic and social ones. The level of literacy, as recorded in the 1926 census, was a mere 2–3 per cent among the Uzbeks and other indigenous peoples of the southern belt, and just over 7 per cent among the Kazakhs. Within a very short period, a network of 'ABC schools' was created to teach the rudiments of literacy. This was later developed into a full educational programme with primary, secondary and tertiary levels. The literacy curve rose steadily until, in the 1970 census, a rate of over 99 per cent was recorded for all the central Asian peoples. By comparison, estimates for the percentage of illiteracy at this period among people aged 15 years and above were: 19.3 per cent in Turkey, 37.1 per cent in Egypt, 46.0 per cent in Iran and 65.2 per cent in Pakistan (UNESCO 1991). Specialized research institutes were established in central Asia, and republican Academies of Sciences were established later. The brightest students were able to pursue their studies in Moscow and other major research centres in the Soviet Union, and through this channel to become members of the international academic community. This was true not only in the natural sciences, but also in many other fields, ranging from archaeology to linguistics.

The educational process was saturated with ideological content. All other interpretations of history were banned. The break with the past was made even more complete by two changes of script, from Arabic to Latin in 1930 and from Latin to Cyrillic in 1940. Vocabularies were reshaped through the introduction of a huge number of Russian and international terms (Kirkwood 1989). The new art forms, sports and other forms of entertainment that were introduced into the region in the 1930s and 1940s further underpinned the Sovietization and, concomitantly, Europeanization of central Asian culture. This was almost always at the expense of local traditions. Thus, for example, traditional acrobats and jugglers were ousted in favour of Soviet-style circus acts. Opera, ballet and theatre companies were established in all the central Asian republics. Local performers were trained, some of whom proved to be prodigiously gifted. Notable examples are Tajik Faroukh Ruzimatov and the Kazakh Altynai Asylmuratova, ranked among the most acclaimed ballet dancers in the world. As part of the wider Soviet cultural elite, they gained international reputations.

The transformation of central Asian society was accelerated by waves of immigrants from the Slav republics. Some Slavs (mostly Russians) had already settled in the region in the pre-revolutionary period, but many more came during the years of Soviet rule. The first and largest period of immigration was 1926–39 when, along with Party officials and bureaucrats, there came doctors, teachers, engineers and other professionals, who contributed to the development of central Asia. Many skilled workers also arrived to work in the newly established industries.

There was another substantial influx of immigrants during the Second World War, when many industrial enterprises and academic institutions were relocated from the western part of the Soviet Union, where they were at risk from the Nazi advance, to the east of the Ural Mountains. The 'punished peoples' added yet another layer of immigration: whole ethnic groups, amounting to hundreds of thousands of people, were accused of collaboration with the enemy and deported *en masse* to central Asia at this time (Nekrich 1978; Minority Rights Group 6 1980). They included Crimean Tatars, Meskhetian Turks, Chechen and Ingush, as well as Germans from the Volga region and Greeks from the Black Sea. Smaller groups of settlers arrived in the 1950s and 1960s, connected with particular economic projects (for example, bringing the 'Virgin Lands' of Kazakhstan under the plough) or natural disasters (to help with the reconstruction of

Tashkent after the earthquake of 1966). Thereafter, there was a fall in the number of incomers.

One of the most important sociocultural changes to take place in central Asia under Soviet rule was the emancipation of women. Previously, women had led relatively secluded lives, especially in urban areas in the southern belt. The *hujum* (attack) campaign, launched in 1927, was aimed at integrating women more fully into society. Wearing the *paranja* (veil) was abandoned; traditionally, it had been worn in the south, in urban centres. Under Soviet law it was not formally banned, but sanctions were often used against women who continued to wear it; their husbands were also sometimes punished.

Education for girls was made compulsory. Women were encouraged to seek employment outside the home and to retain control of their earnings, thus to become independent of their menfolk. Significant changes occurred (for example, by the 1970s the percentage of central Asian women with higher education was not far below that of Russian women). Nevertheless, some traditional patterns of behaviour were maintained. Central Asian women often married at a younger age, on average, than their European counterparts. They also had many more children (families with six or more children are still quite common, especially in rural areas). There was, however, a greater awareness of opportunities outside the home, and a significant proportion of central Asian women began to enter the professions and to take an active part in public life (Massell 1975; Pal'vanova 1981; Patnaik 1989; Akiner 1997).

Together with constructive efforts to build a new Soviet identity, there were also destructive efforts aimed at eradicating any other form of self-definition. The most important target was Islam, the dominant culture of the pre-Soviet era. Muslim institutions were tolerated for the first few years, but towards the end of the 1920s Muslim schools and law courts were phased out. Mosques and *madrasas* (colleges for Islamic instruction) were closed, religious literature confiscated and Muslim clerics persecuted. The assault on Islam coincided with political purges, during which many of the leading intellectuals perished. At the same time, the regime succeeded in co-opting local support, creating vested interests not only for those with political aspirations (that is, within the Communist Party), but also for academics, writers, artists, journalists and other opinion-formers.

The result of these and other changes was a significant reshaping of the public face of society. Yet in the private domain, there was a high degree of conservatism. The power of the old ruling elite was broken, but many members of this group transformed themselves into committed Communist Party functionaries and, in this way, were able to reconsolidate their position in society. At the same time, universal education broadened opportunities for advancement, and there was a relatively high degree of social mobility. Social networks, reminiscent of the traditional clan/tribal structures, continued to play a dominant role, however (Akiner 1996).

These new groupings – colloquially known as 'clans' – were not based exclusively on kinship ties, but included various forms of personal association (formed, for example, at school, work and military service). They were clustered around the Soviet-era khans – that is to say, individuals who had acquired political or economic power within the Soviet system. In many ways, these new clans were not very different from the traditional central Asian client–patron relationships, whereby the leaders had provided rewards and protection in return for allegiance. Such links engendered mutual dependency, which in turn strengthened group solidarity. This provided a covert power base on which to build the personal fiefdoms that flourished within the Soviet system. Arguably, these sub-political loyalties deflected potential nationalist aspirations, with internal clan/regional rivalries taking the place of a challenge to Soviet power.

Soviet development policies

The political and cultural integration of central Asia was accompanied by economic integration. The industrial base of the region in the early 1920s was very low. During the first two five-year plans (1928–33, 1933–38), great emphasis was placed on the development of heavy industry. There was considerable central government investment in the chemical, mining, oil and gas industries, but very little in processing and manufacturing. The needs of the individual republics were always subordinated to those of the Soviet Union. This led to spot developments, whereby major industrial complexes were created that were in no way integrated into the local economy. Even the workforce was imported, mostly from the European republics of the Soviet Union. Most of these enterprises came under direct control from Moscow, not the government of the republic on whose territory they were sited. Throughout the Soviet era, central Asia remained, for the most part, a producer of primary commodities with little value-added benefit.

In the agricultural sector, there was a similar lack of concern for local needs. Collectivization was introduced in central Asia, as in other parts of the Soviet Union, at the end of the 1920s. At the same time, the nomads were 'sedentarized'. Transhumance (of livestock to and from seasonal pastures), an environmental imperative, did continue, but it was subject to bureaucratic regulation. The traditional nomadic way of life, with its skills and rich culture, was lost (Akiner 1995). Allocated areas of specialization were developed to the point that they became monocultures. In Uzbekistan, for example, the land under cultivation for cotton was doubled in the period from 1960 to 1990, severely reducing the republics' capacity for food production. The goal was to ensure cotton independence for the Soviet Union. This overemphasis on a single commodity made the central Asian republics extremely vulnerable, causing them to become dependent on the European parts of the Soviet Union for the supply of such basic necessities as foodstuffs, pharmaceuticals, manufactured goods and machinery. Large subsidies were required from the central government to fund the social services, since the central Asian republics were unable to generate sufficient revenue of their own.

The worst legacy of Soviet rule in central Asia was the widespread incidence of environmental damage. The desiccation of the Aral Sea, once the fourth largest inland sea in the world, was a dreadful example of this. It was caused by the excessive demands for water to feed vast (and often ineffectual) irrigation projects. This diminished the flow of the rivers that emptied into the Aral Sea (the Amu-Darya and Syr-Darya) to such an extent that the level of the sea fell by 14 metres and the surface area diminished by 27,000 km². Local fishing and canning industries were destroyed. The relentless drive to raise agricultural production caused a severe decline in soil fertility, which, in turn, prompted the reckless overuse of chemical fertilizers, herbicides, pesticides and highly toxic defoliants. The result was severe pollution of the soil and water, particularly in Tajikistan, Turkmenistan and Uzbekistan, the main cotton-producing areas.

Industrial pollution also created serious health hazards. Noxious emissions from industrial plants frequently far exceeded accepted safety norms, causing dangerous levels of contamination of air, soil and water. The technology that was used in such installations was frequently inappropriate, and the machinery was poorly maintained and highly inefficient. In Kazakhstan, there was the additional burden of the devastation caused by the space and nuclear arms industries. The region that was most seriously affected was the Semipalatinsk testing zone, where, between 1949 and 1963, 124 atom bombs were detonated in the atmosphere; underground thermonuclear testing continued until 1968.

In brief, the first 60 or so years of Soviet rule brought about radical changes in central Asia. There were major improvements in education, health care and other social services. These advances, however, were achieved through a terrible cultural dislocation. The economic legacy was equally flawed. It achieved impressive development in some fields, but overall was so unbalanced as to cause serious long-term problems for the republics. Far from being assisted towards viable independent statehood, they were ever more tightly tied into all-Soviet Union structures. Moreover, after the initial attempts in the early years of Soviet rule to indigenize the administrative and industrial workforce, there was a tendency to marginalize the local population. Most remained in the rural areas, playing little part in the industrial and technological developments in their respective republics. Qualified professionals and skilled labourers were brought in from other parts of the Soviet Union, thus further increasing central Asia's state of dependence.

Countdown to independence

In the 1980s, President Gorbachev launched a campaign of *perestroika* (restructuring) to improve the economic performance of the Soviet Union. In central Asia, however, the main effect of this exercise was to stimulate a national awakening, prompted in large measure by anger over what was increasingly perceived to be the colonial nature of Soviet rule. There was also bitter resentment of Moscow's high-handed treatment of the local ruling elites; in Kazakhstan, in December 1986, this found expression in a major public demonstration, the first of its kind to be held in the Soviet Union. Sociopolitical movements began to appear in the late 1980s, prompted mostly by local cultural and environmental concerns (for example, the *Birlik* Unity movement in Uzbekistan and the Nevada–Semipalatinsk anti-nuclear movement in Kazakhstan). There was at this time, too, the faint beginning of an Islamic revival in some areas of Tajikistan and Uzbekistan.

There were, however, no calls for national independence in central Asia (very different from the situation elsewhere in the Soviet Union, such as in the

Baltic republics, where there were already powerful separatist movements). Like other Soviet republics, all the central Asian republics made declarations of sovereignty in 1990. Sovereignty in this context did not mean leaving the Soviet Union, but rather it meant greater autonomy within the existing constitutional framework. The emphasis was on establishing the supremacy of republican laws over federal laws. In the nationwide referendum on the future of the Soviet Union held a few months later (March 1991), the central Asian republics voted overwhelmingly to maintain the Union.

In Moscow in August 1991, there was a *coup d'état* to unseat President Gorbachev. The immediate response of many central Asians (including the most senior officials) was to voice support for the coup leaders. However, the coup failed and, in the aftermath, first Uzbekistan, then Kyrgyzstan, Tajikistan and Turkmenistan proclaimed their independence. Yet no formal steps to secede from the Union were initiated. The public at large (who had at no time been consulted and who were for the most part taken by surprise by these announcements) generally supposed that the declarations of independence would remain a mere formality. In fact, within a few weeks the three Slav republics – Belarus, the Russian Federation and Ukraine – had seceded from the Union, thereby signalling the demise of the Soviet era. Thus, it was without a liberation struggle, without even forewarning or preparation, that the central Asian republics achieved independence.

Independence

With independence, the governments of the new states assumed full responsibility for a bewildering array of social, economic and environmental problems. Development in central Asia had always lagged behind that of other Soviet republics, and the region had been heavily dependent on Soviet Union structures and central government subsidies. Consequently, the abrupt termination of budgetary transfers from the central government (one of the principal sources of funding for the welfare services) and the dislocation of inter-republic trade and transport links caused greater distress here than elsewhere.

Yet the newly independent states were initially remarkably successful in coping with these upheavals. Economic reforms were set in motion and there was some attempt to build new institutions. Issues of regional cooperation and integration into the international community began to be addressed. Despite spiralling unemployment and increasing pauperization, there was a high degree of social cohesion and, to some extent, this helped to alleviate the hardships of transition. In Tajikistan, factional rivalries plunged the country into civil war within a few months of independence, but elsewhere stability was maintained.

The central Asian republics possess many assets, not least of which is rich human potential and an impressive resource base. Thus, in 1992, the prospects for a smooth transformation from Soviet rule to independent statehood seemed bright. It soon became clear, however, that there were deep-seated systemic problems in several spheres. Increasingly, these were to hinder attempts at reform. Economic, environmental and social issues are discussed elsewhere in this volume. The remainder of this chapter will focus mainly on political developments.

Post-Soviet political systems

The post-Soviet central Asian states have a formal policy of building democracy, and an official policy has been announced to build post-Soviet institutions in all five states. These have included the drafting of new constitutions and reforms of their parliamentary systems. Turkmenistan took the first steps in this direction, adopting a new constitution and a new system of government in 1992 (Dawisha and Parrott 1997; Capisani 2000). In addition to the *Majlis*, the 50-seat legislative body, two innovative institutions were created: the People's Council, which includes senior ministers and regional administrators (all presidential appointees), and the Council of Elders, made up of respected members of society (selected by the president), whose role is to provide guidance for the leadership. Constitutional reform was introduced in the other four states over the next few years. New, bicameral parliaments were created to replace the one-chamber Supreme Soviets that had existed previously in Kazakhstan in 1994, in Kyrgyzstan in 1995 and in Tajikistan in 1999 (Dawisha and Parrott 1997; Akiner 2000a; Capisani 2000). A similar reform was proposed in Uzbekistan in June 2000 (Central Asia Newsfile 2000b).

The institutional changes have not, Tajikistan apart, seen significant shifts in leadership. Most of today's leaders came to power before the collapse of the Soviet Union (Akiner 2000a). Three of the incumbent presidents were formerly First Secretaries of the Communist Parties of their respective Soviet republics, positions which have been converted to form the basis of independent state governance (Akiner 2000a). All five leaders have now established themselves as powerful central figures within the new states and as the guarantors of national independence and stability (Capisani 2000; Accord 2001).

The constitutional restrictions originally placed on presidential rule, including those regarding age and periods in office, have gradually been amended by decrees and confirmed by referendums leading to the extension of incumbents' terms and in two instances to the presidency or special powers being conferred for life (Central Asia Newsfile 2000a). The central Asian states are typified by a governmental culture of strong presidential rule, supported by family and clan ties and through traditions of patronage and informal or gratitude payments (Akiner 2000a). Current leaders and their networks play the central role in most spheres of public life. It can be argued that this has created stability in central Asia during a period of flux and upheaval, although there have also been concerns expressed about the institutional capacity to ensure an orderly devolution of power in the longer term (Dawisha and Parrott 1997; Akiner 2000a; Jane's Sentinel 2000).

Reflecting past history, most central Asians are distrustful of political activity and thus participation rates are relatively low (Akiner 2000a). Most parties tend to be centred round an individual with a strong personality or sufficient influence to establish a power base (Akiner 2000a). Party membership today remains comparatively small in numbers and restricted in social range, drawing predominantly on a network of personal contacts and acquaintances. Nevertheless, embryonic multi-party systems have begun to emerge. Kazakhstan, Kyrgyzstan and Tajikistan all have several small opposition parties; the only parties of any size tend to be pro-presidential and have official backing (Ruffin and Waugh 1999; Akiner 2000a; Capisani 2000; Central Asia Newsfile 2000a).

As part of the democracy-building process, nationwide referendums and several rounds of elections – presidential and parliamentary – have been held in all the central Asian states. However, many pre-independence practices have persisted with a tendency towards strong press endorsement of incumbents and unanimity of results (Ruffin and Waugh 1999; Freeman 2000; US Department of State 2001).

Civil war in Tajikistan

Tajikistan, the only central Asian state that has so far experienced serious conflict, was arguably also the one where, on the eve of independence, democratization seemed likely to succeed. The presidential elections held in November 1991 offered a broad range of candidates and, by comparison with electoral proceedings elsewhere in the region, this ballot was reasonably free and fair. The winner was Rahmon Nabiyev, a former First Secretary of the Communist Party of Tajikistan. Although he had been well respected during his previous time in office, he proved to be a disastrous choice. By 1991, he had lost touch with the current scene and was unable to maintain a consensus between the different political groupings. By March 1992, the country was slipping towards civil war.

Superficially, the conflict was between three factions: communists, aspiring democrats and Islamic activists. In reality, it was predominantly a power struggle between clan/regional groupings, along a north–south boundary. No single group was strong enough on its own to establish control of the state. The government, based in the capital, Dushanbe, was supported by Russian troops; the governments of the neighbouring central Asian republics were also sympathetic to the Dushanbe regime. Meanwhile, the opposition leaders, who fled to northern Afghanistan, received help from local Afghan field commanders. In September 1992, Rahmon Nabiyev was forced to resign; the office of president was suspended.

The violence escalated rapidly, resulting in a huge loss of life and damage to property. Although the fighting was largely confined to the Tajik–Afghan border region, it caused severe economic and social disruption throughout the republic. The only area that escaped relatively unscathed was the northern province of Khojent. Elsewhere, the economy was devastated, and thousands of refugees were left homeless and destitute. Some fled to Afghanistan, the Islamic Republic of Iran and the neighbouring central Asian republics; others sought refuge elsewhere in Tajikistan. In an attempt to resolve the situation, a peacekeeping force, mandated by the Commonwealth of Independent States, was sent to Tajikistan. This consisted predominantly of troops from the Russian Federation, with some contributions from the neighbouring central Asian republics (excluding Turkmenistan).

The post of president was revived in 1994. Elections were held in November of that year, although much of the country was still racked by strife. International agencies did not send observers, on the grounds that it was impossible to hold free elections under such conditions. Emomali Rahmonov, a southerner representing the Dushanbe government, won by a relatively (in central Asian terms) narrow 25 per cent majority. The government and the armed opposition (known collectively as the United Tajik Opposition) eventually agreed on a ceasefire, which was repeatedly broken by both sides; by 1995, a stalemate had been reached. This eventually prompted the warring factions to heed international peace initiatives (sponsored by the Russian Federation, the Islamic Republic of Iran, the United Nations and other mediators). In June 1997, President Rahmonov and the leader of the opposition, Said Abdullo Nuri, signed a peace agreement and protocol of mutual understanding.

In accordance with the peace settlement, the United Tajik Opposition was allocated 30 per cent of posts in the government. Negotiations over these posts proceeded slowly, but in most cases the outcome was acceptable to both sides. The registration and demobilization of opposition units was also gradually carried out. Most of the refugees have now returned home. Law and order is gradually returning to the country, although cases of assault, kidnapping and murder are still common. The economy of the country was devastated by the war. Since the cessation of hostilities, President Rahmonov's government has, thanks to foreign technical assistance, implemented sound macroeconomic policies. Inflation has been brought under control, and there is now significant economic growth. Increased international confidence in the country has attracted greater flows of economic and humanitarian aid, and this has further helped to stabilize the situation. Today, the situation in Tajikistan is by no means stable, but after 7 years of conflict, there appears to be a general desire on all sides to consolidate the peace settlement.

An Islamic revival?

In the 1980s, after decades of repression and denial of Islam, central Asia began to experience a cautious revival of interest in Islamic culture and belief. This process took on new vigour after independence. Today, however, attitudes towards Islam are marked by ambivalence and ambiguity. On the one hand, there is a general consensus that the faith is an integral part of the national heritage; on the other, there is widespread fear of the rise of Islamic fundamentalism. This dichotomy is born of a lack of genuine familiarity with the religion. Most of the adult population is still largely ignorant of the principal tenets of the faith and the ritual obligations. Yet this is gradually changing. Thousands of mosques and hundreds of part-time and full-time Muslim schools and colleges have been opened since 1989, and religious literature is now widely available throughout the region. Large numbers of central Asians journey to Mecca each year to perform the *haj* (prescribed pilgrimage). Many of the younger generation receive Muslim instruction and attend mosque services regularly. Some girls, as a symbol of their faith, have voluntarily taken to wearing the *hejab* (Islamic headscarf) and loose, all-enveloping outer garments.

There are, however, striking regional variations. The most plentiful signs of a rise in Islamic observance are to be seen in the southern tier, in the densely populated Fergana Valley (where Kyrgyzstan, Tajikistan and Uzbekistan converge). Historically, this was the heartland of Islamic orthodoxy and, even during the Soviet era, the religion retained a stronger hold here than elsewhere in the region. In the northern tier (Kazakhstan and Kyrgyzstan), active adherence to Islam is much less evident. The Islamicization of this part of central Asia occurred much later than in the south, and some would argue that it was always of a rather superficial nature. Today, many Kazakhs and Kyrgyz regard themselves as Muslims – more by culture than by religious conviction.

The constitutions of all the central Asian republics enshrine the division of religion and the state. Throughout the region, however, there has been substantial government support for promoting the role of Islam in public life. Indeed, Islam has to some extent taken the place of Marxist ideology as state dogma. Yet stringent measures to monitor and control Muslim institutions have also been introduced. Clerics must be registered officially; otherwise, they are liable to prosecution. The activities of Muslim missionaries from abroad are subject to rigorous scrutiny. There is an increasingly repressive attitude towards any manifestation of Islam that is not specifically sanctioned by the state authorities. The most extreme instances of state control are in Uzbekistan, where the government is deeply concerned about the spread of Islamic fundamentalism.

Opinions, both within central Asia and abroad, differ greatly as to whether there are genuine grounds for anxiety on this score, or whether the 'Islamic threat' is being used as an excuse to justify the suppression of any form of opposition. It is certainly true that, since the mid-1990s, Islamicist groups in Uzbekistan have been intensifying their activities. Very little reliable information about these organizations is available, however. The two that are mentioned most often are the *Hizbi-Tahrir* (Liberation Party) and the Islamic Movement of Uzbekistan. The size, social composition and sources of funding of these groups can only be surmised. The relationship between them is not clear. Their political goals, likewise, are opaque. It is claimed that they want to establish an Islamic state. According to the state authorities, they are ready to use force to accomplish this aim. They are also accused of having links with organized crime, especially drug trafficking.

Several terrorist attacks have taken place in recent years, in the Fergana Valley and in the capital, Tashkent. The most serious was an assassination attempt on the life of President Karimov in February 1999. Later that same year, there was a hostage-taking incident in southern Kyrgyzstan. Four Japanese geologists who were working in the area were held captive for several weeks. It is rumoured that the Japanese Government eventually paid a handsome ransom for their release. The Uzbek Government has accused the Islamicists of perpetrating these outrages. Thousands of supposed activists and their relatives have been imprisoned. Nevertheless, much of the evidence that has been produced is far from convincing. Human rights organizations, both local and international, claim that incriminating material is often planted on suspects by the police. It is possible that Islamicists were involved in these incidents, but the scale and brutality of the government retaliation has assumed the guise of an indiscriminate witch-hunt. There is no indication that the broad mass of the population is in any way sympathetic to the project to create an Islamic state. However, the current wave of persecution is creating the very discontent that could radicalize elements within the Muslim community, if this has not already happened (Akiner 2000b).

Ethnic minorities

All the central Asian republics have multi-ethnic populations. The proportion of titular people within the population as a whole ranges from over 70 per cent in Turkmenistan and Uzbekistan, to fewer than 50 per cent in Kazakhstan. The number of minority groups in each state is very considerable (over 100 different ethnic groups are to be found in Kazakhstan alone). When the Soviet Union collapsed, many observers feared that there would be an upsurge in ethnic strife. To date, however, there have been no outbreaks of violence comparable to those that occurred during the last years of Soviet rule, when there were ferocious clashes between Uzbeks and Meskhetian Turks in Uzbekistan in 1989, and between Uzbeks and Kyrgyz in Kyrgyzstan in 1990. In both cases, there were hundreds of deaths and much destruction of property. These outbreaks of violence were sudden and unexpected, but they arose from long-standing grievances rooted in ethnic competition over work and housing (Melvin 1995; Smith 1995). There has been a heightening of tension, however, particularly in Kazakhstan and Kyrgyzstan, between the titular people and the ethnic minorities. This is largely the result of the nationalizing policies that have been adopted throughout the region since independence.

The most obvious instance of this trend is the elevation of the language of the titular population to the status of state language (thus, for example, Uzbek is now the state language of Uzbekistan). These languages are increasingly the medium of communication in public life. During the Soviet era, it was Russian that played this role. Today, the use of Russian in the administration, in higher education and in the professions is gradually being phased out. The non-titular peoples, not only Slavs but also representatives of the many other ethnic groups, feel disadvantaged by this process. Their sense of grievance is heightened by the fact that little provision has been made by the authorities to provide dictionaries and teaching materials to help them acquire the necessary linguistic fluency. Some believe that, in the future, measures such as these will be used to exclude ethnic minorities from public service and that, in effect, these minorities will become second-class citizens.

Such fears prompted a major exodus of the non-titular peoples. Soon after the collapse of the Soviet Union, hundreds of thousands of Slavs emigrated. So, too, did large numbers of Germans, Poles and Greeks (all deported to central Asia during the Second World War). Many of the emigrants were highly qualified professionals. This sudden brain drain caused severe problems for the nascent national economies in central Asia. The respective governments of these states have made efforts to reassure the minorities that their fears of discrimination are groundless. This has slowed the outflow somewhat, but it has by no means succeeded in halting it.

Regional integration

During the Soviet era, the republics of the central Asian periphery were tied to the 'centre' rather than to each other. Consequently, intra-regional links were weak. Contacts with neighbouring countries beyond the Soviet frontier were minimal and tightly regulated by Moscow. Since independence, one of the tasks that have confronted these new states is the development of relationships that enhance regional cooperation, particularly with regard to economic activities and the fight against common security threats (for example, drug trafficking and terrorism). To this end, they have joined an overlapping group of organizations aimed at promoting ties within central Asia, and likewise within the wider regional context.

Moves to create a Central Asian Union were initiated in January 1993. As a first stage, a customs union was created between Kazakhstan, Kyrgyzstan and Uzbekistan. In 1996, the Central Asian Bank for Cooperation and Development was formed. Also, free economic zones were established in the border regions of the three countries. In a further move to strengthen regional cooperation, a joint central Asian peacekeeping battalion was created, to operate under the aegis of the United Nations. The Central Asian Union, enlarged by the accession of Tajikistan, was renamed the Central Asian Economic Community (CAEC) in 1998. By 2000, the only central Asian republic still outside the CAEC was Turkmenistan.

The building of intra-central Asian institutions is of prime importance, since many regional matters can only be solved on a multilateral basis (for example, water management, transportation and cross-border trade). Yet progress has been hampered by a lack of organizational experience, as well as by concerns over loss of sovereignty. Increasingly, too, political rivalries have begun to emerge between the central Asian republics; there are fears in some quarters that Uzbekistan, by far the most populous state, is seeking to establish regional hegemony. It is possible that these are merely teething problems and will be overcome with time. Until that happens, however, it will be difficult to achieve effective cooperation.

A parallel development to the formation of the CAEC was the integration of the central Asian republics into the Economic Cooperation Organization (ECO). This developed from a series of earlier regional alliances, dating from the Baghdad Pact of 1955 between Turkey and Iraq, later joined by Pakistan and Iran. Iraq withdrew from the pact, which was renamed the Central Treaty Organization (CENTO) in 1958; in 1984, it became ECO. In February 1992, under the aegis of the Islamic Republic of Iran, the organization embarked on a programme of activities focused on central Asia. The five central Asian republics, as well as Afghanistan and Azerbaijan, subsequently became members of ECO. Regular working meetings and summits between heads of state are held, but the limited financial resources of the constituent members has meant that, to date, the organization has acted more as a forum for debate than as the sponsor of major economic projects.

A regional grouping that at first seemed destined to be little more than a talking shop was the so-called Shanghai Five. In 1996, the heads of state of China and neighbouring Kazakhstan, Kyrgyzstan, Russian Federation and Tajikistan met to discuss cross-border issues, including specific questions of border demarcation. Negotiations proceeded slowly, but for the most part smoothly. Summit meetings between the five became a regular annual event. The sphere of activities of this group now includes active cooperation to combat terrorism and other cross-border security threats.

The forging of new regional networks has diversified contacts, but has not meant the severing of ties with other former Soviet republics. Bilateral relations with ex-Soviet partners have been re-established and strengthened; in particular, the relationship with Russia remains of key importance for all the central Asian republics. On a multilateral level, the central Asian republics are also members of the Commonwealth of Independent States (CIS). All, with the exception of Turkmenistan, acceded to the Collective Security Treaty signed in May 1992 (although Uzbekistan withdrew in 1999). In 1996, Kazakhstan and Kyrgyzstan joined the Russian Federation and Belarus to form an inner core within CIS. A quadripartite agreement on 'The Regulation of Economic and Humanitarian Integration' was concluded, covering such matters as: the creation of a united economic area; the development of common energy, transport and information systems; and the coordination of foreign policy. By 2000, these goals were still far from being realized.

International relations

Before the collapse of the Soviet Union, the central Asian republics had few links with the external world. Today, the central Asian capitals are connected to many cities in Asia and Europe by direct flights. Satellite links have helped to integrate the region into international telecommunication networks. There are now fully operational ministries of foreign affairs and of foreign economic relations in all the central Asian republics. Trade and diplomatic links have been established with over 100 foreign governments; central Asian embassies have been opened in the United States and the main European and Asian centres. Likewise, there are growing communities of foreign diplomats, businessmen and technical advisers in the central Asian republics.

All five central Asian republics were accepted as members of the United Nations on 2 March 1992. They subsequently joined affiliated agencies, such as the United Nations Educational, Scientific and Cultural Organization (UNESCO) and the World Health Organization (WHO). They also joined major international financial institutions, including the International Monetary Fund (IMF), the World Bank, the European Bank for Reconstruction and Development and the Asian Development Bank (ADB). In addition to the regional groupings mentioned in the previous section, these states now belong to diverse international organizations. They include the Organization of the Islamic Conference, the Organization for Security and Cooperation in Europe (OSCE) and the North Atlantic Treaty Organization (NATO) Partnership for Peace programme (Tajikistan is not yet a member of the last organization).

In the first years of independence, the foreign policies of the central Asian republics were mainly reactive, a response to external overtures. Priorities soon emerged, however. One was to secure capital investment and technical assistance from abroad. Some progress has been made in this direction, particularly in the oil, gas and mining sectors. The other priority was to diversify access to world markets. During the Soviet era, all the export routes from central Asia lay through Russia. This created a situation in which Moscow had ultimate control over the foreign economic relations of these republics. To escape this stranglehold, new transport outlets were required – in short, there was an urgent need to revive the ancient Silk Roads. Steps have been taken to open this route. In the east, transport links between Kazakhstan and China are now operational; in the south-west, they are operational between Turkmenistan and the Islamic Republic of Iran. Thus, the main components of a trans-Asian bridge, stretching from the Yellow Sea to the Persian Gulf, have already been re-established. The EU is eager to strengthen ties with the central Asian republics and has embarked on an ambitious project to create a transport corridor between Europe and central Asia (known by the acronym TRACECA). The Economic Cooperation Organization has also proposed the development of a transport system to link central Asia to its southern neighbours.

With regard to external security threats, Afghanistan represents the greatest (and some would argue, only) direct menace. The danger is not so much that of military invasion, but rather the insidious destabilizing influence of on-going turmoil in a neighbouring country. Moreover, huge consignments of drugs are ceaselessly smuggled across the long, porous border that Tajikistan, Turkmenistan and Uzbekistan share with Afghanistan. The central Asian republics are predominantly a transit link in the route to Europe and the Middle East; however, local drug addiction is now increasing, especially among the young. Weapons circulate freely, fuelling crime and violence. The rise of the Taliban movement has exacerbated fears that fanaticism and terrorism, masquerading in the guise of religion, will engulf central Asia. The central Asian republics have repeatedly appealed to the international community to intensify efforts to bring peace and stability to Afghanistan, and hence to the whole region. So far, this has not yielded any significant results.

In the immediate aftermath of independence, there was much speculation about whether the new central Asian republics would emulate the Iranian model of Islamic theocracy, or the Turkish model of secular, Western-style democracy. Initially, the central Asian republics favoured a rapprochement with Turkey. There was an assumption, at official level and popular level, that Turkey would be able to provide unlimited aid. Turkey did indeed provide aid (mostly in the form of credits), but far less than had been anticipated. Relations have remained cordial (apart from some bouts of friction with Uzbekistan) and Turkish business interests are well represented in the central Asian republics, but no pan-Turkic special relationship has emerged.

The Islamic Republic of Iran, like Turkey, does not have sufficient economic resources to provide the investment that the central Asian republics require. This automatically sets a limit to the extent of its active influence in the region. In the religious sphere, the Islamic Republic of Iran (which is Shia Muslim, unlike central Asia, which is almost entirely Sunni Muslim) has pursued a policy of non-interference, emphasizing instead the need for regional cooperation in trade, exploitation of natural resources, environmental protection and the development of the Caspian Sea zone.

The central Asian leaders have repeatedly stressed their intention to avoid being drawn into any ideological or ethnically based alliance. Today, although some differences are emerging in the foreign policy orientation of the individual states, in general the overall thrust is to pursue good working relations with a broad spectrum of countries, while maintaining a non-aligned stance.

Thus, all the central Asian republics are careful to remain even-handed in their relations with, for example, India and Pakistan, or Israel and the Arab states. Turkmenistan has taken this concept furthest, declaring a state of positive neutrality that precludes membership in any military pacts or inter-state unions that require collective responsibility (hence Turkmenistan's limited involvement in CIS and other regional groupings).

Conclusions

The central Asian republics, in their modern form, are still very young. They are in the midst of extremely complex social, political and economic transitions. The magnitude of the upheaval caused by the sudden demise of the Soviet Union is only now becoming apparent. The leaders of these states have made preserving stability a priority. This is understandable, particularly in view of the horrors of the Tajik civil war. Yet there is a danger that fear of instability could lead to a situation in which any form of innovation is regarded as a threat. In the political sphere, this desire to avoid change is already producing a creeping paralysis that is obstructive to democratization and liberalization. Some, especially within the region, insist that this is a price worth paying, since stability is a precondition for orderly transition. Others argue that this approach does not solve problems, but merely postpones, and perhaps intensifies, the possibility of a crisis in the future. There are no easy solutions: hindsight is the only exact science.

References

Accord (2001) An international review of peace initiatives, in K. Abdullaev and C. Barnes (eds) *Politics of Compromise: The Tajik Peace Process*. London: Conciliation Resources.

Akiner, S. (1986) *Islamic People of the Soviet Union*. London: Kegan Paul International.

Akiner, S. (1995) *The Formation of Kazakh Identity: From Tribe to Nation-State*. London: Royal Institute of International Affairs.

Akiner, S. (1996) Ethnicity, nationality and citizenship as expressions of self-determination in central Asia, in D. Clarke (ed.) *Self-Determination: International Perspectives*. London: Macmillan.

Akiner, S. (1997) Between tradition and modernity: the dilemma facing contemporary central Asian women, in M. Buckley (ed.) *Self-Determination: International Perspectives*. London: Macmillan.

Akiner, S. (2000a) Emerging political order in the newly independent Caspian States: Azerbaijan, Kazakhstan and Turkmenistan, in G.K. Bertsch, C.S. Craft, S.A. Jones *et al.* (eds) *Crossroads and Conflict: Security and Foreign Policy in the Caucasus and Central Asia*. London: Routledge.

Akiner, S. (2000b) Islam and central Asia in the 1990s, *Harvard International Review*, 22(1): 62–5.

Capisani, G.R. (2000) *The Handbook of Central Asia: A Comprehensive Survey of the New Republics*. London: Tauris.

Central Asia Newsfile (2000a) Issue no. 86, *Central Asia Newsfile*, 8(1).

Central Asia Newsfile (2000b) Issue no. 91, *Central Asia Newsfile*, 8(6).

Dawisha, K. and Parrott, B. (1997) *Conflict, Cleavage and Change in Central Asia and the Caucasus.* Cambridge: Cambridge University Press.

Freeman (2000) Statement on Elections, US Deputy Assistant Secretary of State Bennett Freeman, OSCE Human Dimension Implementation Meeting, 17 October 2000, Warsaw, Poland.

Goldman, B. (1934) *Red Road Through Asia.* London: Methuen.

Jane's Sentinel (2000) *Security Assessment.* Coulsdon, Surrey: Jane's Information Group.

Kirkwood, M. (1989) *Language Planning in the Soviet Union.* London: Macmillan.

Massell, G. (1975) *The Surrogate Proletariat.* Princeton, NJ: Princeton University Press.

Melvin, N. (1995) *Russians Beyond Russia: The Politics of National Identity.* London: Pinter/ Royal Institute of International Affairs.

Minority Rights Group (1980) *The Crimean Tartars, Volga Germans and Meskhetians: Soviet Treatment of Some Minorities* (new edition), Report No. 6. London: Minority Rights Group.

Nekrich, A. (1978) *The Punished Peoples: The Deportation and Tragic Fate of Soviet Minorities at the End of the Second World War* (trans. G. Saunders). New York: W.W. Norton.

Pal'vanova, B. (1981) *Emantsipatsia Musul'manki* [*Emancipation of the Muslim Woman*]. Moscow: Nauka.

Patnaik, A. (1989) *Perestroika and Women Labour Force in Soviet Central Asia.* New Delhi: New Literature.

Ruffin, M.H. and Waugh, D. (eds) (1999) *Civil Society in Central Asia.* Seattle, WA: University of Washington Press.

Skrine, F.H. and Ross, D.E. (1899) *The Heart of Asia.* London: Methuen.

Smith, G. (1995) *Nationality and Ethnic Relations in the Post-Soviet States.* Cambridge: Cambridge University Press.

UNESCO (1991) *Statistical Yearbook 1991.* Paris: UNESCO.

US Department of State (2001) *Country Reports on Human Rights Practices,* February 2001. Washington, DC: US Department of State, Bureau of Democracy, Human Rights and Labour.

three

Macroeconomic pressures

Richard Pomfret

Introduction

This chapter describes and analyses macroeconomic changes in central Asia during the 1990s and discusses their implications for funding health care in a sustainable manner. After a brief review of the initial conditions, the macroeconomic policies and performance of the central Asian republics since independence are analysed. The third and fourth sections consider the implications of public and private funding of health care.

The starting point

The central Asian republics were among the poorest republics of the Soviet Union (Pomfret 1995). Due to different concepts of output and differing relative prices, comparing income and output levels of centrally planned economies and market economies is problematic. Estimates of per person gross national product in the five central Asian republics on the eve of independence are given in Table 3.1 and, although the dollar value should be treated with caution, these estimates are commonly accepted as reflecting the relative outputs of the Soviet republics. In particular, Kazakhstan had substantially higher output per person than the other four central Asian republics. Although income inequality (measured by Gini coefficients) was moderate in all Soviet republics, the incidence of poverty was higher in central Asia and Azerbaijan than in the other Soviet republics (Atkinson and Micklewright 1992). (The Gini coefficient is a summary measure of inequality: 0.00 implies perfect equality, where every observation has the same income; 1.00 implies perfect inequality, where the last observation has all the income.)

Initially, the break-up of the Soviet Union was expected to have a less adverse trade impact on both Kazakhstan and Turkmenistan. Kazakhstan's higher per person income reflected a better-educated population and a more diversified

Table 3.1 Initial conditions: republics of the former Soviet Union, 1989–90

Republic(s)	Population (millions) mid-1990s	Per person GNP[a] 1990	Gini coefficient 1989	Poverty, % pop[b] 1989	Terms of trade[c]
Soviet Union	289.3	2870	0.289	11.1	
Kazakhstan	16.8	2600	0.289	15.5	+19
Kyrgyzstan	4.4	1570	0.287	32.9	+1
Tajikistan	5.3	1130	0.308	51.2	−7
Turkmenistan	3.7	1690	0.307	35.0	+50
Uzbekistan	20.5	1340	0.304	43.6	−3
Armenia	3.3	2380	0.259	14.3	−24
Azerbaijan	7.2	1640	0.328	33.6	−7
Georgia	5.5	2120	0.292	14.3	−21
Belarus	10.3	3110	0.238	3.3	−20
Moldova	4.4	2390	0.258	11.8	−38
Russia	148.3	3430	0.278	5.0	+79
Ukraine	51.9	2500	0.235	6.0	−18
Estonia	1.6	4170	0.299	1.9	−32
Latvia	2.7	3590	0.274	2.4	−24
Lithuania	3.7	3110	0.278	2.3	−31

Notes: [a] GNP per person is given in US$ and is computed by the World Bank's synthetic Atlas method. [b] Poverty refers to individuals in households with a gross per person income of less than 75 rubles. [c] The impact on the terms of trade of moving to world prices was calculated at the 105-sector level of aggregation, using 1990 weights.

Sources: Columns 1–2 (World Bank 1992: 3–4); columns 3–4 (Atkinson and Micklewright 1992: table U13, based on Goskomstat household survey data); column 5 (Tarr 1994)

economy, endowed with grain exports and a variety of minerals and energy resources and with industrial production, particularly in north Kazakhstan. The Tengiz oil project, involving Chevron as the foreign partner, was the largest foreign investment project in the Soviet Union and promised good export prospects for the 1990s. In the 1980s, Turkmenistan had also become a major energy exporter, as its natural gas resources were developed and pipelines constructed to the western Soviet Union. With the collapse of central planning that accompanied the break-up of the Soviet Union, the shift to world prices was expected to benefit Turkmenistan more than any of the other non-Russian new independent states; it was also expected to have a positive economic impact on Kazakhstan (Table 3.1, last column). In practice, these rosy predictions for energy exporting countries were not realized during the 1990s, as potential exports were inhibited by the decrepit pipeline system that took central Asian oil and gas to stagnating markets in which customers did not have hard currency to pay for their fuel imports.

Central Asia's role in the Soviet division of labour was that of a producer of raw materials, especially cotton, and the cotton economy was most dominant in Uzbekistan. Unlike the energy exports of its neighbours, Uzbekistan's cotton could be sold at world prices and transported to new markets. Uzbekistan's second export, gold, was even easier to transport and sell at world prices. Thus, despite a significant disruption for the manufacturing sector, centred on Tashkent, Uzbekistan was less damaged by the shift to market-based international trade than might have been expected.

The initial prospects for Kyrgyzstan and Tajikistan were grimmer. Both are mainly mountainous countries with few readily exploitable natural resources and small manufacturing sectors. The prospects for the newly independent Tajikistan were further damaged by a civil war that had already broken out before the dissolution of the Soviet Union. Tajikistan was the last country to replace the old Soviet ruble, only introducing a national currency in 1995. Despite several attempts to set economic reforms in motion, serious sustained moves to establish the institutions of a market economy were delayed until 1997 by civil unrest (described by Akiner in Chapter 2).

Economic shocks and economic performance

The central Asian republics faced three major economic shocks in the late 1980s and early 1990s: transition from central planning, dissolution of the Soviet Union and hyperinflation. The central planning system was dismantled and the transition to a more market-oriented economy created severe disorganization (Blanchard 1997). This transition process is usually dated from Gorbachev's reforms, especially those of 1987–88, although the initial impact on the southern republics was muted. In 1991, the unexpectedly rapid dissolution of the Soviet Union created additional problems. Supply links and demand sources were disrupted by new national borders and attempts to retain resources within these borders. In central Asia, the ability of governments to deal with these new challenges was compounded by the difficult process of creating new national institutions in countries with no history of sovereignty, and by the severing of positive net resource flows from the rest of the Soviet Union. The attempt to support existing trade by retaining a common currency in the early 1990s fuelled inflation (Pomfret 1996).

In all of the central Asian republics, the early 1990s were characterized by declining output and hyperinflation. The magnitude of these changes is difficult to measure. One reason is that reporting biases shifted: in a centrally planned economy, state managers often had an incentive to pad their output figures to fill plan targets; after the abolition of central planning, however, producers had an incentive to hide income from tax-hungry states (or they suspected that under-reporting might be in their best interest). In trying to create an index, more important problems are how to compare different bundles of goods, some of which did not even exist before the 1990s, and how to weight goods whose official prices were economically meaningless before the 1990s. The problem of finding appropriate relative prices to aggregate all the goods and services produced into a measure of gross domestic product (GDP) was compounded by hyperinflation, which made it difficult to calculate changes over time in real output.

Some of these data problems are truly insoluble, and we have numbers that are more or less useful, but are in no sense precise measures. Prices increased

Table 3.2 Economic performance indicators in central Asia, 1989, 1993, 1996 and 1999

Country	GDP^a (US$ millions)	Real GDP (% of 1989)			Inflation^b		
	1989	1993	1996	1999	1993	1996	1999
Kazakhstan	40 304	76	61	63	2 169	29	18
Kyrgyzstan	5 357	67	54	63	1 363	35	40
Tajikistan	4 731	58	39	44	7 344	41	31
Turkmenistan	6 318	83	59	64	9 750	446	21
Uzbekistan	20 465	88	85	95	885	64	25

Notes: ^{a} GDP is at market prices in US$ millions. ^{b} Inflation is represented by the annual increase in consumer price index (end of year).

Sources: ^{a} UNDP (1999), European Bank for Reconstruction and Development (2000)

very rapidly in 1992, by more than 50 per cent per month throughout the region. The annual inflation rate in Kazakhstan and Kyrgyzstan, whose governments made little attempt to restrict price increases by artificial controls, was somewhere between 1300 and 3000 per cent over the calendar years 1992 and 1993. In Uzbekistan, whose government placed restrictions on price increases, open inflation was lower in 1992 and 1993, but higher in 1994. Turkmenistan was even stricter in controlling price increases in 1992, but had the highest inflation in the region in 1993 (Table 3.2). During 1992 and 1993, how much lower the latter two countries' inflation was depends on exactly how the regulated prices are weighted, whether one uses the official price or the free market price that existed concurrently for many foodstuffs, and so forth. From an economic perspective, as pointed out by the European Bank for Reconstruction and Development in various *Transition Updates*, there is little difference between annual inflation rates of 2169 and 1363 per cent, but they make a huge difference as deflators of nominal GDP. (Estimates for Kazakhstan and Kyrgyzstan in 1993 were well above the threshold for hyperinflation.)

In 1993, Kazakhstan, Kyrgyzstan, Turkmenistan and Uzbekistan issued national currencies and, in a sense, prices started a new life. With greater stability in the consumption basket's composition after 1993, measures of the consumer price index made more sense, although the problem of how to deal with regulated prices in Uzbekistan and especially Turkmenistan remained. Also, annual inflation rates became increasingly meaningful as the decade progressed. Overall, using domestic inflation rates to deflate nominal GDP to obtain measures of real output growth during the 1990s is fraught with difficulties, especially in making year-on-year and cross-country comparisons.

Nevertheless, indicators of relative performance are needed, even if we know the absolute numbers may be of limited meaning. The best efforts to place the national statistics on a common basis are the national account estimates of the International Monetary Fund (IMF), World Bank and European Bank for Reconstruction and Development. Table 3.2 presents estimates of GDP for the five central Asian republics, as an index based on 1989. By 1996, GDP had fallen by over one-third in Kazakhstan, over two-fifths in Turkmenistan and just under a half in Kyrgyzstan. The decline in GDP was greatest in war-torn Tajikistan and smallest in the more gradually changing Uzbekistan. Uzbekistan had, in fact, started to stand out among all of the former Soviet successor states as the country with the smallest post-transition decline in output.

In the late 1990s, the economies of Kazakhstan, Kyrgyzstan and Tajikistan experienced reasonable growth, which may have reflected the fruits of more thorough economic reforms, but this growth also reflected a rebound from the deeper troughs. Uzbekistan also registered positive, but lower, growth in GDP between 1996 and 1999, and the GDP of Turkmenistan recovered slightly after a severe decline in 1997. Despite recent improvements, real output remains significantly below pre-transition levels. In 1999, real GDP was still below half its pre-transition level in Tajikistan and a third below the pre-transition levels in Kyrgyzstan, Kazakhstan and Turkmenistan. The 1998 fiscal crisis in the Russian Federation had a negative impact on the region's economic performance, especially in Kazakhstan, which still relies heavily on trade with the Russian Federation.

The implications for future economic growth depend on how this past experience is interpreted. Kazakhstan, Kyrgyzstan and, to a lesser extent, Tajikistan are all generally viewed as having made substantial progress in creating market-based economies, which should provide a springboard for future growth. Kazakhstan had a better base, given its higher living standard and human capital endowment, but has suffered from large-scale emigration and corruption. While liberalization in Kyrgyzstan has been supported by international institutions, such as the IMF and World Bank, the ultimate outcomes are not yet clear. Poverty certainly increased markedly in the early 1990s, according to Milanovic (1998) to the highest levels in any transition economy. Rising poverty in the region may inhibit future growth if Kyrgyzstan destroys assets and fails to invest in human capital formation, in order to meet current consumption needs (Pomfret 1999; Anderson and Pomfret 2000). Tajikistan, too, has huge potential problems if the fragile post-1997 peace breaks down.

Uzbekistan and Turkmenistan are usually classified among the least liberalized of the economies in transition, yet they present quite different pictures in terms of outcomes. Uzbekistan has the best real output performance in the former Soviet Union and has enjoyed positive GDP growth since 1996. Its inflation came down more slowly than did inflation in Kazakhstan or Kyrgyzstan, dropping below 50 per cent per year in 1997, compared to 29 per cent in Kazakhstan and 35 per cent in Kyrgyzstan in 1996 (Table 3.2), but a market-based economy has been established. Enterprise reform has moved fairly slowly and the exchange rate has become increasingly artificial since the introduction of exchange controls in the second half of 1996, so that there are major clouds on the horizon. In contrast, Turkmenistan attempted to avoid economic change, at least until 1997, and it is unclear how much has changed since then. There has, however, been positive growth in 1998 and 1999, following agreements over gas exports. In sum, Uzbekistan has been relatively successful with its cautious reform, although future problems may have been stored up, while Turkmenistan has tried to avoid reform, and (together with Belarus) is the least reformed of the former Soviet republics.

In all five central Asian republics, economic transition has been associated with increased inequality and poverty (Milanovic 1998; Falkingham 1999; see also Falkingham, Chapter 4). Unemployment has increased, although it is difficult to measure; the decline in employment, however, has been more defined during the 1990s, especially in Kazakhstan.

Implications for public funding of health care

The end of central planning in the late 1980s, followed by declining real output, dissolution of the Soviet Union and the termination of intra-Union transfers, all severely strained government budgets. The worst case was Tajikistan, where GDP fell by more than 60 per cent and the ratio of government expenditure to GDP dropped from 50 per cent to 16 per cent between 1991 and 1998 (Table 3.3). The combined effect left real public expenditure in 1998 at less than 15 per cent of what it had been in 1990, before independence. In Tajikistan, the negative implications for health expenditure have been exacerbated by the internal security situation, which pulled limited public resources away from social spending, so that public funding on health truly collapsed during the civil war.

The situation in the other central Asian republics has been less extreme, but still dire. Table 3.3 shows that the public sector in all central Asian republics was in financial crisis during the first half of the 1990s, as the real level of resources available to governments declined dramatically. Combining the

Table 3.3 General government spending and balance in the central Asian republics (as per cent of GDP), 1990–99

	1990	1991	1992	1993	1994	1995	1996	1997	1998	1999
General government spending										
Kazakhstan	31.4	32.9	31.8	25.2	18.4	20.8	18.6	20.4	25.8	21.5
Kyrgyzstan	38.3	30.3	33.9	39.0	32.4	33.2	32.7	32.7	35.6	34.7
Tajikistan		49.6	65.7	60.7	61.4	29.4	18.9	17.0	15.8	18.3
Turkmenistan	43.6	38.2	30.3	19.4	19.2	23.1	16.3	25.3	25.9	21.6
Uzbekistan	46.1	52.7	49.7	46.4	35.3	38.7	41.6	32.5	35.9	33.7
General government balance										
Kazakhstan	1.4	−7.9	−7.3	−4.1	−7.5	−2.7	−4.7	−6.9	−7.4	−4.1
Kyrgyzstan	0.3	4.6	−17.4	−14.4	−5.7	−8.4	−8.8	−8.8	−11.2	−10.2
Tajikistan		−16.4	−30.5	−20.9	−5.2	−5.3	−5.8	−3.3	−3.8	−3.2
Turkmenistan	1.2	2.5	−9.4	−4.1	−2.3	−2.6	0.3	0.0	−2.7	0.9
Uzbekistan	−1.1	−3.6	−18.3	−10.4	−6.1	−4.1	−7.3	−2.4	−3.0	−2.2

Note: The general government expenditure in Kyrgyzstan includes net lending and expenditure under foreign-financed public investment programmes. In Turkmenistan, most quasi-budgetary expenditures of the sectoral ministries fell outside the budget. When all state funds are taken into account, the 1998 fiscal deficit is closer to 10 per cent rather than the official figure of 2.7 per cent.

Source: European Bank for Reconstruction and Development (1997, 2000)

decline in real GDP with the ratio of falling government expenditure to GDP implies declines in real public spending. Between around 1990 and 1996–97, public spending declined by about 70 per cent in Kazakhstan, 67 per cent in Kyrgyzstan, 64 per cent in Turkmenistan and 48 per cent in Uzbekistan (Cheasty and Davis 1996; Pomfret and Anderson 1997). The situation appears to have stabilized after 1994 (after 1995 in Tajikistan), but real revenue levels remain considerably below those that existed in the early 1990s.

As the decade progressed, differing national patterns emerged. The data in Table 3.3 suggest that Tajikistan, Turkmenistan and Uzbekistan appear to have made reasonably good progress in controlling their budget deficits since 1995. The experience of Uzbekistan is clearly different from that of the other central Asian republics and, as a consequence, it has been able to sustain considerably higher levels of public spending. Nevertheless, tighter controls on spending were introduced in 1997, following a reversal in its pattern of deficit reduction in 1996. The data for Turkmenistan should be regarded with caution, as less than half of public-sector transactions appear as public expenditures, and the country's progress in fiscal adjustment has been minimal. Indeed, an IMF report suggests that the real public-sector deficit was as much as 24 per cent of GDP in 1997 and was nearly 11 per cent of GDP in 1998 (Craig 1999).

These declines in the level of public spending occurred as societies were subjected to huge shocks, which generated conflicting demands for government expenditures. In the early 1990s, enterprises faced with imminent bankruptcy and consumers faced with rising prices of basic goods and services successfully lobbied for subsidies, to which all five governments acceded to varying extents. Uzbekistan appears to have responded most positively to the need to maintain public spending on education and health, devoting the highest proportion of GDP to these sectors (Table 3.4). In contrast, social spending all but collapsed in Tajikistan following the civil war. In 1998, spending on health care amounted to just 1 per cent of GDP, spending on education to 2.3 per cent of GDP and spending on social security to just 0.2 per cent of GDP (Falkingham 2000b: table 4.1). In Kyrgyzstan, substantial foreign assistance has helped to preserve total spending, and donors have encouraged focusing attention on investment in human capital. In Kazakhstan, health care was one of the first casualties of

Table 3.4 Social spending (as per cent of GDP) for the central Asian republics, 1991–96

	Social security		Education		Health care	
	1991	1996	1991	1996	1991	1996
Kazakhstan	4.9	0.6	7.6	3.2	4.4	2.7
Kyrgyzstan	5.5	3.8	8.0[a]	5.4	5.0	2.9
Tajikistan	3.0[b]	0.2[d]	11.1[b]	3.3	6.0	1.1[c]
Turkmenistan	3.2	0.8	9.6	2.8	5.0	1.5[c]
Uzbekistan	7.7	2.5	10.2[b]	7.4[c]	5.9	3.1

Notes: [a]1990, [b]1992, [c]1995, [d]1997.

Source: Falkingham (2000a: table 2)

independence. The share of the government budget going to health care fell by about a third between 1991 and 1992, and the percentage of GDP spent on health care fell from just over 4 to 2 per cent, where it stayed in subsequent years (Brooks and Thant 1998). In both Kazakhstan and Turkmenistan, the limited long-term commitment to social spending appears to be related to declining standards of governance, either due to prestigious presidential projects or to corruption. Examples of major projects in Turkmenistan are the presidential palace and new Ashgabat airport; in Kazakhstan, it is the new capital city of Astana. Governance in Kazakhstan is analysed more fully by Kalyuzhnova (1998) and Olcott (1998).

Apart from the declining resources available for public spending on health, the new environment of the 1990s has created fresh funding difficulties. Even during the Soviet era, much expenditure on health and education was managed at the local level, albeit following nationally determined norms and with resource transfers managed by central planners. Since independence, all five central Asian republics have faced challenges of managing vertical fiscal imbalance – that is, the gap between national and local revenue and expenditure. Klugman (1999) provides evidence, mainly from Kazakhstan, of the substantial regional disparities in educational services that have emerged during the 1990s as a result of vertical fiscal imbalance.

Thus, not only have the resources available for public spending declined, but geographical equity has also diminished. The most innovative approach to providing decentralized social services has been in Uzbekistan, but significant regional variations have been found even in this case (Coudouel and Marnie 1999).

Implications for private funding of health care

The macroeconomic pressures leading to declining and less equal public provision of health services are also likely to limit the emergence of offsetting private expenditure. According to Falkingham (Chapter 4), sharply declining incomes prevent most people from substituting private spending on health for declining public provision. In the poorer regions of central Asia, most people have little money available after meeting basic housing and food needs. A World Bank survey of 150 households in Bishkek in June 1995 revealed that households spent, on average, 70 per cent of their income on food and 10 per cent on energy; the lowest quartile spent 78 per cent on food and 22 per cent on energy (Finkel and Garcia 1997). Such figures paint a grim picture – inadequate incomes trying to cover basic needs – of a substantial part of the population of the capital city of Kyrgyzstan. Lack of disposable income makes it unlikely that large-scale private health markets will emerge soon.

The traditions of extended assistance and the emergence of a new rich class are the two countering forces to grim poverty. The extended family remains strong in most of central Asia, and local self-help groups also exist in various forms, so that people join together to lend money to a member of the group who is in trouble (Falkingham *et al.* 1997). Thus, although private health care may appear to be beyond the reach of poor individuals, these countering insurance mechanisms might allow people to afford health care when they need it.

The increased inequality in income has created an elite who can afford to buy health care. The number of people in this group is unclear, although some at the pinnacle of the new elite can afford (and choose) to go overseas for major treatment.

One problem in assessing changes in income and wealth distribution is the substantial reduction in the use of financial intermediaries (dis-intermediation). The hyperinflation of the early 1990s and confiscatory currency reforms of 1993 and 1994 led to distrust of domestic currencies. Failure to create well-functioning financial systems during the 1990s has also discouraged the use of financial institutions. The result of these developments is clear, but the magnitude is not. Because barter is highly inconvenient, the general pattern has been to convert the central Asian republics into cash economies, where the national currency and foreign currencies (primarily United States dollars) are the major means of exchange – both leaving little trace of actual trans-actions. This move to a cash economy has been apparent in the health and education services, where it is widely recognized that access to particular insti-tutions or services requires cash payments to teachers, doctors or adminis-trators, but these transactions are largely unrecorded (see also Falkingham, Chapter 4; Kutzin and Cashin, Chapter 8). The ability of the *nouveau riche* to seek treatment abroad is facilitated by the large number of US$100 bills in the economy.

Complicating the analysis of both the demand side and the supply side is the large-scale emigration that took place during the 1990s, especially from Kazakhstan and Kyrgyzstan. The composition of the emigrants is skewed towards the more skilled element, reducing the potential market for private health care and the availability of trained medical practitioners.

Conclusions

The decade of the 1990s witnessed huge economic changes in central Asia. In all five republics, real output was lower in 1999 than it was a decade earlier, inequality and poverty increased, and inflation, although much reduced from the early 1990s, continues. Government expenditures have fallen in real terms and the willingness to maintain the share of public spending going to health care has varied. Problems of governance in some countries exacerbate the decline in public health services. Overall, the need for all countries to continue progress towards fiscal balance suggests that there is little reason to expect significant increases in public funding for the health systems of central Asian republics in the near future. The prospects for private health care offsetting the decline in public provision of such services are also restricted by the macroeconomic pressures. The combination of declining average real income and increasing inequality have left many people with no discretionary income after meeting basic needs for food and shelter. Traditions of mutual assistance through local community groups or the extended family provide some relief among the poor, but the monetary amounts are limited. There is also a class of newly rich, which has cash and can afford private health care locally or abroad, but the number of people involved is probably not very large.

References

Anderson, K. and Pomfret, R. (2000) Living standards during transition to a market economy: the Kyrgyz Republic in 1993 and 1996, *Journal of Comparative Economics*, 26(3): 502–23.

Atkinson, A. and Micklewright, J. (1992) *Economic Transformation in Eastern Europe and the Distribution of Income*. Cambridge: Cambridge University Press.

Blanchard, O. (1997) *The Economics of Post-Communist Transition*. Oxford: Clarendon Press.

Brooks, D. and Thant, M. (1998) *Social Sector Issues in Transitional Economies of Asia*. Oxford: Oxford University Press.

Cheasty, A. and Davis, J. (1996) Fiscal transition in countries of the former Soviet Union: an interim assessment, *MOCT-MOST: Economic Policy in Transitional Economies*, 6(3): 7–34.

Coudouel, A. and Marnie, S. (1999) From universal to targeted social assistance: an assessment of the Uzbeck experience, *MOCT-MOST: Economic Policy in Transitional Economies*, 9(4): 43–58.

Craig, J. (1999) Fiscal adjustment, in E. Gurgen, H. Snoek, J. Craig *et al.* (eds) *Economic Reforms in Kazakhstan, Kyrgyz Republic, Tajikistan, Turkmenistan and Uzbekistan*, Occasional Paper No. 183. Washington, DC: World Bank.

European Bank for Reconstruction and Development (1997) *Transition Report 1997*. London: European Bank for Reconstruction and Development.

European Bank for Reconstruction and Development (2000) *Transition Report Update*. London: European Bank for Reconstruction and Development.

Falkingham, J. (1999) *Welfare in Transition: Trends in Poverty and Well-being in Central Asia*, CASE Paper No. 20. London: Centre for Analysis of Social Exclusion, London School of Economics.

Falkingham, J. (2000a) From security to uncertainty: the impact of economic change on child welfare in central Asia, in K. Vleminckx and T. M. Smeeding (eds) *Child Well-being in Modern Nations*. Bristol: Policy Press.

Falkingham, J. (2000b) *Women in Tajikistan*. Manila: Asian Development Bank.

Falkingham, J., Klugman, J., Marnie, S. and Micklewright, J. (1997) *Household Welfare in Central Asia*. Basingstoke: Macmillan.

Finkel, E. and Garcia, H. (1997) Rehabilitating the Kyrgyz Republic's power and district heating services, in M. Cernea and A. Kudat (eds) *Social Assessments for Better Development: Case Studies in Russia and Central Asia*. Washington, DC: World Bank.

Kalyuzhnova, Y. (1998) *The Kazakstani Economy: Independence and Transition*. Basingstoke: Macmillan.

Klugman, J. (1999) Financing and governance of education in central Asia, *MOCT-MOST: Economic Policy in Transitional Economies*, 9(4): 423–42.

Milanovic, B. (1998) *Income, Inequality, and Poverty during the Transition from Planned to Market Economy*. Washington, DC: World Bank.

Olcott, M. B. (1998) *Kazakhstan: A Faint-hearted Democracy*. Washington, DC: Carnegie Endowment for International Peace.

Pomfret, R. (1995) *The Economies of Central Asia*. Princeton, NJ: Princeton University Press.

Pomfret, R. (1996) *Asian Economies in Transition*. Cheltenham: Edward Elgar.

Pomfret, R. (1999) Living standards in central Asia, *MOCT-MOST: Economic Policy in Transitional Economies*, 9(4): 395–421.

Pomfret, R. and Anderson, K. (1997) *Uzbekistan: Welfare Impact of Slow Transition*, UNU/WIDER WP135. Helsinki: United Nations University World Institute for Development Economics Research.

Tarr, D. (1994) How moving to world prices affects the terms of trade of 15 countries of the former Soviet Union, *Journal of Comparative Economics*, 18: 1–24.

UNDP (1999) *Central Asia Prospects for Development*. New York: UNDP.

World Bank (1992) *Measuring the Incomes of Economies of the Former Soviet Union*, Policy Research Working Paper WPS 1057. Washington, DC: World Bank.

chapter four

Poverty, affordability and access to health care

Jane Falkingham

Introduction

Most countries of former Soviet central Asia have either initiated reform of the health sector or are contemplating it, as is discussed in Part II. With negative real income growth and falling government revenues, a key concern of many governments is to secure additional financing for health care services through non-budgetary sources, such as hypothecated payroll taxes, premium-based insurance and increased private financing through patient cost-sharing. Before such reforms can be debated, however, careful consideration is needed of both the current level and distribution of household expenditures on health care, and of the extent to which increased patient cost-sharing through charges may influence access to health care, especially among the poor. The ability to pay for health care is one of the most important issues facing policy-makers today.

In this chapter, I first examine the impact on living standards of the transition from a planned economy to a market economy in the five republics of former Soviet central Asia: Kazakhstan, Kyrgyzstan, Tajikistan, Turkmenistan and Uzbekistan. With regard to these transitions, I then investigate the growth of out-of-pocket payments for health care within the region. Finally, I evaluate the impact of these payments on household welfare and the extent to which they may impede access to health care among the poor.

Trends in household welfare

At independence, all of the newly formed central Asian republics inherited high levels of human capital. Education and health care were free, and there were extensive social services and transfers. High levels of social expenditures and relatively low wage differentials had resulted in an overall distribution of income that was much more egalitarian than that in most market economies (Atkinson and Micklewright 1992). Under the Soviet system, poverty did not officially exist, although there were *maloobespechenn'* (under-provisioned) families (Braithwaite 1995).

Poverty, however, was not unknown. Atkinson and Micklewright (1992), using a per person income of 75 rubles per month as the national poverty threshold, estimated that, in 1989, 31 million people, or 11 per cent of the total population of the Soviet Union, were living in poverty. The proportion varied considerably across the republics, with over half of those living in Tajikistan having a per person income of less than 75 rubles a month compared to just 2 per cent in Estonia (see Table 3.1 in Chapter 3). Together, the central Asian republics contained just over half of all the poor, while accounting for only 17 per cent of the Soviet population. Thus, even before the turmoil of the early 1990s, a significant proportion of the population of central Asia was surviving on a low income.

In Chapter 3, Pomfret notes that since independence the interruption of inter-republic trade within the former Soviet Union and the impact of tight government stabilization policies, combined with the withdrawal of subsidies from Moscow, have resulted in a severe economic depression across the region. Figure 4.1 shows the change in real gross domestic product (GDP) since 1989. Compiling a consistent series of data on economic performance across time presents considerable problems, both due to changes in definitions and variations

Figure 4.1 Cumulative change in real GDP in central Asia, 1989–2000 (1989 = 100)

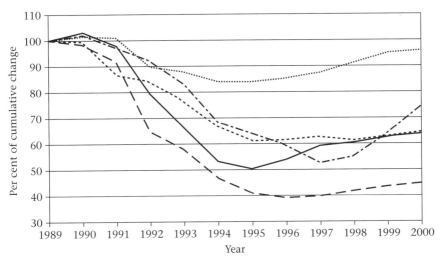

Note: The figures for 1999 are estimates and the figures for 2000 are projections
Sources: 1990 and 1991 (European Bank for Reconstruction and Development 1997);
other years (European Bank for Reconstruction and Development 2000)

in data quality. Absolute numbers should be treated with caution. The overall trends are clear, however. Economic growth was negative in all countries in the region up to 1995, when a gradual reversal of fortunes began, with the exception of Turkmenistan, which experienced a 25 per cent drop in GDP in 1997. Recovery has been slow and, despite recent improvements, real output remains significantly below pre-transition levels. Contributing to this slow progress has been the recent turmoil in the economy of the Russian Federation, with the subsequent loss of the region's export markets to the Russian Federation and exchange rate instability following the collapse of the rouble. In 1999, real GDP was still below half its pre-transition level in Tajikistan and a third below the pre-transition level in Kazakhstan, Kyrgyzstan and Turkmenistan.

Inequality

In common with other countries in transition, the fall in output has been accompanied by a rise in the inequality of incomes. For the years 1987–90, it is estimated that the Gini coefficients for per person income in the central Asian republics, estimated from the family budget surveys, ranged from 0.29 in Tajikistan and Turkmenistan to 0.31 in Kyrgyzstan, with Kazakhstan occupying a middle position of 0.30. (The Gini coefficient is a summary measure of inequality: 0.00 implies perfect equality, where every observation has the same income; 1.00 implies perfect inequality, where the last observation has all the income). By 1993, the Gini coefficient had increased to 0.33 in Kazakhstan, to 0.36 in Turkmenistan and to 0.55 in Kyrgyzstan (Milanovic 1998), and it is estimated that the Gini coefficient for Tajikistan in 1999 was 0.47 (Falkingham 2000a). These increases in inequality are among the highest ever recorded over such a short time interval. With Gini coefficients around 0.5 or above, income inequality in Tajikistan and Kyrgyzstan is now comparable to that observed in some of the most unequal Latin American economies. The unprecedented magnitude and speed of the change in income distribution has left many people disorientated, and the emergence of a small, but highly visible elite has heightened the sense of relative deprivation among people at the bottom.

Poverty

Besides an increase in relative poverty, there has also been a rise in the number of people in central Asia who live in absolute poverty. The economic dislocation of transition has both exacerbated the disadvantage of those groups traditionally thought to be poor (pensioners, families with a large number of children and single-parent families) and given rise to new groups of poor. These include the families of workers on leave without pay, the long-term unemployed, agricultural workers, young people in search of their first job and a growing number of refugees – both economic refugees and persons displaced as a result of civil conflict.

Since independence, World Bank sponsored living standards surveys have been held in four of the Republics: Kazakhstan, Kyrgyzstan, Tajikistan and

Table 4.1 Absolute poverty rates in central Asia and other selected countries of the former Soviet Union

Country	Survey date	Headcount index		1988 GNP (US$ per person)[a]	1998 GNP (US$ PPP 1996 per person)
		US$2.15 per day (% pop.)	US$4.30 per day (% pop.)		
Kazakhstan	1996	5.7	30.9	1340	4317
Turkmenistan	1998	7.0	34.4	502	2875
Kyrgyzstan	1998	49.1	84.1	380	2247
Tajikistan	1999	68.3	95.8	370	1040
Georgia	1999	18.9	54.2	970	3429
Russian Federation	1998	18.8	50.3	2260	6186
Azerbaijan	1999	23.5	64.2	480	2168
Republic of Moldova	1999	55.4	84.6	380	1995
Armenia	1999	43.5	86.2	460	2074

Notes: The poverty headcount numbers are based on the international poverty lines of US$2.15 and US$4.30 purchasing power parity (PPP) per person per day. The PPP was calculated using 1996 estimates, which take into account recent changes in the price structure following periods of hyperinflation in the early 1990s, trade liberalization and real exchange rate realignment. No comparable data were available for Uzbekistan. [a] World Bank Atlas method.

Source: World Bank (2000)

Turkmenistan. The results from the most recent survey in each of the central Asian republics, together with comparable data from selected other countries in the Commonwealth of Independent States (CIS), are presented in Table 4.1.

According to the US$2.15 per day absolute poverty line used by the World Bank, the proportion of the population living in poverty in central Asia varies from 6 per cent in Kazakhstan to 68 per cent in Tajikistan. Using the US$4.30 per day poverty line results in significantly higher poverty rates in both Kazakhstan and Turkmenistan, with around a third of the population in both countries living below this standard, while in Tajikistan poverty by this standard is an almost universal experience.

There is no comparable data available for Uzbekistan. Analysis of a household survey conducted by the European University Institute in 1995, however, suggested that around 30 per cent of the population were poor (Coudouel 1998). Of course, poverty rates depend both on the poverty line chosen and the definition of income (or expenditure) against which this line is compared. Nevertheless, the above data indicate that a significant proportion of people in central Asia survive on few material resources.

Who are the poor?

To develop effective policies to alleviate poverty, it is important to identify those groups that comprise the majority of the poor in each country. To compare

Figure 4.2 Composition of the poor by age group in four central Asian republics

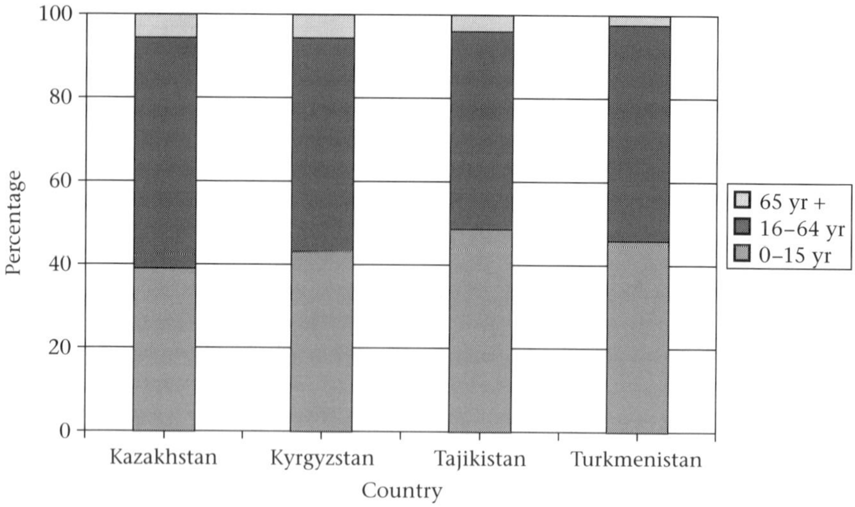

Source: Based on Figure 13 in World Bank (2000: Chapter 2)

the pattern of poverty across countries, the poverty line in each country is set at 50 per cent of median per person consumption. This allows us to look at the characteristics of the poor, relative to others in the same country.

As Figure 4.2 clearly shows, children account for around half of the poor in central Asia. This is not surprising, as children also account for between 35 per cent (in Kazakhstan) and 48 per cent (Tajikistan) of the population in the central Asian republics. If, however, one examines the risk of being poor relative to the national average, children in central Asia do experience an elevated risk of poverty. Children in Kazakhstan are 24 per cent more likely to be poor than on average, while in Turkmenistan children are 14 per cent more likely, in Kyrgyzstan 12 per cent more likely and in Tajikistan 7 per cent more likely. In all central Asian republics where data are available, the relative risk of a family being poor increases with the number of children in the family (Table 4.2). Together with the elderly, children are also more likely to suffer from acute ill health problems and have greater health care needs than other groups.

Table 4.2 shows how the relative risk of poverty (that is, the ratio of the poverty rate for a particular subgroup to the average poverty rate) in the central Asian republics varies by selected household characteristics. If a particular subgroup has a relative poverty rate greater than 1, this implies that the group has a higher incidence of poverty than the average and that the characteristic defining that group may be a correlate of poverty that can be used in policy design.

Poverty is associated with labour market participation. Households headed by an unemployed or retired person are more likely to be poor than the general population, except in Tajikistan. Although there is an elevated risk of poverty, this risk is not as great as might be expected. This is because being employed does not necessarily result in higher income, as wages are often low and are frequently in arrears. As such, the labour market affords little protection against

Table 4.2   Relative poverty risks for households with selected characteristics within the central Asian republics

Relative risk of poverty for households where:	Kazakhstan 1996	Kyrgyzstan 1997	Tajikistan 1999	Turkmenistan 1998
No children	0.65	0.36	0.32	0.38
Two children	0.93	0.82	0.81	0.66
Three or more children	2.20	1.34	1.11	1.36
Head is retired	1.10	1.30	0.93	1.10
Head is unemployed	1.29	1.12	0.71	1.76
Rural	1.21	1.23	1.02	1.39
Access to a private plot	0.80	1.02	0.99	1.18

Note: Poverty is defined as below 50 per cent median per person consumption.

Source: Derived from World Bank (2000: Appendix D)

households falling into poverty. Similarly, although poverty is generally higher in rural areas, access to a private plot of land on which to grow food is no guarantee against being poor, although it may be critical in some households' survival.

Other dimensions of poverty

Material resources (or a lack of them) reflect just one, albeit very important, dimension of poverty. Monetary measures fail to capture other important aspects of an individual's well-being, such as public goods, community resources, social relations, culture, security and the natural environment. Alternative indicators of poverty, or well-being, are provided by measures that focus on an individual's capabilities – that is, a person's capacity to live a healthy life, free of avoidable morbidity, having adequate nourishment, being informed and knowledgeable, being capable of reproduction, enjoying personal security, and being able to freely and actively participate in society. Such measures are included in the Human Development Index and the Human Poverty Index calculated by the United Nations Development Programme.

Table 4.3 presents information on the components of the Human Development Index for both 1991 and 1998. Over the last decade, there has been deterioration in most indicators of human development. The most fundamental measure of the well-being of a population is how long, on average, its members can expect to live. Life expectancy at birth has fallen in all central Asian republics, with the exception of Kyrgyzstan, where it has remained stable. This snapshot, however, masks large fluctuations within the decade (as discussed by McKee and Chenet in Chapter 5).

The countries of central Asia began the transition with almost universal literacy. Over the last decade, however, there have been serious reversals in several countries, and it is likely that the high literacy rates of the past will not be sustained in future generations. One of the most worrying trends is the decline in the proportion of children aged 3–6 years enrolled in pre-primary

Table 4.3   Human development indicators in central Asia, 1991 and 1998

	1991			1998			Rank HDI (of 174)
	Life expectancy at birth (years)	Adult literacy rate (%)	Real GDP per person (PPP US$)	Life expectancy at birth (years)	Adult literacy rate (%)	Real GDP per person (PPP US$)	
Kazakhstan	69.0	97.5	4490	67.9	99.0	4378	73
Kyrgyzstan	68.0	97.0	3683	68.0	97.0	2317	98
Tajikistan	70.0	96.7	2180	67.5	99.0	1041	110
Turkmenistan	66.0	97.7	3540	65.7	98.0	2550	100
Uzbekistan	69.0	97.2	2790	67.8	88.0	2053	106

Note: HDI = Human Development Index.

Sources: Falkingham *et al.* (1997: Table 1.1) and UNDP (2000)

Table 4.4   Changes in school enrolment rates (per cent of the relevant age group) in central Asia, 1989 and 1998

	Kindergarten net enrolment rate (% 3–6-year-olds)			General secondary enrolment rate (% 15–18-year-olds)		
	1989	1998	% change 1989–98	1989	1998	% change 1989–98
Kazakhstan	52.2	11.0	−79	30.4	21.0	−31
Kyrgyzstan	31.3	8.7	−72	36.6[b]	36.2	−1
Tajikistan	16.7	7.7[a]	−54	41.5	16.0	−61
Turkmenistan	36.0	19.0	−47	39.0	25.0	−36
Uzbekistan	38.5	16.1	−58	37.5	28.6[c]	−24

Notes: [a] 1996, [b] 1990, [c] 1997.

Source: TransMONEE database (UNICEF 2000)

school education (Table 4.4). Before independence, attendance at kindergarten was widespread. About a half were enrolled at kindergartens in Kazakhstan and around a third in Kyrgyzstan, Turkmenistan and Uzbekistan. Enrolment was lowest in Tajikistan, at less than a sixth of the children in the target age group. Since independence, rates have fallen dramatically by a half to three-quarters in all countries, with consequent implications for child development.

Basic education continues to be compulsory throughout the central Asian republics, and the enrolment of 7- to 15-year-olds generally has remained high, although there is evidence of a growing problem of absenteeism (Falkingham 2000b). Post-compulsory education enrolments, however, have fallen dramatically. The proportion of 15- to 18-year-olds attending general secondary schools has declined by over 60 per cent in Tajikistan, by a third in Kazakhstan and Turkmenistan, and by a quarter in Uzbekistan.

In summary, the human costs of transition within central Asia have been high. The proportion of the population living in absolute poverty has increased and the achievements of the past, in terms of human development, are now under threat.

The funding gap and the growth of private payments

During the Soviet era, the health care systems throughout central Asia were characterized by widespread access and high levels of service use. Health care provision was extensive and free at the point of delivery. Since independence, health services have deteriorated rapidly in the face of severe financial constraints, exacerbated in Tajikistan by extensive damage to the infrastructure during the civil war.

As Pomfret has discussed in Chapter 3, government expenditure as a share of GDP in Tajikistan fell by nearly two-thirds from 50 per cent to 17 per cent between 1991 and 1997. Elsewhere, proportionate declines ranged from around a third in Uzbekistan to a fifth in Kyrgyzstan. The steep decline in real government expenditures has eroded the capacity of the health system to provide effective and accessible medical care to the public. The collapse in GDP, combined with lower government spending, has meant that real spending on health has declined sharply to between only a quarter to a third of that before independence.

The widening gap between the health care budget and the actual costs of care has resulted in an increased burden on the household, both in terms of official charges and, more commonly, under-the-counter or informal payments. Informal payments have been defined as 'payments to individual and institutional providers in-kind or cash that are outside the official payment channels, or are purchases that are meant to be covered by the health care system' (Lewis 2002). Anecdotal and empirical evidence suggests that informal payments for health care are extensive in central Asia. Although in principle medical supplies and drugs required as part of inpatient treatment remain free, the scarcity of such items in medical facilities has led to an increasing number of patients having to purchase them. Furthermore, local budgetary constraints and petrol shortages have eroded the capacity of the ambulance service, and often patients have to provide their own transportation to medical facilities. Importantly, informal user charges for consultations are frequently being imposed to help subsidize salaries, despite the official position that such consultations remain free of charge.

Health workers are among the lowest paid workers in the region. For example, in 1998 in Tajikistan, the average monthly salary among employees in the health sector was US$4.80 compared to the workforce average of US$11 and an average of US$33 for workers in key enterprises, such as the state mining, electricity and manufacturing companies (Rahminov *et al.* 2000). Data from the National Statistical Committee of the Kyrgyz Republic (2000) also indicate that health workers are poorly paid; their official salaries fell from 79 per cent of the average salary in 1995 to just 59 per cent in 1998. As well as being low, salaries in the public sector are often paid late, with arrears of several months being common. Given this, many physicians and nurses in the region are increasingly reliant on informal payments and in-kind gifts from patients. An in-depth study undertaken in a rural district of Turkmenistan found that over a half of all respondents had paid a health care professional for services in addition to the customary 'thank-you gifts' (Ladbury 1997).

Although there is a tradition in central Asia and the Caucasus of presenting monetary or in-kind gifts as a mark of gratitude, there is evidence that, over time, this voluntary tradition is being supplanted by provider-generated demands for payment as a precondition for treatment. Since independence, the practice of charging patients for consultations or hospital admission has increased in Kyrgyzstan (Falkingham 1998). In 1993, of those people consulting a doctor, 11 per cent reported making a payment. By 1994, this had risen to 25 per cent and, by 1996, over half of patients reported making some payment in connection with a consultation. Paying for inpatient admission in Kyrgyzstan was non-existent in 1993. By 1994, 24 per cent of inpatients paid for admission and, of those paying, nearly a third (31 per cent) had not expected to pay (Abel-Smith and Falkingham 1995). By 1996, however, payments related to hospital admissions had become widespread, with three-quarters of the people admitted reporting some payment.

In neighbouring Kazakhstan, a study of informal payments for health care suggests that virtually all patients now make some payment to practitioners for ostensibly free services. Patient payments for medicines in hospitals account for between 25 and 30 per cent of the total health budget for material items (Ensor and Savelyeva 1998).

In Tajikistan, in 1999, of those persons who reported seeking medical assistance 2 weeks before the survey, nearly a half (48 per cent) reported making payments for their last consultation and 18 per cent gave gifts. The proportion making a payment for the consultation varied according to the household's financial status, with 38 per cent of the poorest households making such a payment compared with 53 per cent of the richest. The proportions reporting a gift were 9 per cent and 17 per cent, respectively (Falkingham 2000a).

There is also evidence that informal payments in the form of in-kind contributions are widespread and constitute a significant resource input for inpatient care. In a household survey conducted in two *oblasts* of Kyrgyzstan in 1997, Blomquist (1997) found that most inpatients had to provide many of their own inputs, including medicines (65 per cent), bedding and towels (55 per cent), laundry (90 per cent) and food (84 per cent). In Tajikistan, recent evidence indicates that these contributions have extended into services that are normally the responsibility of health professionals. In the lowest income group, 66 per cent of inpatients from poor households reported that family members administered medicines, and 43 per cent reported that family members had administered injections. The corresponding figures for the richest fifth of the population were still high: 54 per cent for drugs and 24 per cent for injections (Falkingham, in press).

Poverty and access to health care

There is a small, but growing, body of evidence that the growth of out-of-pocket payments is beginning to affect access to health care. Evidence from

Table 4.5 Reasons for non-use of medical services by area of residence, Kyrgyzstan, 1996

Main reason for non-use of medical services	Urban (%)	Rural (%)	Republic (%)
Self-medicated	**56**	**47**	**50**
Not needed	12	9	10
Too far	2	5	4
Poor service	5	5	5
Too expensive	**20**	**29**	**25**
Other	7	7	7

Source: Author's own analysis of the Kyrgyzstan Living Standards Measurement Survey (1996)

the 1996 Living Standards Measurement Survey in Kyrgyzstan shows that, among those people either injured or sick in the month before the survey, and who either chose or were forced not to seek medical attention, the cost of treatment was the second most important reason cited (Table 4.5). Not surprisingly, rural residents were more likely than urban residents to report not seeking medical attention due to the distance involved. Rural residents were also more likely than urban residents not to receive medical attention due to cost constraints. It should be noted that poverty in Kyrgyzstan has also been found to be higher in rural areas.

A similar analysis for Tajikistan shows that the cost expected was cited as the main reason for not using health care by a third of the respondents. The proportion varied according to the economic status of the household, with those living in the poorest fifth being nearly twice as likely to report affordability as the main reason for not seeking health care than the richest fifth (Table 4.6). Even among the richest fifth, a lack of resources was cited by a quarter of the respondents. This is not surprising, given that an estimated 96 per cent of

Table 4.6 Reasons for not seeking medical assistance by economic status of the household, Tajikistan, 1999

Main reason for non-use of medical services	Poorest 20%	Next poorest quintile	Third poorest quintile	Next richest quintile	Richest 20%	Republic
Self medicated	**42**	**49**	**50**	**55**	**65**	**52**
Believed problem would go away	11	3	16	5	6	8
Too far/facility closed/poor service	1	2	4	5	3	3
Too expensive	**42**	**41**	**28**	**30**	**24**	**33**
Other	5	5	2	5	2	4

Note: Using chi-squared statistics, all values are significant at $P < 0.001$.

Source: Author's own analysis of the Tajikistan Living Standards Survey (1999)

Table 4.7 Percentage of persons ill in the 4 weeks before the survey, reporting all required drugs obtained and, if not, the reasons for not obtaining them, Kyrgyzstan, 1993–96

Category	1993 (%)	1994 (%)	1996 (%)
Obtained all	50	66	74
Obtained only a part	—	23	—
None obtained at all	50	11	26
Why not obtained?			
Not in stock	78	49	9
Too expensive	17	35	73
Other	5	72	18

Note: In 1994, percentages for why medicines were not obtained do not sum to 100%, as respondents were allowed to give more than one answer.

Sources: Kyrgyzstan Multi-Purpose Survey (1993); Kyrgyzstan Health Financing Survey (1994); Kyrgyzstan Living Standards Survey (1996)

the population of Tajikistan are currently living below the official minimum subsistence basket (Falkingham 2000a).

Similar concerns are also present in other areas of health care. Table 4.7 shows the percentage of persons in Kyrgyzstan who were or were not able to obtain all the medicines required. It illustrates two points. First, immediately following independence, a large proportion of people were unable to obtain all the drugs necessary, the key reason being a lack of availability. Since 1993, however, the problems of drug supply have eased considerably and, in 1996, three-quarters of people were able to obtain all the medicines needed. Second, of those people who did not, the main constraint now appears not to be availability, but the ability to pay. In 1993, just 17 per cent of those unable to obtain all the medicines required reported the main reason to be 'they could not afford them'. By 1996, this had risen to a staggering 73 per cent. Clearly, the high cost of drugs and other medical services is an impediment to use for some sections of the population.

In other countries in the region, access to pharmaceuticals was also significantly affected by household economic status. From the 1996 Living Standards Survey in Kazakhstan, Sari *et al.* (2000) found that the poor were less likely than the non-poor to have purchased medicine 30 days before the survey. Although the poor are more likely to have access to the limited subsidies for medications that are available for vulnerable groups, these subsidies have been reduced dramatically, and it is likely that the high cost of medicines deters the poor from purchasing necessary medications. In Tajikistan, individuals from the poorest households were significantly less likely than other groups to receive a prescription from the physician and, of those who did, most (70 per cent) were unable to buy the prescribed medications (Table 4.8). This has implications for any revolving drug schemes to be developed in Tajikistan, and elsewhere in the region, and underscores the importance of establishing careful exemption policies that protect the poor, especially children and women – the most frequent consumers of essential pharmaceuticals.

Table 4.8 Medication use in the 2 weeks before the survey in Tajikistan, by household economic status

Category	Poorest 20%	Richest 20%	All of Tajikistan
Of those who consulted a doctor, % who received prescription	14	21	20
Of those with a prescription, % unable to buy prescribed medication	70	24	36
Reasons why unable to buy prescription			
Too expensive	**90**	**80**	**84**
Could not find	10	10	7
Other	—	10	9

Note: Using chi-squared statistics, all values are significant at $P < 0.001$.

Source: Author's own analysis of the Tajikistan Living Standards Survey (1999)

In summary, official and informal payments are acting both to deter people from seeking medical assistance and, once advice has been sought, to deter them from receiving the most appropriate treatment.

The impact of health payments on household welfare

There is also evidence that, besides acting as a deterrent to use, the need to make payments for health care imposes a substantial financial burden on families unfortunate enough to experience illness or injury and that these burdens have probably grown worse as the need to pay for health care services (often informally) has grown. In Kyrgyzstan, in 1994, the total cost of an illness episode for one member of a family exceeded household monthly income in 20 per cent of households experiencing an illness; furthermore, almost 50 per cent of inpatients reported severe difficulties in finding the money to pay for their stay. Many had to borrow money or sell assets, such as farm animals, to obtain the money needed (Abel-Smith and Falkingham 1995). From 1996 to 1997, monthly per person expenditures for chronic illness rose by about 40 per cent in real terms. On average, these expenditures were about 125 per cent of monthly per person consumption expenditures. For chronic illness, among the poorest 20 per cent of persons surveyed, expenditures were more than three times per person consumption levels (Dorabawila 1999).

Evidence from the 1999 household survey in Tajikistan reveals a situation similar to that in Kyrgyzstan, although one that is undoubtedly more severe in its consequences. The median amount reported to be paid for an ambulatory visit and associated services (including standard fees, informal gifts, travel costs and the costs of prescribed medicines) exceeded median monthly per person income (Table 4.9). Although poorer persons paid less than richer persons, median consultation (and associated) expenditures of persons in the poorest quintile exceeded median monthly per person income, whereas such

Table 4.9 Mean (median) value of out-of-pocket payments for consultations and associated medications by quintile, Tajikistan, 1999

Category	Poorest 20%	Richest 20%	All of Tajikistan
Official payments	2047 (1000)	10 682 (2000)	5 006 (1500)
Informal gifts (inc. money)	2125 (1500)	21 882 (5000)	9 423 (3000)
Cost of travel to consultation	1326 (200)	1 355 (500)	1 217 (400)
Prescription medication	819 (800)	15 740 (9250)	6 439 (3000)
Other medicine	990 (500)	6 514 (1000)	3 034 (1000)
Per person monthly household income	1890 (2054)	28 372 (22 504)	11 036 (7794)

Note: Values are expressed in Tajik roubles (TR). In May 1999, US$1 = TR 1200.

Source: Author's own analysis of the Tajikistan Living Standards Survey (1999)

expenditures by persons in the richest quintile, while high, did not. The costs associated with inpatient care were much greater and were a significant financial burden for all families, although the likely out-of-pocket expenditures for a person from the poorest quintile could easily exceed annual income. To cope with these high costs, many families unfortunate enough to suffer a hospitalization are compromising their future financial well-being and possibly becoming impoverished. Nearly a third of the families surveyed went into debt (or increased their debt) to meet hospital costs, and just over a quarter sold household assets (Falkingham, in press).

Similarly, the Kazakhstan Living Standards Measurement Survey found that the cost of a physician visit was as high as 21 per cent of monthly income for the poor, compared with 6 per cent for the rich. Among those people who purchased medicine, the expenditure represented nearly 40 per cent of monthly household income for the poor and 10.8 per cent for the non-poor (Sari *et al.* 2000). Hospitalization also poses a significant threat to the economic well-being of the poor in Kazakhstan, since Sari *et al.* (2000) found that expenditures for hospital stays were on average more than 2.5 times monthly income in poor households.

Conclusions

It is clear that the human cost of transition in central Asia has been high. The percentage of the population living in absolute poverty has increased and the achievements of the past, in terms of relatively high life expectancy and near universal literacy, are now being threatened. During reform, it is essential to protect universal access to basic social services for the poor. If fiscal expediency makes it necessary to introduce charges for any of these services, including health care, then it is essential that these charges are explicit rather than informal, and that they are accompanied by targeted exemptions for low-income families. The present system of unregulated prescription charges and payments for consultations is both inefficient and inequitable. The costs falling on the users of the health services vary widely and arbitrarily. The ability to pay for health care is now a major problem among the poor, and there is growing evidence that, despite informal systems of targeting, access to health care is being affected.

The challenge facing policy-makers is how to take them into account *and* to ensure that equity in access to health care is achieved. This is important from both a human development and a human rights perspective. The long-term development prospects of the central Asian republics rest on their human, intellectual and social capital. What is clear is that a growing proportion of the poor in these countries can no longer afford 'free' health care.

References

Abel-Smith, B. and Falkingham, J. (1995) *Financing Health Services in Kyrgyzstan: The Extent of Private Payments*, LSE Health Working Paper. London: London School of Economics.

Atkinson, A. and Micklewright, J. (1992) *Economic Transformation in Eastern Europe and the Distribution of Income*. Cambridge: Cambridge University Press.

Blomquist, J. (1997) *Results and Recommendations from the Social Services Household Survey of Jalal-abad and Osh Oblasts, Kyrgyz Republic*, Report prepared for the Asian Development Bank. Bethesda, MD: Asian Development Bank.

Braithwaite, J. (1995) The old and new poor in Russia: trends in poverty, in J. Klugman (ed.) *Poverty in Russia: An Assessment*, Vol. 2, Report No. 14110-RU. Washington, DC: World Bank.

Coudouel, A. (1998) Living standards in Uzbekistan, PhD dissertation. Florence: European University Institute.

Dorabawila, V. (1999) *Health Status and Private Health Expenditures in the Kyrgyz Republic*. Washington, DC: World Bank.

Ensor, T. and Savelyeva, L. (1998) Informal payments for health care in the former Soviet Union: some evidence from Kazakhstan, *Health Policy and Planning*, 13(1): 41–9.

European Bank for Reconstruction and Development (1997) *Transition Report 1997*. London: European Bank for Reconstruction and Development.

European Bank for Reconstruction and Development (2000) *Transition Report Update*. London: European Bank for Reconstruction and Development.

Falkingham, J. (1998) Barriers to access? The growth of private payments for health care in Kyrgyzstan, *Eurohealth*, 4(6): 68–71.

Falkingham, J. (2000a) *A Profile of Poverty in Tajikistan*, CASE Discussion paper. London: Centre for Analysis of Social Exclusion, London School of Economics.

Falkingham, J. (2000b) From security to uncertainty: the impact of economic change on child welfare in central Asia, in K. Vleminckx and T.M. Smeeding (eds) *Child Well-being in Modern Nations*. Bristol: Policy Press.

Falkingham, J. (in press) Poverty, out-of-pocket payments and inequality in access to health care: evidence from Tajikistan, *Social Science and Medicine*.

Falkingham, J., Klugman, J., Marnie, S. and Micklewright, J. (1997) *Household Welfare in Central Asia*. Basingstoke: Macmillan.

Ladbury, S. (1997) *Turkmenistan Health Project: Social Assessment Study*. Washington, DC: World Bank.

Lewis, M. (2002) Informal health payments in eastern Europe and central Asia: issues, trends and policy implications, in E. Mossialos, A. Dixon, J. Figueras and J. Kutzin (eds) *Funding Health Care: Options for Europe*. Buckingham: Open University Press.

Milanovic, B. (1998) *Income, Inequality, and Poverty during the Transition from Planned to Market Economy*. Washington, DC: World Bank.

National Statistical Committee of the Kyrgyz Republic (2000) http://nsc.bishkek.su

Rahminov, R., Gedik, G. and Healy, J. (2000) *Health Care Systems in Transition: Tajikistan*. Copenhagen: European Observatory on Health Care Systems.

Sari, N., Langenbrunner, J. and Lewis, M. (2000) Affording out-of-pocket payments for health services: evidence from Kazakhstan, *Eurohealth*, 6(2): 37–9.

UNDP (2000) *Human Development Report 2000*. New York: Oxford University Press.

UNICEF (2000) *TransMONEE Database*. Florence: UNICEF.

World Bank (2000) *Making Transition Work for Everyone: Poverty and Inequality in Europe and Central Asia*. Washington, DC: World Bank.

chapter five

Patterns of health

Martin McKee and Laurent Chenet

Introduction

Central Asia has an unusual pattern of mortality and struggles with the double burden of infectious and non-communicable disease. Yet, in contrast to the Russian Federation and the Baltic republics, there is remarkably little published research on patterns of health and its determinants in the region. Although aggregate data on mortality from major disease categories are published by the World Health Organization (WHO), access to more detailed information (such as regional or socioeconomic differences, or to evidence about the validity of the data) has been difficult to obtain. In part, this reflects the very limited capacity for data analysis and interpretation within health ministries and universities in the region. There is also a persisting culture of secrecy in some places, with concerns about exposing perceived national failings to international scrutiny. For example, in at least one country there have been discussions by senior policy-makers about the possibility of refusing to provide data on notifications of syphilis to WHO, because of fears about the impact on the embryonic tourist industry.

Changes in life expectancy at birth

Although it has many limitations, life expectancy at birth, as a measure of overall health in a population, has the benefit of simplicity. Before 1991, life expectancy at birth was broadly similar to that in Russia, with the exception of female life expectancy in Turkmenistan, which was consistently about 4 years lower than in other republics. In particular, most of the republics exhibited similar changes to those seen in the Soviet Union in the mid-1980s, at the time of Gorbachev's anti-alcohol campaign. Kazakhstan and Kyrgyzstan behaved most like Russia, with only small changes in Tajikistan and Turkmenistan, and Uzbekistan occupied an intermediate position. Although these trends have

Figure 5.1   Life expectancy at birth, in years, for central Asian men

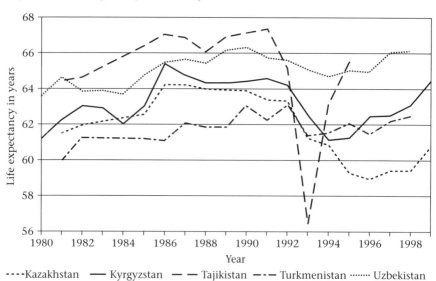

Source: WHO (2000)

not been subjected to detailed analysis, the close similarity to those seen in Russia, which are well understood, strongly suggests that alcohol has been a major cause of premature mortality, at least in Kazakhstan and Kyrgyzstan.

After 1990–92, life expectancy at birth fell in all countries. Tajikistan, however, requires separate consideration. The dramatic decline in life expectancy in the early 1990s coincided with the civil war. In addition to the estimated 60,000 deaths from communal violence (Rahminov *et al.* 2000), the war also led to mass movements of population and major weaknesses in death registration, so that meaningful analysis of the available data is impossible.

The decline in life expectancy among men was greatest in Kazakhstan and Kyrgyzstan, both of which followed trajectories that were very similar to that seen in the Soviet Union, with rather more gradual declines in Turkmenistan and Uzbekistan (Figure 5.1). The decline in female life expectancy was much more consistent (Figure 5.2), with Uzbekistan experiencing a steep fall similar to that seen in its northern neighbours. As with the changes seen in the 1980s, the similarity to the changes observed in the Soviet Union suggests the importance of alcohol as a proximate risk factor in the observed trends (Walberg *et al.* 1998). This is supported by the observation that countries such as Kazakhstan, which experienced a substantial increase in life expectancy during the 1985 anti-alcohol campaign, also saw a large decline in the early 1990s, whereas those where the 1985 improvement was less, such as Uzbekistan, experienced a small subsequent decline. The already low female life expectancy in Turkmenistan fell even further in 1994 to 66.5 years, before improving.

Differences in life expectancy by gender between countries in the former Soviet Union offer some important insights into determinants of disease. Compared with life expectancy in Russia, life expectancy of males in central

Figure 5.2 Life expectancy at birth, in years, for central Asian women

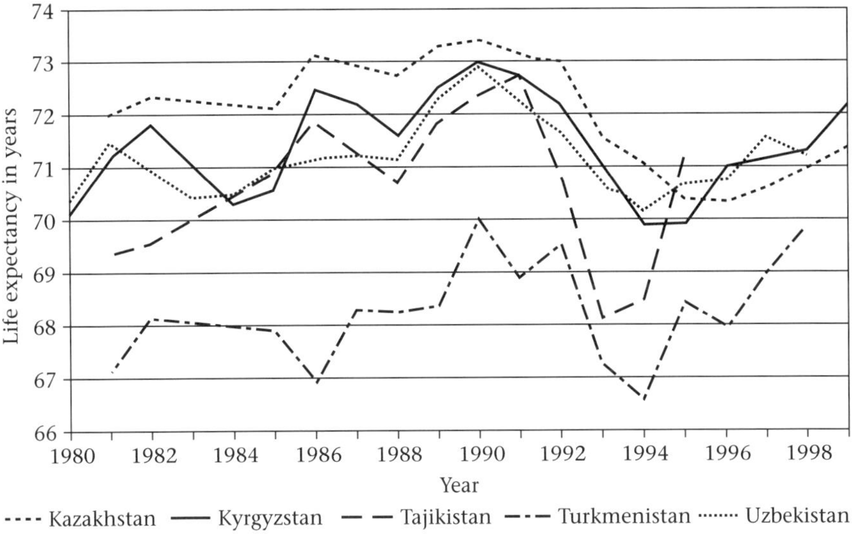

Source: WHO (2000)

Asia has tended to be better, while that of females has been worse. Anderson and Silver (1997) argued that this is because female life expectancy reflected the general level of economic development of the republics, whereas male life expectancy reflected the presence of particular risk factors, most notably alcohol consumption. Thus, Tajikistan and Turkmenistan, both less developed than the other central Asian republics and with relatively low rates of alcohol consumption, reflected the persistence of a traditional Islamic culture.

One of the major limitations of life expectancy at birth as a summary measure is the extent to which it is driven by infant mortality rates, especially where these rates are relatively high, as is the case in this region. In particular, changes in the way in which infant mortality is recorded can have a disproportionate impact on life expectancy at birth.

During the Soviet era, infant mortality in central Asia was always much higher than in Russia, with the highest rates found in Tajikistan and Turkmenistan. Rates have, however, fallen in all countries since independence, with particularly spectacular declines in Kyrgyzstan and Uzbekistan.

Validity of data

Before proceeding to examine specific causes of premature death, it is necessary to review what is known about the quality of data in this region. Reconstruction of life tables based on published data from countries in the region has identified several concerns (Anderson and Silver 1997). Possible explanations for the deviations from expected patterns include erroneous reporting of age, with heaping (which creates peaks) at 5 year intervals, and simple non-recording.

As already noted, there must be concern about the data for Tajikistan, but this is also the case for data for adjacent parts of neighbouring countries, given the large, but poorly quantified movements of population that resulted from its civil war and from events in neighbouring Afghanistan.

Turning to specific causes, during the Soviet era, Goskomstat (the State Statistical Committee) undertook regular investigations of the quality of data collection, including certification of cause of death. Published results of such studies are, however, largely limited to urban centres or to some of the European parts of the Soviet Union. There is, consequently, little direct evidence about the quality of data at that time, although it is probable that some of the problems reported elsewhere, such as a tendency to overestimate deaths from cardiovascular disease, would also apply. Since independence, such limited evaluations as may have been conducted appear to have received an even lower priority. In other former Soviet countries, there has been a marked increase in the use of non-specific diagnostic codes – in particular, at the expense of deaths from suicide or homicide – and it is likely that this is also true in the central Asian countries. In the Russian Federation and Ukraine, there has been a decline in recorded deaths from cancer among the elderly in rural areas; this is most probably a consequence of weaknesses in data collection (Shkolnikov *et al.* 1999).

The one area where there is a reasonable understanding of the weaknesses of the data is infant mortality. The Soviet Union used its own definition of a live birth. This had the effect of reducing the infant mortality rate below that which would have been reported had the WHO definition been applied. The magnitude of the difference has been estimated by several researchers, both during the Soviet era and, by observing the changes that occurred when the Baltic states changed to the WHO definition, after independence. These researchers estimated that the Soviet definition would underestimate the true figure by about 20 per cent (Anderson and Silver 1990).

There is more direct evidence from several countries in this region, from a series of demographic and health surveys, in which large household surveys (approximately 4000 women) asked, among other things, about births and child survival. The results of these surveys indicate that the official data from Kazakhstan, Kyrgyzstan and Uzbekistan, where surveys have been conducted, underestimate the true values by between 30 and 50 per cent. Consequently, it is probable that the use of the Soviet definition of a live birth is not sufficient to explain the difference, and there is likely to be considerable, underregistration of births and infant deaths in some areas. This situation is likely to deteriorate further in the countries that have introduced charges for registration.

Specific causes of death

For the reasons outlined above, it is necessary to interpret data on causes of death with some caution. By confining analysis to those under the age of 65, where it is plausible that certification of cause of death would be less of a problem than among those dying at older ages, it is possible to draw some tentative conclusions.

Cardiovascular disease is the largest contributor to the gap in mortality between this region and industrialized countries, with rates about five times higher than in western Europe. Since the early 1990s, rates have increased steeply among men in each country, but this has been especially dramatic in Kazakhstan, where it has risen by almost 50 per cent. Among women, increases are again apparent, but are less marked. The speed of these changes, which are also apparent in the Russian Federation, have caused some to challenge the validity of the data, because of the inconsistency with the time scale over which changes in classical risk factors exert their effects. Although there are certainly reasons for concern in this region, it is now apparent that such rapid changes can be explained by the major role that alcohol consumption (in particular, binge drinking) plays in the aetiology of ischaemic heart disease in former Soviet states (McKee and Britton 1998). While changes in alcohol consumption can explain the rapid fluctuations observed, other factors are likely to contribute to the underlying gap between this region and the West. These include traditional factors, such as smoking, a diet high in fat and, probably, poor detection and treatment of hypertension, as well as (at least in some areas) diets that are extremely low in antioxidants. As in other former Soviet republics, there has been some improvement in cardiovascular mortality since the mid-1990s.

Some of the same factors, such as inadequate detection and treatment of hypertension and a diet low in antioxidants, can probably explain the vast difference in cerebrovascular disease mortality between central Asia and western Europe.

Cancer is also a major contributor to the East–West gap in mortality. In central Asia, Kazakhstan, with much higher death rates than in western countries, stands out. This is due to both smoking-related cancers and other cancers, with death rates from lung cancer among men being twice that seen in western Europe. Although, at present, this cause of death is falling slightly, research in the Russian Federation (where the same phenomenon has been observed) has shown that this reflects changes in smoking rates in the post-war period, so that rates can be expected to rise again in about 2003. To date, smoking-related cancers are still relatively low in other central Asian countries, particularly among women, but this is likely to change considerably in view of the extremely intensive marketing efforts by transnational tobacco companies. Their symbols are almost ubiquitous in many cities, and they are actively targeting young people by, for example, sponsoring discos, admission to which is conditional on presenting a used cigarette pack.

In contrast to the apparent lack of concern about the risks posed by smoking, there has been considerable political discussion of the potential risks of cancer arising from Soviet era nuclear testing at Semipalatinsk, in Kazakhstan. A study of childhood cancers found about 70 per cent more cases of childhood leukaemia among those living within 200 km of test sites, compared with those living over 400 km away. There may also be a small increase in brain tumours in those close to the sites (Zaridze et al. 1994). The contribution of such cancers to the overall burden of mortality in the region is, however, small.

The third leading contributor to the East–West mortality gap is injuries and violence. As with cardiovascular disease, alcohol consumption is often an important proximate cause. Several countries experienced very dramatic increases in road-traffic accidents in the period after independence, but these have now fallen to levels much closer to those seen in western Europe – albeit with a much lower density of traffic. In some places, police enforcement of laws on speeding has been strengthened markedly, although road conditions remain extremely poor.

Deaths from other causes of injury and violence are, however, much more frequent than in the West. There have been spectacular increases in deaths in Kazakhstan and Kyrgyzstan since independence, while rates in Turkmenistan and Uzbekistan (although high) have remained relatively stable. Kyrgyzstan has, however, experienced a small reduction in deaths from injuries since 1994. The causes of the high number of injuries are inadequately understood, but some features are known. Drowning, especially in summer and among young children, is much higher than in the West, as are scalds from domestic cooking accidents. The extensive design features that have been adopted in the West to enhance safety are largely absent. These include such diverse factors as making steps on stairs the same height, covering exposed electrical wiring and even placing barriers around (or covering) holes in the road. In many cities, there is a high level of violence, often associated with alcohol. Ambulance services are often inadequate and levels of first-aid training poor.

Maternal mortality, which remains at about six to eight times the level in the EU, must also be mentioned. A detailed study of these deaths in Kazakhstan, where there has been no improvement in maternal death rates since the 1980s, showed that most were attributable to illegal abortions (Kaupova *et al.* 1998).

While the pattern of mortality among adults is often similar to that in the European part of the former Soviet Union, there is persisting high childhood mortality from diseases such as diarrhoea and respiratory infections.

Measures of morbidity

While there are concerns about data on mortality, these are even greater for data on morbidity. Very limited information is available, and it is essentially limited to infectious disease. Thus, certain issues will receive prominence simply because they are measured, while others, which may be as important, are not. Nonetheless, some issues do emerge. The incidence of tuberculosis has risen sharply everywhere, returning to rates last seen in the early 1980s (Dzhunusbekov *et al.* 1997). There has been little direct research on the underlying causes in central Asia but, as the same phenomenon has also been seen in the Russian Federation, it is probable that similar factors apply (Viljanen *et al.* 1998). In the Russian Federation, a key factor is the growth of the prison population, with large numbers of predominantly young men being held under grossly inadequate conditions. Failings in the system of care provided (Keshavjee and Becerra 2000), the existence of corruption and weak systems of follow-up treatment have led to a marked increase in multidrug-resistant tuberculosis that is proving extremely difficult to control.

Another infectious disease that is causing increasing concern is syphilis, the rates of which have exploded (Illiev *et al.* 1999). Although not yet apparent in published data, these trends are clearly a harbinger of a major epidemic of acquired immunodeficiency syndrome (AIDS). Future increases in human immunodeficiency virus (HIV) infection are also likely because of the dramatic increase in intravenous drug use. Afghanistan is the source of up to 80 per cent of the heroin supplied to Europe, and much of it is transported through Kyrgyzstan and Tajikistan. The number of addicts in Kyrgyzstan is estimated to have increased four-fold in the 1990s. A survey undertaken by the United Nations and the Open Society Institute, which funds a large harm-reduction programme in the region, estimated that up to 18 per cent of addicts in Bishkek and 49 per cent in Osh were infected with HIV (Frantz 2000). The co-existence of AIDS and drug-resistant tuberculosis is obviously a matter of grave concern.

As in the Russian Federation, a breakdown in immunization programmes in the early 1990s contributed to outbreaks of diphtheria, although these have again been brought under control (Glinyenko *et al.* 2000; Kembabanova *et al.* 2000; Niyazmatov *et al.* 2000). The failure of immunization programmes also contributed to some outbreaks of poliomyelitis (Sutter *et al.* 1997).

There is also some evidence from Uzbekistan that, despite chlorination at water-supply plants, leakage from sewers is contributing to the continuing high rates of diarrhoea in some areas (Semenza *et al.* 1998).

The only other cause of morbidity for which there are reasonable data is the very high level of anaemia among many women in the region, and of anaemia and failure to thrive among children (Giebel *et al.* 1998). These problems are attributed largely to nutritional iron deficiencies and to the absence of factors promoting iron absorption, such as vitamin C. This level of anaemia, in large part, appears to reflect the distribution of food within traditional families, exacerbated by factors such as heavier menstrual loss due to the widespread use of the intra-uterine device as a form of contraception. Anaemia tends to be somewhat more common among Kazakh and Uzbek women than among Russians in either Kazakhstan or Uzbekistan (National Institute of Nutrition 1996; Institute of Obstetrics and Gynaecology 1997; Research Institute of Obstetrics and Paediatrics 1998).

Much of the region is also susceptible to endemic goitre, due to iodine deficiency. Although this was largely controlled during the Soviet era by means of iodine-enriched salt, there has been a rapid growth in imports of non-enriched salt that is sold at a much lower price than the enriched salt.

There have been a few other studies of particular diseases. For example, a study in the Fergana Valley in Uzbekistan found a low prevalence of hypertension, compared to other countries, but relatively high rates of obesity and diabetes, which was present in 9 per cent and 5 per cent, respectively, of semi-rural men and women and 13 per cent and 9 per cent, respectively, of urban men and women (King *et al.* 1998).

Sub-national patterns of disease

The data discussed so far have been at the country level. Unlike other former Soviet states, it has been extremely difficult to obtain access to data at the sub-national level, so that regional variations have received little attention. It is likely, however, that large variations, especially between urban and rural areas, do exist. This can be seen clearly in a comparison of mortality from various causes in the *oblasts* of Turkmenistan, based on mortality data from 1995. Death rates among men from nearly all causes were lower in Ashgabat, the capital, than in more rural *oblasts*. Among women, however, the difference is very marked, with overall death rates about 50 per cent higher in rural areas. This equates to a difference in life expectancy at birth of about 10 years. Much of this difference is due to the lower survival of female infants in rural areas, raising concerns about cultural attitudes on the value of male and female lives (Tohidi 1994).

Similar differences are also apparent in the results from the demographic and health surveys. For example, in Kyrgyzstan in 1997, infant mortality was 70 per 1000 in rural areas but 54 per 1000 in urban areas. The corresponding figures for mortality under 5 years of age were 82 and 58, respectively (Research Institute of Obstetrics and Paediatrics 1998).

There is even less information available on other parameters, such as education or ethnicity, which may be associated with differences in mortality, although, again, the demographic and health surveys do provide some information with regard to children. In general, in Kyrgyzstan, survival to 5 years of age is somewhat better among children of Russian descent than among children of other nationalities (mortality of 37 per 1000 compared to 79 per 1000 in Kyrgyz families and 77 per 1000 in Uzbek families). Also, there is less mortality among people whose parents had completed higher education (56 per 1000 compared with 93 per 1000 in people with only a primary or secondary education in Kyrgyzstan) (Institute of Obstetrics and Gynaecology 1997).

Summary and implications

In terms of their patterns of health, the former Soviet republics of central Asia exhibit some similarities, but also considerable differences. Tajikistan has been ravaged by a civil war. The health of women in Turkmenistan, especially in rural areas, stands out as being much worse than in any other part of the former Soviet Union. Kazakhstan and Kyrgyzstan are in many ways rather similar, although Kazakhstan stands out in terms of its high mortality from cancer.

The region exhibits some of the worst features of both developed and developing countries, with high rates of heart disease and, in some cases, cancer, but also high rates of childhood infections. These findings stress the importance of developing effective mechanisms for health promotion and for integrated primary care, especially in rural areas. Perhaps the main implication of this brief review is the need for a much greater emphasis on the collection and analysis of routine data and a better understanding of the determinants of disease and premature death in the central Asian republics.

References

Anderson, B.A. and Silver, B.D. (1990) Trends in mortality of the Soviet population, *Soviet Economy*, 3: 191–251.

Anderson, B.A. and Silver, B.D. (1997) Issues of data quality in assessing mortality trends and levels in the new independent states, in J.L. Bobadilla, C.A. Costello and F. Mitchell (eds) *Premature Death in the New Independent States*. Washington, DC: National Academy Press.

Dzhunusbekov, A.D., Khazhibaeva, Z.I. and Dametov, U.S. (1997) Epidemiologicheskaia situatsiia po tuberkuezu v Respublike Kazakhstan [Epidemiologic situation of tuberculosis in the Republic of Kazakhstan], *Problemy Tuberkuleza*, 1: 25–7.

Frantz, D. (2000) Heroin and needles: battling AIDS in central Asia, *New York Times*, 16 October, p. 8.

Giebel, H.N., Suleymanova, D. and Evans, G.W. (1998) Anaemia in young children of the Muynak District of Karakalpakistan, Uzbekistan: prevalence, type, and correlates, *American Journal of Public Health*, 88(5): 805–7.

Glinyenko, V.M., Abdikarimov, S.T., Firsova, S.N. *et al.* (2000) Epidemic diphtheria in the Kyrgyz Republic, 1994–1998, *Journal of Infectious Diseases*, 18 (suppl. 1): S98–S103.

Illiev, S.K.H., Gaipova, M.B. and Karmanova, G.A. (1999) Epidemiologicheskie osobennosti VICh-infektsii v Turkmenistane [The epidemiological characteristics of HIV infection in Turkmenistan], *Zhurnal Mikrobiologii Epidemiologii Immunobiologii*, 1: 19–21.

Institute of Obstetrics and Gynaecology, Ministry of Health of the Republic of Uzbekistan (1997) *Demographic and Health Survey 1996*. Calverton, MA: Macro International Inc.

Kaupova, N., Nukusheva, S., Biktasheva, H., Goyaux, N. and Thonneau, P. (1998) Trends and causes of maternal mortality in Kazakhstan, *International Journal of Gynaecology and Obstetrics*, 63: 175–81.

Kembabanova, G., Askarova, J., Ivanova, R. *et al.* (2000) Epidemic investigation of diphtheria, Republic of Kazakhstan, 1990–1996, *Journal of Infectious Diseases*, 181 (suppl. 1): S94–S97.

Keshavjee, S. and Becerra, M.C. (2000) Disintegrating health services and resurgent tuberculosis in post-Soviet Tajikistan: an example of structural violence, *Journal of the American Medical Association*, 283: 1201.

King, H., Abdullaev, B., Djumaeva, S. *et al.* (1998) Glucose intolerance and associated factors in the Fergana Valley, Uzbekistan, *Diabetic Medicine*, 15: 1052–62.

McKee, M. and Britton, A. (1998) The positive relationship between alcohol and heart disease in eastern Europe: potential physiological mechanisms, *Journal of the Royal Society of Medicine*, 91: 402–7.

National Institute of Nutrition, Academy of Preventative Medicine of Kazakhstan (1996) *Demographic and Health Survey 1995*. Calverton, MA: Macro International Inc.

Niyazmatov, B.I., Shefer, A., Grabowsky, M. and Vitek, C.R. (2000) Diphtheria epidemic in the Republic of Uzbekistan, 1993–1996, *Journal of Infectious Diseases*, 181 (suppl. 1): S104–S109.

Rahminov, R., Gedik, G. and Healy, J. (2000) *Health Care Systems in Transition: Tajikistan*. Copenhagen: European Observatory on Health Care Systems.

Research Institute of Obstetrics and Paediatrics, Ministry of Health of the Kyrgyz Republic (1998) *Demographic and Health Survey*. Calverton, MA: Macro International Inc.

Semenza, J.C., Roberts, L., Henderson, A., Bgan, J. and Rubin, C.H. (1998) Water distribution system and diarrheal disease transmission: a case study in Uzbekistan, *American Journal of Tropical Medicine and Hygiene*, 59: 941–6.

Shkolnikov, V.M., McKee, M., Vallin, J. *et al.* (1999) Cancer mortality in Russia and Ukraine: validity, competing risks and cohort effects, *International Journal of Epidemiology*, 28: 19–29.

Sutter, R.W., Chudaiberdiev, Y.K., Vaphakulov, S.H. *et al.* (1997) A large outbreak of poliomyelitis following temporary cessation of vaccination in Samarkand, Uzbekistan, 1993–1994, *Journal of Infectious Diseases*, 175 (suppl. 1): S82–S85.

Tohidi, N. (1994) *Gender, Identity and Restructuring in the Muslim Countries of the Former Soviet Union.* Los Angeles, CA: International Sociological Association.

Viljanen, M.K., Vyshnevskiy, B.I., Otten, T.F. *et al.* (1998) Survey of drug resistant tuberculosis in northwestern Russia from 1984 through 1994, *European Journal of Clinical Microbiological Infectious Diseases,* 17: 177–83.

Walberg, P., McKee, M., Shkolnikov, V., Chenet, L. and Leon, D.A. (1998) Economic change, crime, and mortality crisis in Russia: a regional analysis, *British Medical Journal,* 317: 312–18.

WHO (2000) *WHO European Health for All Database.* Copenhagen: WHO Regional Office for Europe.

Zaridze, D.G., Li, N., Men, T. and Duffy, S.W. (1994) Childhood cancer incidence in relation to distance from the former nuclear testing site in Semipalatinsk, Kazakhstan, *International Journal of Cancer,* 59: 471–5.

chapter SIX

The Soviet legacy:
the past as prologue

Mark G. Field

Introduction

It is impossible to interpret the evolution of health care in the central Asian republics without an understanding of the system of socialized medicine that was in place in the Soviet Union for over 70 years. That evolution is both a reaction against the previous structure as well as a continuation of some of the patterns shaped during the Soviet era.

The Soviet health care system was often considered one of the few redeeming aspects of an otherwise bleak totalitarian society. It constituted an important ideological element, both domestically and abroad, similar to the notion that Italian fascism was somehow redeemed (or justified) because Mussolini made the trains run on time! Mrs Melita Norwood, the Englishwoman who recently was revealed as having spied for the Soviet Union for 40 years, mentioned the benefits of health care as one of the reasons she wanted to protect the Soviet regime (Hoge 1999).

Historically, it is important to note that the Soviet Union was the first nation in the world to make a constitutional pledge of universal, although not necessarily equal, entitlement to medical care to its entire population, to be paid by society and thus free at the point of service. This was meant to emphasize the ideological and emotional significance of lifetime health security, with the state offering medical care from the cradle to the grave. It also removed the cash nexus between provider and patient.

In the Soviet Union, attitudes towards socialized medicine were at the centre of the debate on health care reform. The collapse of the Soviet system provided an opportunity to reshape the existing health care system and to remove some of the many structural problems that had hobbled it in fulfilling its promises. In Russia, much discussion and some experiments (in Kemerovo, Samara and Leningrad) had taken place in the years that preceded the fall of the regime (Twigg 1998). But these experiments were abandoned after the collapse, often replaced by efforts to build an anti-model to Soviet-style socialized and state medicine, paralleling the more general transition from a communist, centralized command economy to a more democratic, decentralized, more efficient, market-oriented structure. These reforms were also promoted by Western consultants (Wedel 1998). This meant dissociation from former patterns and, in some instances, wholesale rejection. But to understand such changes as they took place in all the republics of the former Soviet Union, it is important to have a precise idea of the departure point at the end of 1991 (the legacy). This is because that departure point necessarily shaped the new system – if only in the negative sense of a model to be modified, if not abandoned.

In health care, as in most human affairs, one cannot proceed *de novo*, since one must utilize, reshape or, as the case may be, retain certain elements of the past system. Although this chapter draws on writings about health care in Russia, it should be noted that the organization of Soviet socialized medicine was, in most aspects, similar in each one of the constituent republics or autonomous regions due to the highly centralized and standardized nature of the Soviet polity. Thus, while there were minor differences, it would be redundant to describe the health care system in each one of the constituent republics. In fact, this uniformity determined, to a large extent, the rigidity of the Soviet health system and its inability to react to different regional and local conditions. The reaction against such inflexibility has informed, to a large extent, many aspects of post-Communist health policy and reform, and has often led to devolution of power and decentralization of health care (at the expense of national concerns) in the post-Communist world.

The evolution of the Soviet system

The ideology, nature and structure of Soviet socialized medicine were born in the cauldron of the Revolution, and large-scale epidemics and pandemics, including typhus. Lenin recognized the gravity of the situation. He stated shortly after the revolution, 'Typhus among a population [already] weakened by hunger without bread, soap, fuel, may become such a scourge as not to give us an opportunity to undertake socialist construction. This [must] be our first step in our struggle for culture and for (our) existence' (Tretyakov 1944). In 1919, at the height of the typhus epidemic, Lenin declared, 'either the louse [carrier of typhus] conquers socialism or socialism conquers the louse' (Vinogradov and Strashun 1947). Thus, stemming epidemics was a first priority, but those who forged the Soviet system of health care were influenced by German hygienists of the nineteenth century and had well-defined ideas of the kind of health care they wanted to establish. Marxist ideology also emphasized the social aetiology of illness, particularly the exploitation of labour that was characteristic of a capitalistic society. Moreover, the new system built on the strong Russian populist tradition of *zemstvo* (land) medicine that arose after the middle of the nineteenth century (Field 1957); in it, physicians devoted themselves to bringing a modicum of medical care to the peasant population, rather than engaging in private medicine and enriching themselves. It also drew on the fairly powerful professional associations of physicians, which were corporate bodies even under a Tsarist regime, with their political views often getting them into trouble with the authorities.

The history of Soviet socialized medicine may be divided broadly into two parts: 1918–28 and 1929–91. The first part (sociological and preventive) was in line with the Marxist and hygienist views mentioned above; the second part (clinical and remedial) was shaped by the immediate needs of the industrialization, collectivization and militarization drive launched by Stalin, which gave Soviet society its defining characteristics.

Nikolai Semashko, a physician and Lenin's companion in exile, formulated the concept of Soviet socialized medicine; it was greatly influenced, as mentioned above, by the German hygienists of the nineteenth century who saw a link between social and economic conditions and illness and by the French socialists. He was also influenced by the Marxists and, in particular, by Friedrich Engels and his seminal work on *The Condition of the Working Class in England*. Semashko was appointed the first Commissar of Health, in July 1918, in a decree signed by Lenin. The Russian term for health, as in the name of the Commissariat, is not an exact translation of the Russian expression *zdravookhranenie*, which combines health (*zdorovie*) with protection or maintenance (*okhranenie*). Thus, the Russian expression (meaning perhaps the first national Health Maintenance Organization) also reflects an important duality, that of prevention as well as treatment.

This duality is found in Greek mythology. Asclepius, the Greek (and Roman) father of medicine, had two quarrelsome daughters. Hygeia, the goddess of health, was known for *preventing* illness through a balanced style of life. Panacea, her sister, was the goddess of *cures*; her role was to *treat* illness. They began life as equals, but eventually the demand for Panacea's services grew so much that it exceeded her capacity to heal everyone. Unfortunately, the price for her services soon outstripped many people's ability to pay (Smith 1994).

Originally, Soviet socialized medicine was meant to redress the imbalance by emphasizing that society was the main aetiological factor in the production of illness. The introduction of socialism, therefore, would permit (in contrast to capitalism) the creation of social and economic conditions that would greatly limit illness and premature mortality. Socialism would reduce or eliminate poverty and the exploitation of the working class, would build decent housing, and would emphasize public health and other elements of a preventive nature. By the same token, this meant a gradual de-emphasis on clinical services. This approach, however, lasted only about 10 years. At the end of the 1920s, Stalin decided to embark on a policy of rapid industrialization and militarization, and the collectivization of agriculture. As the country embarked on a process of forced capital accumulation at the expense of the working population, Semashko and Hygiea moved to the background (Semashko was actually fired as Commissar of Health). Stalin's policies created the very same social and economic conditions that Engels had excoriated as causing illness and premature mortality. Panacea moved to centre stage and remained in that position until the fall of the regime – and, to a large extent, until today. Critics of the Ministry suggested it should be renamed the Ministry of Medicine!

What, then, were the major structural features of socialized medicine? It was not an insurance or indemnity scheme: it was state or public medicine, a service provided directly by the polity, operating on the following basic principles: Health protection was enshrined in the Constitution, which states that health care was a right of citizenship. That right was implemented by a series of basic principles that constituted the legal (and ideological) underpinnings of socialized medicine. Specifically, Article 42 of the 1977 Constitution (the one in force at the time of the collapse) states that:

> Citizens of the USSR have the right to health protection. This right is ensured by the development and improvement of safety and hygiene in industry; in carrying broad prophylactic measures; by measures to improve the environment; by special care for the health of the youth including the prohibition of child labour, excluding the work done by children as part of the school curriculum; and by developing research to prevent and reduce the incidence of disease and ensure citizens a long and active life.

Health, medicine and public health became a public responsibility of the state, with no room for the private sector or initiative, or for religious activity or charity. The state became the provider of all health services.

In principle, health policy (that is, the development of all health measures) took place within the comprehensive framework of a national plan and was, thus, part and parcel of the development of the Soviet system as a whole. Since the polity (or more accurately the Communist Party) controlled, among other things, the flow of financial resources allocated to health care, it could control the priority allocated to health services. Thus arose the planned (or integrated) nature of health care as part of the Soviet system.

The health service was highly centralized, hierarchical and organized administratively, with a top-down decision process. The Health Minister (always a physician) was a member of the Cabinet (the Council of Ministers of the USSR) and was thus the chief officer responsible for the health of the nation. The health ministry operated through its counterparts in the republics: health ministries and health departments down to the lowest administrative levels. The entire structure was financed from the state budget at the different administrative levels. Health personnel were state employees – educated, deployed and salaried by the state.

In principle, there was unity of theory and practice – that is, a close connection between the ideology of Marxism–Leninism and praxis. In actuality, this meant a de-emphasis on basic research in medicine and an emphasis on solving immediate health problems, particularly as they affected the working or fighting capacity of the population. Although the official rhetoric held prevention as the keystone of the health service, most human and financial resources flowed to the clinical services. Health promotion and education – directed at school children and the general population, and aimed at encouraging a healthy lifestyle – were marginal.

Equality of access (as against universality) was shelved as long as general and medical resources remained scarce, so that access and quality of care were calibrated to the regime's evaluation of the importance of the role and the rank of the individual (and his immediate family). Thus, medical care followed precisely the contours of the stratification of Soviet society, from the luxurious facilities reserved for the Kremlin elites to the spartan and primitive care earmarked for the lower orders. Equality was relegated to that distant and mythical future of full communism and a society of abundance.

Socialized medicine

One of the distinctive and strong points of Soviet socialized medicine was that, in theory, everyone was assigned to a medical facility, not as a result of personal choice, but as a function of residence, occupation or rank. Organizationally, the population was served by two networks of medical facilities: the territorial or residential network and the occupational or departmental network, including 'closed' medical facilities.

In the territorial or residential network, which served the majority of the population, residence determined the outpatient polyclinic to which the individual (and his family) was assigned. For this purpose, the population was divided into catchments (known as medical districts) of about 40,000 persons (10,000 children and adolescents and 30,000 adults), although the numbers could vary. The physical size of the districts depended on population density, being quite small in the cities and very large in the countryside. The district was thus not a geographical area, but instead was an administrative and medical one. It, in turn, was subdivided into micro-districts of about 4000 persons, each of which was served by two or three *terapevti* (physicians), preferably including a paediatrician, a nurse and other support personnel. The medical centre of a district was a polyclinic, an outpatient facility. In the countryside, however, where distances were great and the roads often impassable, a polyclinic might include a small (ten beds or less) inpatient unit. The district polyclinic thus served as the portal of entrance into the medical care system. Each one also had a complement of specialists, who covered more than one micro-district, and each was affiliated with hospitals (again serving several medical districts) to which patients could be referred. In addition, there were specialized outpatient dispensaries for specific conditions or population groups (for example, prenatal care, tuberculosis, cancer and diseases of the nervous system).

The territorial or residential principle (inspired, in part, by certain aspects of pre-Revolutionary *zemstvo* medicine) meant that each inhabitant knew precisely where to turn for medical attention. In that scheme, patient and physician were automatically assigned to each other, so there was little or no choice. More latitude, however, was available in choosing a specialist. Physicians saw patients at the polyclinic for about half of their working day and made house calls for the other half. Clinic consultations were usually limited to a few minutes (often less than ten), and half of the time was consumed by paper work. Dr G. Ivanov, in a letter to *Izvestia* in 1986, complained that he was so pressed for time that he had to make diagnoses and prescribe treatment as speedily as a 'jet pilot in aerial combat' (Ivanov, cited by Tutorskaia 1986). Another doctor reported that she went through her appointments without looking up at her patients. Her workload was 36 patients in 4 hours, thus 7 minutes per patient, with more than half of that time consumed by paperwork (Paikin and Silina 1978).

The closed, departmental or occupational network encompassed a variety of medical systems, access to which was determined either by occupation or rank, rather than residence. Departmental health care systems were reserved for the members of certain administrations or ministries, as well as a number of organizations, such as the Academy of Sciences or even the employees of large department stores. They were not available to the general population, hence the use of the word 'closed' to describe these networks. In addition, industrial enterprises had their own medical hospitals and clinics – the larger the enterprise, the more comprehensive these facilities. In factories and plants, the physician in charge of the health of the workers in a shop or department was the functional equivalent of the micro-district physician, so that the individual often had a choice between a residential or occupational physician. There were, in addition, a whole range of closed facilities reserved for the members of the different elites, culminating in the hospitals, clinics and rest homes of the Kremlin (called the *Kremlinovka*), where the highest officials (and their families) had access to the best medical care, equipment and buildings. In some instances, patients could also be sent abroad for treatment. These facilities, the equivalent of private hospitals and clinics in the West, were considered perquisites of rank, although part of 'socialized medicine', and were financed from the budgetary allocations for health protection.

It can thus be seen, as mentioned earlier, that medical care reflected the highly stratified nature of Soviet society, and promotion or demotion changed one's medical category. The closed facilities, in particular, reflected higher status, and the quality of care was presumably better than in the territorial network used by ordinary people. The closed networks employed a disproportionate amount of personnel and financial resources available for health care, at the expense of the territorial network that suffered shortages of all sorts. In a country that boasted more doctors and hospital beds per person than anywhere else in the world, ordinary people received minimal assistance, with long waits and poorly equipped hospitals. In 1987, for example, about half of all doctors in Moscow worked in special or closed polyclinics or hospitals (Borich 1987). It has been estimated by Davis (1979) that about 0.1 per cent of the population received superlative care (in Soviet terms), and that 25 per cent received relatively high-quality care in departmental and capital cities facilities. Another 24 per cent received acceptable services in medium city and industrial subsystems, while about half of the population received poor or substandard care in the countryside and low-density areas.

Unlike the West, education, training and research were separate, with most research being undertaken in specialized centres outside the university system. Education was considered mediocre in comparison with international standards, and there was an emphasis on early specialization, with a neglect of general practice. The basic medical qualification was awarded after a 6 year course at a medical institute, followed by an internship. Higher degrees were also available, including the Candidate and Doctor of Medical Sciences. With very few exceptions, research was weak and depended to a large extent on findings from abroad. Most Soviet medical literature did not conform to Western standards in terms of clear specification of methods or presentation of results, and instead contained extensive subjective interpretation and so-called expert judgement. No Nobel Prize in Medicine was awarded to a Soviet citizen during the entire Soviet era.

The balance sheet: strengths and weaknesses

Soviet socialized medicine scored several important achievements, however. There were decreases in mortality and morbidity and a corresponding increase in life expectancy, particularly dramatic after the Second World War and the introduction of antibiotics. The major epidemics that had been a feature of the first part of the century were effectively eliminated in the post-war period. Of course, this is not entirely due to the health care system, as improvements in the environment and the general standard of living accounted for most of it. But socialized medicine did receive a great deal of the credit for such improvements, whether justifiably or not. This optimistic picture, however, began to fade in the mid-1960s, with a sudden and unexpected rise in infant mortality, increases in other vital indices (mortality, morbidity) and, indicative of an official recognition of the emerging problems, an embargo on the publication of such statistics (Field 1995). Thus, by the time the Soviet regime collapsed, it was recognized that this was a major area for reform and restructuring.

There are many possible reasons for the weakening of the Soviet health care system. These include increased expenditures on defence to match those of its main adversary, the United States. As the gross national product (GNP) of the Soviet Union was only a fraction of that of the United States, the regime was faced with the dilemma of guns versus butter (with the former gaining). In addition, expenditures were rising for the space programmes; and inefficiencies were growing in the command economy system geared mostly to the military–industrial complex. Furthermore, corruption, particularly under Brezhnev, was becoming more pervasive. At the time of the collapse, the amount of money earmarked for health care was about a third of what it had been in the mid-1960s.

By the end of the Soviet era, the weaknesses of health care had become apparent. The expectation by the population that health services were their due, as a right of citizenship, clearly was not being met.

One well-recognized problem was that, while there had been an enormous increase in the number of physicians and of hospital beds, the emphasis had been on quantitative, rather than qualitative, indices. In addition, there were other important concerns. An underlying issue was that health care was assigned a low priority in the Soviet scheme: it was not a 'productive' area and it simply took resources. Thus, it was consistently underfunded according to the 'residual principle' (Chazov 1990).

The health care system contained many perverse economic incentives; for example, hospitals were funded according to the number of beds they possessed, whether needed or not. The over-centralized, top-down command system was often unable to address new problems and situations, most graphically illustrated by the response to the Chernobyl nuclear accident. It could not adapt to local conditions and exhibited a pervasive inertia. This was particularly problematic as the major threats to health were making a rapid epidemiological transition, from infectious to chronic diseases.

The Soviet medical profession was highly stratified, with a small number of elite, almost entirely male doctors at the top and an enormous, predominantly female and poorly paid workforce at the local level. In particular, there was a failure to develop primary care, as mentioned earlier; instead, there was a concentration on the creation of a large number (over 100) of specialities, operating at a low level. The lack of an autonomous (or semi-autonomous) medical profession as a corporate group that could articulate the needs of both practitioners and patients, when coupled with the gender stratification of a highly sexist society, conspired to further weaken the prestige of medicine and health care.

There were other problems. The health care system suffered from a perennial shortage of equipment, supplies and, in particular, pharmaceuticals (including dependence on foreign east European producers), and also from under-capitalization of domestic production. Also, the promotion of healthy lifestyles was neglected, with Soviet paternalism denying personal responsibility for one's health. Widespread corruption and inefficiency, with extensive under-the-table payments or 'envelope passing medicine', made the promise of free care a sick joke. Finally, the medical profession was isolated from trends in international medicine; this, when combined with the weak Soviet research base, led to the persistence of obsolete clinical practices.

Conclusions

The legacy of the Soviet system is a heavy one, particularly in the context of other major economic and political problems. First, there is the question of the persistence of institutional memory – that is, patterns inherited from the past that may be difficult to shake off, for example the patterns of long-term hospitalization for tuberculosis. An observer wrote recently: 'The money from Moscow may be gone, but the network designed by the Soviet government – grand, cumbersome, repetitive and blind to the perverse and often baffling economics of medicine – lives on' (Specter 1998). The final verdict on Soviet socialized medicine could be summed up by: 'Noble purpose, grand design, flawed execution, mixed results' (Field 1990).

In many respects, Soviet central Asia was like a part of a colonial empire: Moscow supplied (in exchange for raw materials) medical equipment and pharmaceuticals, so that local production did not develop to meet local needs. After the collapse of the Soviet system, the government was blamed for many of the problems of health care. Initially, this led to a rejection of the polity as the source of adequate care, and the infatuation with the anti-model of privatization, decentralization and competition, with the market seen as the solution to the various problems. This soon led to a polarization between the few who could afford private care and the majority who could not. Nonetheless, the population still expects that the state must provide medical care to those who need it and cannot afford it, at no cost (or marginal cost) at the point of service. Failure by the state to ensure this medical care is seen as state desertion – that is, as a violation of the social contract and of the obligation that society has towards each individual. This has important ideological and political implications.

References

Borich, T. (1987) For a limited circle – polemical remarks on special polyclinics and special hospitals, *Current Digest of the Soviet Press*, 39(32): 21.

Chazov, E.I. (1990) In search of the new, obstacles on the way. *Meditsinskaia Gazeta* (in Russian), 16 February, pp. 1–2.

Davis, C. (1979) *The Economics of the Soviet Health System: An Analytical and Historical Study, 1921–1978*. Cambridge: Cambridge University Press.

Field, M.G. (1957) *Doctor and Patient in Soviet Russia*. Cambridge, MA: Harvard University Press.

Field, M.G. (1990) Noble purpose, grand design, flawed execution, mixed results: Soviet socialized medicine after seventy years, *American Journal of Public Health*, 80: 144–5.

Field, M.G. (1995) The health crisis in the former Soviet Union: a report from the 'post-war zone', *Social Science and Medicine*, 41: 1469–78.

Hoge, W. (1999) The great-grandmother comes in from the cold, *New York Times*, 13 September, p. A4.

Paikin, A. and Silina, G. (1978) The district physician (in Russian), *Lituraturnaia Gazeta*, 27(11): 11.

Smith, D.R. (1994) Porches, politics and public health, *American Journal of Public Health*, 84(5): 725–6.

Specter, M.A. (1998) Citadel of Russia's wasteful health system, *New York Times*.

Tretyakov, A.F. (1944) *Protection of the Peoples' Health in the RSFSR*. Moscow: Ogiz.

Tutorskaia, S. (1986) Frankly (in Russian), *Izvestia*, 7 February, p. 3.

Twigg, J.L. (1998) Balancing the state and the market: Russia's adoption of obligatory medical insurance, *Europe–Asia Studies*, 50(4): 583–602.

Vinogradov, N.A. and Strashun, I.D. (1947) *Health Protection of the Workers in the Soviet Union*. Moscow: Medgiz.

Wedel, J. (1998) *Collision and Collusion: The Strange Case of Western Aid to Eastern Europe*. New York: St Martin's Press.

part two

Health systems and services

chapter seven

The reform process

Serdar Savas, Gülin Gedik and Marian Craig

Introduction

This chapter is concerned with the health sector reform process in central Asia, including both the planning and implementation phases. We argue that these two phases represent an integral and continuous process and that the process followed during policy development is as important as the content of the policy itself. Utmost attention is required to understand fully the context in which reforms take place, the process of policy formulation, implementation and evaluation, and the actors who are involved, as well as those who will be affected by the policy itself. The reform process in central Asia, therefore, is explored from these perspectives.

What were the pressures for reforming health care?

The 1990s witnessed a changing environment in central Asia: politically, economically and socially. There was enthusiasm for change of any sort; anything different from the old system was considered good. Initially, in the health sector, change was quite simply equated with the introduction of health insurance, and the development of democracy was seen as synonymous with privatization. The understanding of these concepts, however, was weak or even non-existent. Since health insurance was perceived as the method of financing and organizing health services in Western countries, it was seen as the best way forward. Privatization was understood as freedom, availability of consumer goods and access to a better life, and was thus mystified.

Besides the general enthusiasm for change, the main triggers for reforming health care can be thought of as external (arising from outside of the health sector) and internal (from within the health sector) (Savas and Gedik 1999).

External pressures

Need for new systems for new countries

After the disintegration of the Soviet Union, each of the newly independent central Asian republics comprehensively reviewed all of its systems. As policies were no longer dictated from Moscow, the political imperative arising from independence made this process more urgent and substantial reforms were initiated across sectors of the economy. Since the condition of the health care sector was regarded as less urgent, health reform proposals did not gather momentum until the mid-1990s.

Economic transition

The economic recession, which started in the 1980s under Soviet rule, was exacerbated by the circumstances following the downfall of the Soviet regime. After independence, the central Asian republics underwent a sharp economic decline. The reasons for this included the withdrawal of subsidies from Moscow, the breakdown of inter-republic trade and the impact of government stabilization policies (Falkingham et al. 1997). Gross domestic product had fallen by approximately half in the central Asian republics by 1996, with a significant decline in public spending, fiscal imbalance and widespread poverty (Mills 1998). The inherited social programmes were not sustainable. An increasing trade imbalance caused shortages of drugs and other consumables. This coincided with deterioration in the health and well-being of the population.

Changes in production and allocation mechanisms

In the Soviet Union, the production and distribution strategy was centrally planned, with tasks allotted to particular republics (Pomfret, Chapter 3). Central Asia's role was mostly to produce raw materials. After the break-up of the Soviet Union (and thus the distribution system), the new republics had to address any production deficits in supply through external trade or internal production. Market forces succeeded central planning as the determining factor in production. These changes had an impact on the health sector in terms of both goods (for example, medical equipment, pharmaceuticals and vaccines) and services (for example, highly specialized medical care and medical and nursing education).

Increasing international relations

The interaction with Western countries increased with independence, coinciding with an increasing debate about health care systems in the West. This debate has echoed through the central Asian republics. Health policy in welfare states was being influenced by concerns about escalating costs that exceeded levels of economic growth. Pressures to contain costs were major factors in health care system reforms in Western countries. Although the drivers of cost escalation were different in the central Asian republics, the cost-containment debate has also influenced the agenda. Many external agencies have also been active in the region, with each agency bringing its own agenda and expertise.

Internal pressures

For governments and health ministries, the most pressing force for reform was the substantial decline in resources during the initial years of independence, coupled with the difficulty of running the existing system. Other shortcomings identified by international and bilateral agencies, such as a lack of managerial skills, inadequate medical knowledge and skills and excess capacity, were not perceived as problems by local officials. These concerns were only later recognized by governments when confronted with implementation problems. The internal pressures for reform are summarized in the following sections.

Deterioration in health status

An epidemiological transition was being experienced in the central Asian republics before independence. This transition included not only the characteristics of developing countries (high infant and maternal mortality and increasing infectious diseases), but also a shift to those of developed countries (increasing non-communicable diseases, such as cardiovascular disease and cancer) (McKee and Chenet, Chapter 5). This situation, when combined with fiscal constraints, led to a further deterioration in the health status of the population, including an increase in communicable diseases, such as tuberculosis, sexually transmitted infections, malaria and diphtheria. The rapidity of social change is also likely to have an impact on levels of mental health, although there has been no specific analysis of this issue.

Inefficiencies in the system

The allocation of resources between sectors and within the health sector was heavily skewed, with major regional disparities and with most resources spent on inpatient care. The system was technically inefficient, with excess provision and inappropriate use of health care. In particular, the role of hospitals was over-emphasized and primary care was used ineffectively. Moreover, the development of the health care system has been driven by quantitative norms, such as beds/physicians/facilities per thousand population. These norms formed the basis for planning and budgeting, resulting in an excessively high hospital capacity, high admission rates, unnecessary hospitalization, long hospital stays and a large number of health personnel, but a low quality of services. The lack of a management culture, coupled with low levels of skills, has been an obstacle to improving efficiency.

Treatment protocols and procedures are also outdated, as exemplified by the treatment of tuberculosis and sexually transmitted infections. There is a great need for retraining and continuing education.

Poor infrastructure

The physical infrastructure is poorly maintained. The poor layout of buildings, poor structural conditions and shortage of functioning equipment restrict the activities that health facilities can undertake (Hopkinson 1994, 1997; Amori 1997).

Changing expectations of citizens

There has been a worldwide trend towards empowerment of the patient, with citizens demanding a more patient-oriented approach to health care. In the central Asian republics, independence and the new market economy have brought with them a demand for better health care. Realizing this has been difficult, however. The general public has begun to express its concern about the lack of medicines at affordable prices, of basic facilities in hospitals and of transport to health facilities, as well as the competence of health personnel (Ladbury 1997).

Who are the players in the reform process?

The actors involved in health care reforms in the central Asian republics cover a wide range of groups: from government to private sector, from professionals to general public, as well as international and bilateral agencies. The importance and influence of each group varies from country to country, but the state maintains strong control and influence. Within the government, various institutions are involved in the reform process.

Health ministries

The health ministries, in general, retain the lead policy responsibility. In the early years of independence, they were ill-equipped to assume this responsibility, since policy-making and planning were carried out by the central Ministry of Health in Moscow. The republican ministries had been regional ministries, simply acting as a channel for policies developed centrally. They were confronted with a spectrum of new tasks, including formulating policy, preparing legislation, monitoring the health of the population, commissioning research, developing reform strategies, supervising the implementation of plans and ensuring the training of health personnel. They also control the national-level health budget and supervise the research institutes and national hospitals.

The ministries of health in Kyrgyzstan, Tajikistan and Uzbekistan adapted to the new circumstances relatively rapidly and have taken the lead in health sector reform. The Ministry of Health in Kazakhstan has experienced public-sector reorganizations, initially being established as a health committee accountable to the Minister of Education, Culture and Health, then a state health agency with autonomous status. Such internal restructuring distracted attention from its policy-making function. In Turkmenistan, the Ministry of Health has only a marginal role in policy-making due to a very centralized presidential rule; although the ministry develops policies, their adoption and implementation depends upon decisions made at higher levels.

The trend in the central Asian republics is to decentralize management and empower the *oblast* administrations. Almost all of them adopted laws on self-governance between 1991 and 1996, which increased the responsibility and authority of local administrations. *Oblast* governors are appointed by the president, collect most of the government's revenue and keep a significant portion at the *oblast* level. Consequently, they play an important role in determining local health budgets. The *oblast* health administrations have a dual responsibility to both ministries of health and *oblast* governors.

Oblast *health administrations*

Oblast health administrations are responsible for managing health facilities in the *oblast*. Their involvement in policy-making and strategic planning is limited. Where demonstration projects were developed, the role of *oblast* administrations has been more significant, as in Kazakhstan, Kyrgyzstan and Uzbekistan.

Advisory bodies

Advisory bodies are attached to the government or presidential apparatus. Their health policy advisers sometimes exert considerable power, due to their direct access to vice-premiers, prime ministers or presidents. In some countries, their formal role is purely advisory, but in others, such as in Turkmenistan, they are closely involved in policy- and decision-making.

Finance ministries

The finance ministries formulate the budget to be approved by the parliament and allocate funds to the health ministries. The finance ministries also deal directly with *oblast* administrations and provide indicative allocation figures, but the final decisions on local health budgets are made by the local administrations. Consequently, the health ministries have no involvement in the budget process. Thus, reforms of health care financing depend to a great extent on the finance ministries. In some cases, health ministries have attempted to develop strategies on health care financing, but these have stalled in the finance ministries. For example, a comprehensive health care strategic plan has been drawn up in Kyrgyzstan, but delays in financing reforms have occurred. These delays have affected proposals for the *oblast*-level pooling of funds, the introduction of a single payer system and changing the budgeting system to introduce financial incentives for providers (Adams *et al.* 1998; Gedik and Kutzin 1998). These changes would facilitate health care reform implementation, but await decisions by the Ministry of Finance.

Health insurance

Health insurance is on the agenda of all central Asian republics. All republics have drafted insurance laws, some of which have been implemented. Turkmenistan has introduced voluntary insurance, but this remains of marginal significance. In Kazakhstan, the health insurance fund was a partner in the health reform implementation based on a purchaser–provider split between 1996 and 1998. The autonomous fund, however, was converted into a purchasing department of the Health Committee in 1999 because of a mounting budget deficit and failures of coordination.

The Health Insurance Fund established in Kyrgyzstan in 1997 is an important actor, as a facilitating agency, in reform implementation. Its autonomous budget, while still part of the Ministry of Health, allowed the fund to initiate new provider payment mechanisms in line with Ministry of Health policies, without waiting for decisions by the Ministry of Finance.

Trade unions

Union membership was, in practice, compulsory under the Soviet system. The main functions of the unions were to represent the employees to the employers (the state), but they also controlled substantial benefits for workers (such as holidays, resort treatment and sick leave). The unions were financed through a payroll tax. Although the unions were powerful under the Soviet system, their involvement in the reform process was marginal. They are, however, still important, since they control certain benefits, such as resort treatments that consume considerable resources, which could be used more efficiently for health.

Health professionals

Health professionals are not major policy players, given the lack of power of professional organizations and, in many cases, lack of interest. Associations for physicians were established after 1991 in almost all central Asian republics. So far, these are not influential bodies, having no statutory standing or formal representation in policy-making. Nursing associations are being established and are developing steadily in some countries. A strengthened role for professional organizations could be expected to increase the involvement of professionals.

The general public

The general public might be expected to be an important actor, as the users of the services, but it traditionally remains silent in the central Asian republics. The lack of a democratic culture leads to an assumption that lay people have nothing to say on policy issues. Furthermore, people believe it to be the responsibility of government to provide health care. Mobilizing public opinion brings great challenges.

International and bilateral agencies

International and bilateral agencies have been active in the region since independence. These include the United Nations Development Programme (UNDP), the World Health Organization (WHO), the World Bank, the United Nations Children's Fund (UNICEF), TACIS (a European Union programme), the European Community Humanitarian Office (ECHO), the Asian Development Bank (ADB), the Department for International Development (DFID) in the United Kingdom, the Danish International Development Agency (DANIDA), the German Technical Cooperation Agency (GTZ), the Swiss Development Cooperation, the Turkish International Cooperation Agency (TICA) and the US Agency for International Development (USAID). These organizations participate in the policy reform process and, in some countries, contribute to the government agenda, as in Kyrgyzstan. In some countries, donors have set up demonstration projects where a donor-driven reform agenda has taken place, as in Kazakhstan. Tajikistan was different, since support concentrated on emergency assistance during the civil war, with structural reforms starting somewhat later.

Although all external agencies share common values and principles, each emphasizes particular principles. For example, WHO promotes the concept of equity and emphasizes the need for a strategic vision and the development of a process for change. The World Bank invests in health care reform through ongoing projects in Kazakhstan, Kyrgyzstan, Tajikistan and Uzbekistan. These have focused on improving efficiency, introducing changes in provider payment mechanisms and strengthening primary health care. Substantial USAID funds support a range of projects, including some experiments in forms of privatization, and also support local demonstration projects and institutional twinning between United States and central Asian institutions.

Coordination of all actors

There is potential for greater coordination between all the actors. The government reform teams (discussed later) need to assume more responsibility for coordinating the various health-sector reform efforts and ensuring wide participation.

How has the process of change been managed?

The process of managing health-sector change varies from country to country within central Asia. Two types of approach have been followed. Some countries followed a rational comprehensive approach, developing a strategic vision, with a clear identification of problems, setting of objectives, analysis of different options and an informed decision on the most appropriate option. Other countries followed an incremental approach, focusing on small changes to existing policies and responding to specific problems through *ad hoc* interventions.

Kyrgyzstan

Kyrgyzstan offers an example of a rational comprehensive approach, in its MANAS Health Care Reform Programme (WHO 1997). Somewhat similar processes have been adopted in Tajikistan and Turkmenistan. In Kyrgyzstan, the development of the master plan followed a process that started with a situation analysis and identification of challenges and constraints. Four broad policy options for health care reform were developed: a preservation strategy, a prioritization strategy, a contract strategy and a *laissez-faire* strategy. The purpose was to initiate a debate on an appropriate strategy and, following wide discussions, the Ministry of Health decided the main directions of health care reform called for a combination of options. A detailed draft was then worked out and distributed for comment, and the master plan was revised and adopted in 1996.

In 2000, pilot implementation is underway in Issyk-Kul, Chui *oblasts* and the city of Bishkek. Despite serious financial constraints with little prospect for improvement, the political commitment of the President ensured steady progress and helped mobilize resources from the international community. Implementation of the MANAS plan is supported by various international and bilateral agencies and is accompanied by a communication strategy targeted at both health professionals and the general public.

At the beginning, a team of 46 professionals, including representatives of central government and *oblasts*, was established within the Ministry of Health to coordinate the process. Their responsibilities have covered both the content of reform (developing policy options and implementation plans) and the process of reform (undertaking a central coordinating function, within the Ministry of Health, and between the ministry, other public bodies and international and bilateral agencies). Training in management and computer skills and technical subjects, as well as opportunities to improve competency in the English language, was provided to the members of the team. The team has been maintained during the implementation period as a department of the Ministry of Health. The initial team members created a critical mass to disseminate knowledge and team spirit throughout the country.

Tajikistan

In Tajikistan, interventions had focused on meeting emergency needs, such as supplying emergency drugs and vaccines, during the armed conflict. The government is now moving towards structural reform. A health for all policy was developed (Ministry of Health Tajikistan 1996) and a plan for reform was initiated under the SOMONI Health Project. Following the approach in Kyrgyzstan, a master plan was developed through a participatory process. A team was established to coordinate the process, supported by appropriate training, and it is envisaged that the team members will coordinate the implementation of the master plan.

Turkmenistan

Turkmenistan has also attempted a systematic approach. The State Health Programme of the President adopted in 1995 defined a broad policy framework, and The Plan for the Realization of the Presidential Health Programme was developed through the LUKMAN health project. Simultaneously, a pilot project in Tedzhen district was prepared to be financed by the World Bank loan, but was suspended before implementation. *Ad hoc* decisions (not in line with the plans) have continued and, although some projects were developed, they have had little impact. This reflects a lack of leadership in the health sector, a lack of informed decision-making and the slower development of democratic mechanisms compared to the other central Asian republics. Furthermore, many decisions require high-level involvement, often by the President. A team was established within the Ministry of Health to implement the LUKMAN health project, but was disbanded after the development of the master plan, due to lack of commitment.

Kazakhstan

Kazakhstan initiated pilot projects in several *oblasts* on an *ad hoc* basis, but these local and donor-driven innovations did not establish adequate links with national policies. After this fragmented approach, the need for a comprehensive strategic plan was discussed, but was slow to be initiated, while uncertainty about the status of the Ministry of Health also hampered strategic development.

Uzbekistan

Uzbekistan is moving to introduce changes in different areas, such as health care finance, privatization, health insurance and new provider payment systems. Some vertical health programmes have been developed, such as tuberculosis and mother and child health. All these interventions lack a uniting strategy. A pilot project in Fergana financed through a World Bank loan started in 1999 and aims to implement a range of reforms.

All the central Asian republics

The financial crisis experienced since independence continues in all central Asian republics. Although some improvement in the economic situation has been achieved, the region has yet to achieve financial stability. National resources are insufficient for the required investments, especially for the improvement of infrastructure and the training of health personnel. Consequently, the implementation of reform has relied on grants, soft loans and credits.

Lessons learned from the experience of reform

In the early 1990s, the pressures on these health care systems produced widespread agreement that reforms were necessary. Some believed the only problem was a lack of funds, whereas others called for system-wide change. The problem for the governments was *what* to change and *how* to get started on the reform path.

It is often argued that system-wide approaches consume too much time and resources (Walt 1994). Savas (2000) has argued, however, that the case of Kyrgyzstan shows the benefits of this approach. Although more time is required to evaluate the outcome, comprehensive planning was important for the following reasons:

- Each country has undergone a comprehensive political, social and economic transition, so that the impact of *ad hoc* minor changes to the health care system have had marginal or even no impact without changes in the other components of the system.
- Policy-making and management capacities were not well developed in the central Asian republics, since these functions were carried out in Moscow. A systematic planning approach in each of these republics has helped to develop these capacities.
- A comprehensive and participatory process has contributed to the development of a democratic culture.

The experiences of the different countries highlight the main issues for a reform process. These include the need for a strategic vision, high-level commitment, a participatory process, a change management team, a capacity-building strategy that draws on the synergy between individual and organizational development, and well coordinated donor inputs.

Need for a strategic vision

Once the need for system-wide change is recognized, a strategic vision for health care reform is needed. The development of a master plan serves as a useful tool to develop such a vision. If a participatory and transparent process is followed within an adequate time frame, the following benefits may flow from the *planning process*:

- The preparation of a plan enables all those involved to learn about the health sector and so contributes to capacity-building.
- The development of the plan provides a forum for coordinating national and international agencies.
- This process ensures that the various programme components are integrated in a comprehensive plan.

Once developed, the master plan can serve as a tool to facilitate the implementation of health care reforms. Commitment to reform, however, must exist at the national level. The following benefits stem from the *existence* of a plan:

- The plan provides direction and guidance for the relevant institution.
- It provides a reference point against which progress may be measured.
- Publicizing the plan creates a visible national agenda for health.
- Dissemination of the plan increases support by contrasting the vision of an improved future with the reality of the problematic present.

Establishing a managerial structure

Health care reform requires efforts that go beyond the daily routine of existing institutions. This extra commitment has been organized in different ways in the central Asian republics. In some countries, different departments in the health ministry, in an institute or in an *oblast* administration have taken responsibility for certain reform tasks. With no central body to oversee the process, this often created fragmentation and competing agendas. The health ministries in Kyrgyzstan, Tajikistan and Turkmenistan established a permanent team, staffed with individuals working full time and not distracted by routine operational matters, to manage the process of change.

Such policy units have provided a recognized locus for policy development. These units have been an important source of career development opportunities, and so have played an important role in capacity-building. Some risks are associated with the creation of such a management team, however. It may be perceived as an elite group whose members receive preferential treatment and who, therefore, may encounter resistance in their dealings with other health professionals. It may be difficult to extend capacity-building beyond the change management team; indeed, there may be incentives to prevent this from happening. The team may concentrate most of its activity on one well-financed project (for example, a World Bank financed project), although this may provide an opportunity for wider coordination, as happened in Kyrgyzstan.

Capacity-building

There is no scarcity of ideas in central Asia on what might be done to reform health care. Lengthy discussions have been held on many occasions, and many documents canvas the various options. The main problem, however, lies in the lack of national capacity to implement the reforms, a problem not well recognized by national governments. Some governments considered that staff capacity was adequate and that resources would be better spent on physical infrastructure. The donor community, however, believes that the institutional capacity needed to implement change and to manage a modern health service must be enhanced. Each donor has included strategies for capacity-building in its projects, but there is no overall policy.

The World Health Organization has emphasized the importance of simultaneous policy development and capacity-building. In addition to various training activities, it has sought to improve the sustainable supply of trained staff. The Kazakhstan School of Public Health was established in 1997 as the sole school of public health in the region, and a health management training centre was established in Kyrgyzstan. These two institutions have the potential to contribute to the training of public health professionals in the region.

International agency collaboration

Since the early 1990s, relations between international and bilateral agencies have improved. The early years were characterized by co-existence, where each agency worked independently of one another, but good collaboration has subsequently been achieved in some countries.

International and bilateral agencies need to play an intrinsic role in the democratic process of policy development. With all parties involved openly expressing their concerns and expectations, the agenda of contributors to the process can be far better placed to further the national agenda. Coordination of activities within a well-defined framework will also be enhanced. To maximize the impact of the work undertaken, it is vital that efforts should not only be coordinated to avoid duplication, but should also be specifically designed to be complementary – combining to create a synergetic effect – and thus truly maximizing the impact on the health of the population.

Ownership is a key issue. People must feel a true sense of pride and ownership in the overall programme of health-sector reform in their country. The coordination role must be placed in the hands of nationals of the country, and international and bilateral agencies must respect this.

Conclusions

This chapter aimed to provide a short account of the reform process and to identify the factors for success derived from experience in the region. Experience suggests that governments must invest more resources in strengthening the reform process. Our understanding of the process of change is still limited, and there is need for further research, not only on what to do but also on how to do it.

References

Adams, O., Apfel, F., Gedik, G. and Kuzin, J. (1998) *Report on the Implementation of Health Care Reforms in Kyrgyzstan for the Period May–November 1998*, Document EUR/KGZ/ CARE 07 04 10 (B). Copenhagen: WHO Regional Office for Europe.

Amori, E. (1997) *Development of a Technology Management Programme (Turkmenistan)*, Document EUR/ICP/CARE 0702 02 (E). Copenhagen: WHO Regional Office for Europe.

Falkingham, J., Klugman, J., Marnie, S. and Micklewright, J. (eds) (1997) *Household Welfare in Central Asia*. Basingstoke: Macmillan.

Gedik, G. and Kutzin, J. (1998) *Report on the Implementation of Health Care Reforms in Kyrgyzstan for the Period December 1997–April 1998*, Document EUR/KGZ/CARE 07 01 01 (C). Copenhagen: WHO Regional Office for Europe.

Hopkinson, M. (1994) *Kyrgyzstan Health Sector Reform Project: Buildings and Equipment*, unpublished internal document. Washington, DC: World Bank.

Hopkinson, M. (1997) *Proposed Turkmenistan Health Project: Buildings and Equipment*, unpublished internal document. Washington, DC: World Bank.

Ladbury, S. (1997) *Turkmenistan Health Project: Social Assessment Study*. Washington, DC: World Bank.

Mills, M. (1998) *Tajikistan: Health Sector Note*, unpublished internal document. Washington, DC: World Bank.

Ministry of Health Tajikistan (1996) *State Programme for Health Protection (1996–2005)*. Dushanbe: Ministry of Health.

Savas, S. (2000) *Becoming a Lion*, Document EUR/00/5017691. Copenhagen: WHO Regional Office for Europe.

Savas, S. and Gedik, G. (1999) Health care reforms in central Asia, in UNDP (ed.) *Central Asia 2010: Prospects for Human Development*. New York: UNDP Regional Bureau for Europe and the CIS.

Walt, G. (1994) *Health Policy: An Introduction to Process and Power*. London: Zed Books.

WHO (1997) *MANAS: Health Care Reform Programme of Kyrgyzstan*, Document EUR/KGZ/CARE 07 01 11. Copenhagen: WHO Regional Office for Europe.

chapter eight

Health system funding

Joe Kutzin and Cheryl Cashin

Introduction

This chapter is concerned with the ways in which health systems are funded in central Asia, the consequences of different alternatives, and the possibilities for policy action to diversify funding sources in contexts of low growth, high expectations and diminishing public revenues. We begin with a description of the ways in which health systems are funded in these five countries. Where possible, this includes information on levels and trends in total health finance and the mix of finance sources, and an assessment of the effects on health system objectives. We then turn to an assessment of options and strategies for health system funding in the central Asian republics within the context of low economic growth and highly constrained government expenditures (as highlighted by Pomfret in Chapter 3). Because resource allocation, including provider payment, is the subject of Chapter 9, the present chapter is focused narrowly on resource mobilization issues. Where relevant, however, interactions of revenue collection methods with the other health financing functions are described.

Description of health system financing

Although the introduction states that this chapter is primarily concerned with the different funding *sources* for the health system, a more precise description of its scope is the sources of funds *and* the mechanisms by which funds are contributed, as depicted in Figure 8.1. In many cases, the discussion of funding sources jumps immediately to public and private contributors, but this obscures the reality that a country's population (including individuals and corporate entities) is the initial source of all funds (apart from foreign sources, which are not addressed in this chapter). The health funding source categories identified in this section are based on combinations of funding

Figure 8.1 Health system funding sources and contribution mechanisms

Initial funding sources	Contribution mechanisms	Collecting institutions
Individuals/ families/ employees	1 Direct taxes 2 Indirect taxes 3 Payroll taxes 4 Other compulsory contributions (mandates) 5 Voluntary prepaid contributions 6 Direct payment to providers at time of use 7 Grants 8 Loans	Central government
Employers/ corporate entities		Local government
		Social security agency
Foreign and domestic NGOs and charities		Commercial insurance fund
		Other insurance fund
Foreign governments and multilateral agencies		Employers
		Earmarked savings fund
Foreign and multinational companies		Health care provider

sources and contribution methods that are mutually exclusive and policy relevant. The latter implies that changes in the relative size of each category have implications for public policy objectives (for example, equity, efficiency and sustainability). The categories of relevance to the central Asian republics are:

- *public sources*: government budgets (general revenues) and social insurance (payroll taxes); and
- *private sources*: voluntary prepayment by employers, employees or self-employed individuals and direct out-of-pocket payment to providers.

Although the main distinction among these categories is public/private, it is also useful to make the distinction between sources of funding that are compulsory or voluntary and between sources that involve prepayment or payment at the point of service use. All these dimensions are discussed below.

Levels and trends in health finance from public sources

During the Soviet era, government budget allocations (the state budget) were the predominant source of revenues for the health system. Social health insurance contributions (payroll taxes earmarked for a health fund) constitute another source of public funding, although the revenues and expenditures of such funds do not generally appear in a government's consolidated budget. This is the case with Kazakhstan and Kyrgyzstan, the only central Asian republics to have implemented such mandatory health insurance funds (MHIFs). This section examines levels and trends in funding from these public sources.

It is well known that health and other forms of public spending have declined during the transition to independence; available data make it possible to disentangle the elements of this decline. Levels and trends in government health spending reflect the patterns of real gross domestic product (GDP), real public revenues and expenditures, and government priorities in the allocation of available public resources across sectors. The fall in both GDP and government revenue that has accompanied the transition has been discussed in some detail in Chapter 3. Figure 8.2 shows the share of total government spending allocated to health by each country. Reliable data or estimates are available for 1994–98 for each of the countries, and for earlier years in Kyrgyzstan and Uzbekistan. These data reveal quite different patterns among the countries, in both the share of public spending devoted to health and the trends in these shares.

Figure 8.2 Health as a percentage of total state budget spending

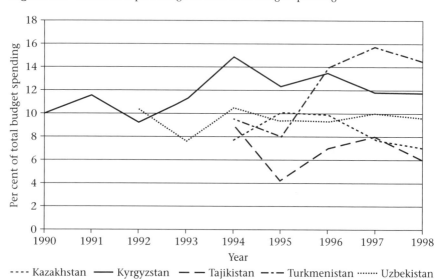

Sources: Kazakhstan: Agency for Health Care, Kazakhstan (2000) for 1994–98, except IMF (2000b) for total government spending in 1994; Kyrgyzstan: National Statistical Committee of the Kyrgyz Republic (2000) and Kutzin (2000); Tajikistan: Thompson (2000); Turkmenistan: IMF (1999a); Uzbekistan: World Bank (1999)

Uzbekistan shows the most stable trend, with relatively little variation in its health allocation since 1994. Conversely, the health share of the Tajik budget was reduced by more than half from 1994 to 1995. It recovered somewhat since then, but has fluctuated. On average, Tajikistan's government allocated less of its revenues to health than the other governments. Turkmenistan also showed a dramatic change in its allocation patterns. The 1996 allocation to health absorbed 6 percentage points more of the government budget than did its 1995 allocation, an increase of about 75 per cent. Moreover, it has maintained the high priority of the health sector; by 1998, it was the clear leader among the countries in its budget allocation patterns. Kyrgyzstan has had, after Uzbekistan, the most stable pattern of budget allocations to health, but these have declined from a high of nearly 15 per cent in 1994 to under 12 per cent in 1998. Finally, Kazakhstan had a rapid decline in the health share of budget allocations, from 10 per cent of public spending in 1996 to 7 per cent of spending in 1998. The period of decline corresponds to the emergence of the Kazakh MHIF (Kulzhanov and Healy 1999), and the Kazakh data in Figure 8.2 include transfers from the budget to the MHIF. Transfers to the MHIF represented about 9 per cent of state budget health spending in 1996, but about 40 per cent of this spending in 1997 and 1998 (Agency for Health Care, Kazakhstan 2000). This suggests that the government reduced budgetary commitments to the health sector in response to the emergence of payroll tax contributions earmarked for health care.

Table 8.1 presents data on the share of government health spending as a percentage of GDP. These data include the value of expenditures from payroll tax contributions to the MHIFs in Kazakhstan and Kyrgyzstan. They show similar, but not identical, trends to those in Figure 8.2. Differences in trends occur when, for example, total public spending moves in one direction but the share of spending on health moves in the other, as in Kyrgyzstan from

Table 8.1 Public spending on health as a percentage of GDP

Country	1990	1991	1992	1993	1994	1995	1996	1997	1998
Kazakhstan	3.3	4.2	2.1	2.4	2.0	2.6	2.4	2.1	1.9
state budget							2.0	1.5	1.4
MHIF							0.4	0.6	0.5
Kyrgyzstan	4.1	3.6	3.2	2.6	3.5	4.0	3.1	2.8	2.8
state budget								2.7	2.7
MHIF								0.1	0.1
Tajikistan	5.0	4.7	5.7	4.9	6.2	1.3	1.8	1.6	1.4
Turkmenistan	3.7	3.7	2.0	1.8	1.8	1.8	2.3	4.0	3.7
Uzbekistan	4.6	4.6	4.7	4.1	3.5	3.6	3.7	3.3	3.3

Note: For Kazakhstan, MHIF only includes payroll tax and self-employed contributions; budget transfers to the MHIF are included as part of state budget health spending.

Sources: Klugman and Schieber (1999) for 1990–94 data for Kazakhstan and 1990–93 data for all countries except Tajikistan. For 1994–98, the following sources were used: Kazakhstan: Agency for Health Care, Kazakhstan (2000); Kyrgyzstan: Kutzin (2000); Tajikistan: Thompson (2000); Turkmenistan: IMF (1999a); Uzbekistan: World Bank (1999)

Figure 8.3 Trends in real health spending from public sources (index: 1999 = 100)

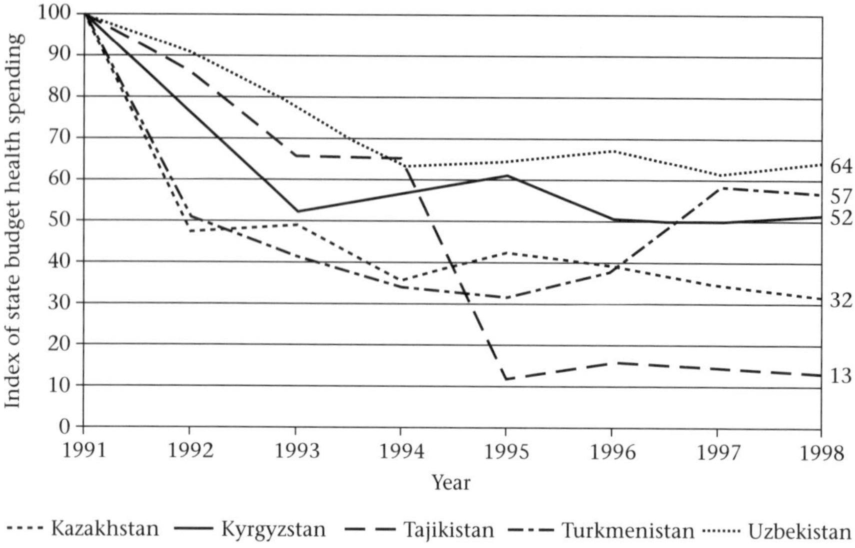

---- Kazakhstan —— Kyrgyzstan — — Tajikistan —·— Turkmenistan ······· Uzbekistan

Note: The trends were constructed from data on health spending, as a percentage of GDP (see sources in Table 8.1) and data on real GDP for each country.

Sources: GDP data came from: IMF (1999a), Izvorski and Gurgen (1999), World Bank (1999), National Statistical Committee of the Kyrgyz Republic (2000)

1994 to 1995. The data for Kazakhstan show clearly that the introduction of a new source of funding did not compensate for the reduction in state budget funding. From 1996 to 1998, real state budget funding (both direct financing and transfers to the MHIF) declined by nearly 70 per cent, while MHIF payroll tax revenues increased by less than 30 per cent. In contrast, in Kyrgyzstan, the funding raised through the MHIF was much less than that in Kazakhstan, but there was no compensatory decline in state budget funding.

By comparing the share of government health spending as a percentage of GDP to data on GDP growth during the 1990s, it is possible to construct the trend in real levels of public funding for health systems. As shown in Figure 8.3, real public spending on health declined dramatically in all the central Asian republics during the first half of the 1990s. This was almost certainly due to the overall decline in the availability of government revenues (associated with the decline in GDP) and the consequent need for public expenditure cuts in the pursuit of fiscal balance. From the mid-1990s, the central Asian republics began to diverge in their health spending patterns, reflecting a combination of different public revenue and growth performance (see Chapter 3) and different public spending priorities.

In Turkmenistan, the change in public-sector priorities in favour of the health sector, which began in 1996, led to a change in health spending that, by 1998, matched the decline in real GDP. Since 1995, however, Kazakhstan has witnessed a steady decline in the share of GDP absorbed by government health spending. The fall from 1995 to 1996 is explained by a decline of over

Table 8.2   State budget health spending per person, in US dollars, 1998

Country	Official exchange rate (US$)	Market exchange rate (US$)	GNP per person, US$, 1998
Kazakhstan	28.7	Same	1310
Kyrgyz Republic	9.8	Same	350
Tajikistan	2.7	Same	350
Turkmenistan	21.4	16.2	575
Uzbekistan	19.7	13.6	870

Note: For Uzbekistan, the market exchange rate for 1998 was calculated by applying the premium over the official rate derived from the calculation of the weighted average of official and unofficial curb market rates for 1997 (World Bank 1999: Annex 2).

Sources: GNP per person data from World Bank's *World Development Indicators* (www.worldbank.org) and population data from WHO (2000), except as indicated. Kazakhstan: health spending from Agency for Health Care, Kazakhstan (2000), exchange rate from IMF (2000b). Kyrgyzstan: health spending and population from Kutzin (2000), exchange rate from IMF (2000b). Tajikistan: health spending from Thompson (2000) and IMF (1999a), exchange rate from McHugh and Gurgen (1999). Turkmenistan: health spending, exchange rate and GDP per person (not GNP) from IMF (1999a). Uzbekistan: market exchange rate from World Bank (1999: Annex 2)

2 percentage points of GDP in total government spending, even as the share of health in the budget increased. The decline from 1996 to 1998 reflects a continued decline in real public spending on health, even as GDP began to show positive growth in 1996. Remarkably, the introduction of the MHIF in Kazakhstan (funded from a mix of payroll taxes and transfers from public budgets, all of which are included in the data) in 1996 was associated with a steady decline in total public spending on health. This stands in contrast to the payroll tax-financed MHIF in Kyrgyzstan, which was associated with a very slight increase in real total public spending on health after its introduction in 1997.

Unlike the other central Asian republics, the decline in real health spending (relative to the change in GDP) in Tajikistan from 1991 to 1994 was less than the decline in GDP. In 1995, however, government health spending declined precipitously. Given that real GDP did not decline rapidly in that year, this fall is probably the result of a sudden shift in public-sector resource allocation priorities. It is also likely that there was a substantial reduction in overall public spending in Tajikistan in 1995 – the result of a three-fold drop in real public revenues in 1995 compared to 1994. Given the fall in total public spending between 1995 and 1996 (by 7 per cent of GDP) and a decline in real GDP of 6.7 per cent, it is remarkable that Tajikistan actually increased its real level of health spending in 1996. This increase was due to an almost 3 per cent increase in the share of government spending devoted to health, reflecting a strong commitment to protect the health sector in the face of budget cuts.

Using 1998 estimates of total public spending on health and US dollar exchange rates, a comparison across countries can be made of per person public spending on health (see Table 8.2). In this kind of comparison, the expectation is that levels of per person spending would reflect country differences in

Figure 8.4 Trends in real per person public spending on health (index: 1995 = 100)

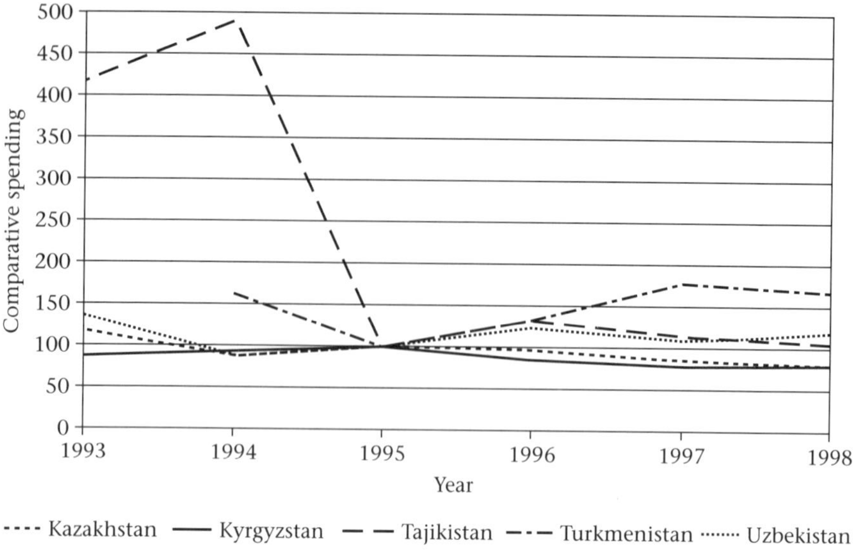

Note: Nominal per person expenditures are deflated by the consumer price index for all countries.

Sources: Kazakhstan: CPI from IMF (2000b), health spending from Agency for Health Care, Kazakhstan (2000). Kyrgyzstan: CPI from National Statistical Committee of the Kyrgyz Republic (2000), health spending from National Statistical Committee of the Kyrgyz Republic (2000) and (Kutzin 2000). Tajikistan: CPI from IMF (2000a), health spending from Thompson (2000) and IMF (1999a). Turkmenistan: CPI from IMF (1999b), health spending from IMF (1999b). Uzbekistan: CPI from World Bank (1999), health spending from World Bank (1999)

per person income. This appears to be only partially true for the central Asian republics, however. Certainly, Kazakhstan, with the highest per person GNP, had the highest per person spending level, and Kyrgyzstan and Tajikistan had the lowest. Turkmenistan, however, stands out for its remarkably high level of spending relative to its income. Even after adjusting for the country's over-valued official exchange rate, health spending is remarkably high for a country of its income level. This can only be explained by the combination of the country's high share of public expenditure devoted to health (over 14 per cent) and its high level of public expenditure relative to its GDP. As discussed by Pomfret in Chapter 3, it is likely that Turkmenistan's real fiscal deficit is considerably greater than that implied by its official figures, which suggests that its current level of public expenditures is not sustainable. Even if the government maintains its current resource allocation priorities that favour the health sector, the need to bring overall public spending in line with public revenues means that the current real level of state budget health spending is not likely to be maintained.

Presenting a trend in dollar per person spending would be misleading, because this would be more a reflection of exchange rate changes than of changes in real levels of resource allocation to the health sector. It is more appropriate to compare changes in real per person spending denominated in national currencies

Figure 8.5 Trends in real per person public spending on health (index: 1995 = 100)

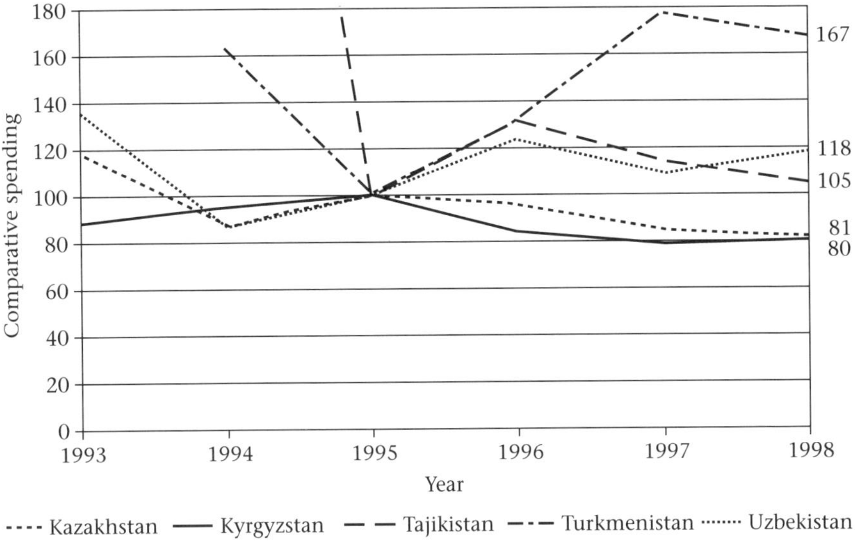

Note: This is the same information as in Figure 8.4, but on a different scale and excludes data for Tajikistan for 1993–94.

Sources: See notes for Figure 8.4

and converted to index values (Figures 8.4 and 8.5). Figure 8.4 is dominated by the nearly four-fold decline in real per person spending experienced by Tajikistan between 1994 and 1995. While dramatic, this is consistent with the other health expenditure indicators already presented. Figure 8.5 presents the same information as in Figure 8.4, but on a different scale, so that differences between the other countries can be seen. Here again, Turkmenistan stands out for its allocations, which have apparently increased real per person state budget health spending by 67 per cent between 1995 and 1998. Uzbekistan and even Tajikistan show more modest increases over this same period, whereas Kazakhstan and Kyrgyzstan experienced reductions. Kazakhstan experienced a steady decline since 1996, whereas Kyrgyzstan reversed its declining trend in 1998.

Voluntary prepayment

Typically, a distinction is drawn between social health insurance and private health insurance (see, for example, Wagstaff *et al.* 1999) in the analysis of health financing. Social health insurance is considered public and private insurance private. When analysing health finance sources, however, the real distinction that should be drawn is between situations or schemes in which the government mandates prepayment or does not mandate it. This allows the classification of voluntary health insurance schemes that are government owned, as with Thailand's voluntary Health Card scheme (Nitayarumphong and Pannarunothai 1998). Of more relevance is the existence, since 1996, of a government-run voluntary health insurance scheme in Turkmenistan (Ensor and Thompson 1998).

The health insurance scheme in Turkmenistan is available to all economically active persons, with contributions set at 4 per cent of the insured's gross income (for private-sector and state enterprise employees), the national average wage (for the self-employed) or a stipend (for students). In its first year of operation, 66 per cent of those eligible elected to join the scheme. The main benefit is a 90 per cent discount on prescribed outpatient drugs. Other benefits are a 25 per cent discount on the cost of dentures, guaranteed hospitalization within 7 days of inpatient referral and free choice of family doctor (Ensor and Thompson 1998).

Although the health insurance scheme has drawn a remarkably high percentage of eligible participants, it does not appear to have mobilized a substantial level of resources. The IMF (1999b) includes the MHIFs on the revenue side of the 'State Budget Operations' table. By comparing the level of these revenues to the total state budget health expenditures included in the same table (assuming that expenditures from the fund are included in the latter), the estimated share of fund revenues in total government health spending was 6.3 per cent in 1996 and 7.4 per cent in 1997. In 1998, the figure dropped substantially to only 1.7 per cent. The reason for this decline is unclear. In net terms, however, the health insurance scheme may be exacerbating the financial problems of the sector, because its fee-for-service reimbursement of drugs has induced cost escalation (Ensor and Thompson 1998). This is a function of the scheme's purchasing methods rather than its revenue raising methods, but it is a risk inherent in many insurance schemes.

Although information is limited, private voluntary insurance is legal and does exist in at least some of the central Asian republics. In those republics for which information exists (Kazakhstan and Kyrgyzstan), the coverage and financial role of private insurance is so minimal as to be unimportant (Kulzhanov and Healy 1999; Sargaldakova et al. 2000). Current economic circumstances and the absence of any history of private health insurance mean that there is simply not much of a market for this in the central Asian republics.

Out-of-pocket payment

'Direct payments by users at the time services are provided' is the last main category of domestic health financing. During the Soviet era, health care services were ostensibly free to all at the point of delivery, apart from outpatient drugs – for which all but some designated vulnerable populations were required to pay. It is likely, however, that some unofficial payments did exist (Ensor and Savelyeva 1998; Falkingham 1998). In central Asia, there has also been a tradition of voluntary gratitude payments (in cash or kind) to care-givers (Falkingham, in press). As Falkingham discussed in Chapter 4, evidence from several sources suggests that the role of out-of-pocket payments in financing health services in central Asia has grown during the transition to independence, and governments are developing policies on official user charges as a part of their health reforms. This section summarizes the information available on the level and trends in these forms of payment in the central Asian republics. In these republics, there are four main forms of direct private payments for health services at the time of use. Two of these may be characterized as official, or at least legal. The first of these is the payment and collection of official user fees in government health facilities for both health and non-health (for example, rental of buildings, transportation and fees for postgraduate education) items. Official fees are levied not only for personal health care services but also for some public health services that involve a transaction, such as the public health certification of industries, food production and restaurants. Other forms of legal out-of-pocket payments are those made to private providers of services (for example, private pharmacies, doctors, hospitals and other practitioners) in a purely private market transaction.

Two other types of direct payments can be categorized as unofficial or informal, which are defined as 'payments to individual and institutional providers in-kind or cash that are outside official payment channels, or are purchases that are meant to be covered by the health care system' (Lewis 2002). The first of these includes payments made directly to health workers for services delivered in publicly owned health facilities. The second includes purchases or in-kind provision of inputs (for example, drugs and food) and services (for example, feeding, bathing and nursing services) that are meant to be funded and provided by the government health system (Ensor and Savelyeva 1998). In most cases, the second kind of informal contributions is made during hospitalizations.

For use in policy decisions, it is important to understand the differences between these forms of payment. Much of the evidence on the magnitude and trends in private health spending does not allow for these to be quantified separately, however. As noted by Falkingham (2001), most of the available survey-based data cannot distinguish between informal payments, formal payments and payments to private providers. Similarly, it is difficult to quantify consistently the value of in-kind provision of services. Thus, in most of the central Asian republics, information available is not adequate for generating a reliable estimate of total private health spending. The best evidence on levels and trends in out-of-pocket payment is presented below and, where possible, this analysis incorporates an assessment of the different forms of direct payment.

Levels and trends in out-of-pocket payments

The most reliable estimate of the total direct private payments for health care comes from an analysis of 1999 living standards survey data in Tajikistan. From these data, Falkingham (2001) estimates that out-of-pocket health spending constituted about 70 per cent of total health spending in 1999 (US$8.58 per person as compared to US$3.75 per person by government). If government health spending equalled 1.5 per cent of GDP in that year (an average of the 1997 and 1998 figures from Table 8.1), this would mean that private spending was about 3.4 per cent of GDP, and total health spending was about 5 per cent of GDP.

Using drug expenditures for standard treatment protocols combined with hospital admission rates, and a small survey of hospitalized patients, Ensor and Savelyeva (1998) estimated private spending for medicines in hospitals in Kazakhstan. From these two methods, they estimated that such payments were between US$40 and US$48 per patient and US$8.5 and US$10.4 per person. At the national level, this would imply that payments for hospital medicines alone represented between 25 and 30 per cent of the 1996 government health budget. Alternatively, Sari *et al.* (2000) used the results of a nationally repres- entative household survey to impute *total* per person private expenditures, leading to an estimate that private expenditures accounted for 32.5 per cent of total health spending in 1996. If, however, the estimates of Ensor and Savelyeva (1998) are accurate, these estimates suggest that total private payments ac- count for substantially more than the 32.5 per cent of total health spending found by Sari *et al.* (2000).

A partial estimate of private spending exists for Kyrgyzstan, where official data on the level of official fee revenues in government facilities have been recorded since 1996. The share of such revenues in government health spend- ing (including MHIF spending) increased from 3.3 per cent in 1996 to 8.4 per cent in 1998. In addition, it is possible to construct an estimate of direct payments for drugs from private pharmacies (the main source of private pro- vision in Kyrgyzstan) in 1998. About half of the total sales of 520 million som by licensed pharmacies in 1998 comprised sales to individuals (that is, out- of-pocket payment). This amount, however, understates the actual volume of drug purchases by individuals, because of the existence of a black market in pharmaceuticals. Staff of the Kyrgyzstan Ministry of Health Pharmaceutical Department estimated that black market sales might add another 25 per cent to total out-of-pocket expenditures for drugs. When added to total recorded health spending (budget, official fees and MHIF) for 1998, it raises the share of health in GDP from 3.1 to 4 per cent. This amount of private expenditure on drugs would represent almost 24 per cent of total health spending. When added to official fees, the share of private spending in total health expend- itures for 1998 would come to about 30 per cent. These remain substantial underestimates of the true level of private and total spending, because informal payments and payments for private health services other than drugs are not included (Kutzin 2000).

Although it is difficult to estimate the level of informal payments, the data presented above suggest that it is both high and increasing (see also Falkingham, Chapter 4). In Tajikistan, it is estimated that private payments accounted for nearly three-quarters of total health spending in 1999. The partial nature of the estimates from Kazakhstan and Kyrgyzstan suggests that it is reasonable to conclude that private spending constitutes at least half of total health expenditures in each country. Such estimates are probably conservative, especially in the case of Kyrgyzstan, given the international evidence showing that the share of private spending is greater in lower in- come countries (Schieber and Maeda 1997). Given the importance of private payments, better data on the extent of the various forms of private health spending are needed for each of the central Asian republics to make informed policy decisions.

Effects of direct payment on individual access to care and economic well-being

Direct out-of-pocket payment at the time of service use has particular effects on access to care, the efficiency with which services are provided and the economic well-being of families that make such payments (Kutzin 1998). This is in marked contrast to the prepaid forms of contribution (general taxation, social insurance contributions and voluntary insurance contributions) described earlier in this chapter. While prepaid forms of contribution do have certain effects (depending on the progressivity of the contribution structure, for example), they do not contain any inherent incentives for the organization or use of health services. These depend on resource allocation (including provider payment) methods described in Chapter 9. Moreover, because they are prepaid, they do not entail an unexpected financial shock to families in the way that direct payments can (because these sometimes cannot be anticipated).

Ensor and Savelyeva (1998) suggest that direct payments can have a number of effects. These include creating or exacerbating differences in access to care between rich and poor households, shifting the focus of providers towards revenue-generating rather than health-improving services, and reducing the efficiency with which inputs are purchased. Because policy-makers in central Asian republics have not addressed informal payments, the possibility exists that these can undermine certain types of reforms (for example, in provider payment) or at least diminish the potential effects of such reforms. Finally, the authors note that informal payments have enabled health service provision to continue even in the context of dramatic falls in public funding. By failing to address informal payments, policy-makers may be able to avoid making explicit and, therefore, politically difficult decisions to prioritize the use of public funds in the health sector.

The survey data from Kazakhstan, Kyrgyzstan and Tajikistan, presented by Falkingham (Chapter 4), provide an indication of the kinds of effects that private payments are having. This evidence suggests that the need to pay for health care places a substantial financial burden on families and is preventing or delaying some from seeking care. These harmful effects on access to care and economic well-being are, as might be expected, felt most severely by poorer families. The extent of poverty in these countries means that these effects are widespread.

It is fair to conclude that arrangements for financing health care in Kazakhstan, Kyrgyzstan and Tajikistan (and probably the other central Asian republics, although to different extents) do not protect individuals and families from falling into poverty as a consequence of health care expenditures. Many people must make a difficult choice between their short-term physical and financial well-being, and many forego needed care because of its expected cost. Overall, the impact of these expected and actual costs falls disproportionately on the poorest families that are least able to cope with them.

Is there a role for compulsory insurance?

The introduction of payroll-tax financed social health insurance has been on the policy agenda of most countries of the former Soviet Union (FSU countries).

As noted by Ensor and Thompson (1998), the desire to obtain earmarked funding for health systems was an important motivation for the consideration of such policies in these countries. As suggested by the transitional pattern of economic decline, growing unemployment and downward pressure on wages, the central Asian situation has not been supportive of compulsory health insurance as a significant source of funds. This conclusion is borne out by country experience, both in terms of revenue generation and even the mere existence of compulsory insurance funds. Tajikistan, Turkmenistan and Uzbekistan have not introduced social health insurance, and Kazakhstan's MHIF existed for only 3 years (1996–98) before its earmarked payroll tax was eliminated and the functions of the organization were transformed. Kyrgyzstan's MHIF has added only a small increment to total public spending on health, and Kazakhstan's MHIF was associated with a net reduction in funding for health. At the present time, Kyrgyzstan has the only functioning MHIF among the central Asian republics.

This does not mean, however, that there is no role for compulsory health insurance funds in the central Asian republics; it just means that raising revenues should not be viewed as a prime objective of such schemes. Because social health insurance funds typically implement several functions of the health care system, in addition to raising revenues (for example, paying providers and monitoring performance), they can have far-reaching effects on the health system (Borowitz et al. 1999). In the case of the central Asian republics and other FSU countries where compulsory insurance is being added as a funding source to an existing budget-financed network of health providers, these effects are likely to differ from those where social health insurance systems have their own separate provider network, as is the case in several Latin American countries (Londo and Frenk 1997).

Theoretically, there is no clear advantage or disadvantage to introducing compulsory insurance into a budget-funded health system. The performance of a health financing system depends on how efficiently and fairly revenues are pooled and on the incentive environment created by provider payment methods. Of course, the method by which revenues are contributed does have implications for social objectives. Although there is evidence from several OECD (Organisation for Economic Co-operation and Development) countries that raising health revenues through general taxation is more equitable than doing so through payroll taxation (Wagstaff et al. 1999), it is not at all clear that this finding can be generalized to the central Asian context. Certain practical or administrative issues that exist in some countries suggest, however, that the source of funds can, in fact, affect how the funds are pooled and how services are purchased. Although a detailed treatment of this is beyond the scope of this chapter, the experiences of Kazakhstan and Kyrgyzstan suggest how the introduction of compulsory insurance into a budget-funded health system can differ.

In both countries, the MHIF was established as a separate national institution that collected its own revenues in an off-budget fund. Both MHIFs duplicated some of the functions of the health ministries (pooling funds and allocating to providers). From its inception, Kazakhstan's MHIF received both payroll taxes and transfers from the state budget, so that local government health authorities saw themselves in competition with the fund for control of the health system (Wickham and Simidjiyski 2000). A substantial share of total public funding was moved through the fund. This comprised 25, 57 and 57 per cent of total public spending on health in 1996, 1997 and 1998, respectively, with about half of this amount coming from payroll taxes (the rest coming from local government budget transfers) (Agency for Health Care, Kazakhstan 2000). Kyrgyzstan's MHIF proceeded much more gradually and only received funds from payroll taxes during its first 3 years. Thus, the revenues that it provided to the health system were viewed as additional; as a result, Kyrgyzstan's MHIF was viewed very positively by the rest of the health system (Gedik and Kutzin 1998). Ironically, therefore, one factor that appears to have contributed to the downfall of Kazakhstan's MHIF was that it became too big, too fast. It was introduced rapidly before the legal and regulatory base was adequately in place or sufficient institutional capacity had been developed. As a result, the MHIF made some important missteps early on and frequently changed its policies, contributing to an initial scepticism and overall lack of trust in the system, which were never overcome.

Even though Kyrgyzstan's MHIF manages a comparatively small amount of resources, its ability to pool funds and distribute these to providers, by using new payment methods, has had far-reaching effects on the organization of service delivery. Conceptually, such changes would have been possible to implement through changes in the way state budget resources are used. In practice, however, government rules on the use of budget funds (for example, strict line-item budgeting) constrained the ability of the Ministry of Health to innovate on its own. Having a health fund with its own source of revenues gave impetus to the implementation of reform. Most important for the potential of this process (and perhaps the lesson for other countries considering the introduction of an MHIF) has been the close coordination of policies and implementation between Kyrgyzstan's MHIF and its health ministry (including the incorporation of the MHIF under the Ministry of Health in 1999). A government decree to include all children as MHIF beneficiaries in 2000 provides the first step in a possible expansion of the role of the fund, as this is meant to be funded by budget transfers (Kutzin 2000). Hence, Kyrgyzstan's MHIF is poised to play a much more important, but politically vulnerable, role in the health system. Time will tell whether this will lead to the same result as that which occurred with Kazakhstan's MHIF or if this is an important step towards the MHIF becoming the health ministry's single payer for health care services for the entire population. If so, its responsibilities for health service purchasing will be of far greater importance than its role as a source of funds (Kutzin 2000).

Although both Kazakhstan's and Kyrgyzstan's MHIF were established as off-budget organizations, there is considerable pressure from the International Monetary Fund to place all such funds on-budget as part of overall macro-economic stabilization and policies to improve fiscal responsibility and transparency. The off-budget status of health insurance funds in Kazakhstan and Kyrgyzstan contributed to the ability to pool funds geographically and to implement new payment systems (because off-budget organizations are not tied to strict line-item budget rules), but it also raised issues of accountability and corruption in Kazakhstan. Countries need to explore other mechanisms, such as a special purpose on-budget fund, that can be as flexible as off-budget funds and achieve the same goals, but that still maintain budgetary accountability.

Conclusions

This chapter contains very few surprises and little good news. The economic and fiscal context of the central Asian republics will not allow for any significant increase in funding for health systems. The same factors that constrain the growth of general revenues also limit the potential of payroll-tax-financed social health insurance. Expansion of voluntary insurance is unlikely and is fraught with problems, even if it were a serious option. Increasingly, health systems are being sustained by (mostly informal) out-of-pocket payments, but these have very harmful consequences for equity in financing, poverty prevention and access to care. All of this suggests that the only realistic reform strategies must focus on cost reductions and efficiency gains, rather than on new forms of generating revenue. The level of health system funding is largely outside the control of health-sector decision-makers, whose attention should instead be focused on improving the use of current resources.

References

Agency for Health Care, Kazakhstan (2000) *Health Expenditure Data.* Almaty: Agency for Health Care.

Borowitz, M., O'Dougherty, S., Wickham, C. *et al.* (1999) *Conceptual Foundations for Central Asian Republic Health Reform Model*, Technical Report of the ZdravReform Program. Almaty: Abt Associates.

Ensor, T. and Savelyeva, L. (1998) Informal payments for health care in the former Soviet Union: some evidence from Kazakhstan, *Health Policy and Planning*, 13(1): 41–9.

Ensor, T. and Thompson, R. (1998) Health insurance as a catalyst to change in former communist countries, *Health Policy*, 43(3): 203–18.

Falkingham, J. (1998) Barriers to access? The growth of private payments for health care in Kyrgyzstan, *Eurohealth*, 4(6): 68–71.

Falkingham, J. (in press) Poverty, out-of-pocket payments and inequality in access to health care: evidence from Tajikistan, *Social Science and Medicine*.

Gedik, G. and Kutzin, J. (1998) *Report on the Implementation of Health Care Reforms in Kyrgyzstan for the Period December 1997–April 1998*, Document EUR/KGZ/CARE 07 01 01 (C). Copenhagen: WHO Regional Office for Europe.

IMF (1999a) *Tajikistan: Enhanced Structural Adjustment Facility Policy Framework Paper (1999–2002)*, prepared by the Tajikistan authorities in collaboration with the staffs of the IMF and World Bank, 18 June. Washington, DC: IMF.

IMF (1999b) *Turkmenistan: Recent Economic Developments*, IMF Staff Country Report No. 99/140. Washington, DC: IMF.

IMF (2000a) *IMF Concludes Article IV Consultation with Tajikistan*, Public Information Notice No. 00/6, 14 February. Washington, DC: IMF.

IMF (2000b) *International Financial Statistics Yearbook 1999*. Washington, DC: IMF.

Izvorski, I. and Gurgen, E. (1999) Growth, employment and real incomes, in E. Gurgen, J. Snoek, J. Craig *et al.* (eds) *Economic Reforms in Kazakhstan, Kyrgyz Republic, Tajikistan, Turkmenistan and Uzbekistan*, Occasional Paper No. 183. Washington, DC: IMF.

Klugman, J. and Schieber, G. (1999) A survey of health reform in central Asia, in Z. Feachem, M. Hensher and L. Rose (eds) *Implementing Health Sector Reform in Central Asia*, papers from an EDI Health Policy Seminar held in Ashgabat, Turkmenistan, June 1996. Washington, DC: World Bank.

Kulzhanov, M. and Healy, J. (1999) *Health Care Systems in Transition: Kazakhstan*. Copenhagen: European Observatory on Health Care Systems.

Kutzin, J. (1998) The appropriate role for patient cost sharing, in R.B. Saltman, J. Figueras and C. Sakellarides (eds) *Critical Challenges for Health Care Reform in Europe*. Buckingham: Open University Press.

Kutzin, J. (2000) Review of Kyrgyz social expenditures, health chapter, in *Report to the Department for International Development*. London: Institute for Health Sector Development.

Lewis, M. (2002) Informal health payments in eastern Europe and central Asia: issues, trends and policy implications, in E. Mossialos, A. Dixon, J. Figueras and J. Kutzin (eds) *Funding Health Care: Options for Europe*. Buckingham: Open University Press.

Londo, J. and Frenk, J. (1997) Structured pluralism: toward an innovative model for health system reform in Latin America, *Health Policy*, 41(1): 1–36.

McHugh, J. and Gurgen, E. (1999) External sector policies, in E. Gurgen, H. Snoek, J. Craig *et al.* (eds) *Economic Reforms in Kazakhstan, Kyrgyz Republic, Tajikistan, Turkmenistan and Uzbekistan*, Occasional Paper No. 183. Washington, DC: IMF.

National Statistical Committee of the Kyrgyz Republic (2000) http://nsc.bishkek.su

Nitayarumphong, S. and Pannarunothai, S. (1998) Achieving universal coverage of health care through health insurance: the Thai situation, in S. Nitayarumphong and A. Mills (eds) *Achieving Universal Coverage of Health Care*. Notaburi, Thailand: Ministry of Public Health, Office of Health Care Reform.

Sargaldakova, A., Healy, J., Kutzin, J. and Gedik, G. (2000) *Health Care Systems in Transition: Kyrgyzstan*. Copenhagen: European Observatory on Health Care Systems.

Sari, N., Langenbrunner, J. and Lewis, M. (2000) Affording out-of-pocket payments for health services: evidence from Kazakhstan, *Eurohealth*, 6(2): 37–9.

Schieber, G. and Maeda, A. (1997) A curmudgeon's guide to financing health care in developing countries, in G. Schieber (ed.) *Innovations in Health Care Financing*, Proceedings of a World Bank Conference, 10–11 March 1997, World Bank Discussion Paper No. 365. Washington, DC: World Bank.

Thompson, R. (2000) *Financial and Economic Analysis of the Health Sector in Tajikistan 1999*, Report prepared for the Somoni Project. Dushanbe: WHO.

Wagstaff, A., van Doorslaer, E., van der Burg, H. *et al.* (1999) Equity in the finance of health care: some further international comparisons, *Journal of Health Economics*, 18: 263–90.

WHO (2000) *WHO European Health for All Database*. Copenhagen: WHO Regional Office for Europe.

Wickham, C. and Simidjiyski, J. (2000) *National Health Insurance Systems: A Review of Selected International Experience*. *ZdravReform Program*. Almaty: Abt Associates.

World Bank (1999) *Uzbekistan: Social and Structural Policy Review*, Report No. UZ-19626. Washington, DC: World Bank.

chapter nine

Allocating resources and paying providers

Tim Ensor and Jack Langenbrunner

Introduction

In eastern Europe and other parts of the former Soviet Union, methods of obtaining funding for the health sector have often dominated the health system reform agenda. From the point of view of system efficiency, the allocation of financial resources is often more important in bringing about change within the health sector. Financial incentives, supported by strong quality control, can yield improvements in the way services are provided. Similarly, ill-conceived incentives can encourage patterns of treatment that conflict with best medical practice and waste resources on inappropriate care.

In this chapter, we examine resource allocation at two levels: first, the allocation of resources to geographic regions and, second, the allocation to health service providers through provider payments mechanisms. The issues involved are closely connected with others addressed in this book. In particular, the preferred method of provider payment is likely to be strongly influenced by the strategy chosen for primary and secondary care restructuring.

Historic situation

During the Soviet era, resources were allocated according to a consolidated national plan (see Field, Chapter 6). This plan was developed before the beginning of the year and based on a bottom-up assessment of need. On the expenditure side, the source of information on needs was an expert assessment of the number of units of input required for a given population at each level of the system. A similar procedure was in place for all publicly financed services. For health care, the norms were defined by the network of health institutions, based on the Semashko model of health service provision and

Table 9.1 Basis of norms used to compute expenditure on line items

Chapter (line item)	Basis of norm
1 & 2 Salaries and social security	Number and grade of staff in post
3 Operating expenditures	Last year's budget
9 Meals	Bed-days
10 Medicines	Bed-days
12 Equipment	Number of beds
14 Furniture and fixtures	Number of beds
16 Maintenance	Number of beds

finance. The model ensured that the country was served by a tiered system of health facilities, starting with the rural feldsher station and ambulatory clinic, through district and city hospitals and polyclinics, and up to regional and national level specialist hospitals, clinics and dispensaries.

These norms led to specific budgetary requirements for each health care institution. The number of beds in an inpatient institution determined the number and type of staff required. Staff numbers in a polyclinic were based on the size of the population served by the area. The total budget for an institution was obtained by multiplying staff numbers by the appropriate national pay scale. This reflected the experience of staff, the specialty and a small number of adjustment coefficients. Adjustments were made for geographic region and for working in areas of environmental degradation. Funding for other line items was based on facility- and population-specific norms (see Table 9.1). Food expenditure in hospitals, for example, was based on the number of bed-days provided in the previous year.

The administrative level above approved finance plans for an area; the national finance ministry approved proposals made by regions, and regional finance departments approved district proposals. Until the break-up of the Soviet Union, the budget proposals of each republic were approved in Moscow. Approval was dependent on whether sufficient revenue was available to finance plans and on adherence to state standards. Revenue was collected at each level of government and then shared between that level and higher levels. Since health and other social sectors were considered unproductive, they were only allocated funding once the productive sectors were financed. This makes the creation of such an extensive health system infrastructure all the more remarkable.

Although the basic population norms encouraged a certain degree of input-dominated equity, the actual distribution was inevitably and inexorably influenced both by the initial distribution of facilities and by political, social and economic factors. Areas that generated more revenue had greater influence over their share than those with a smaller revenue base. In Tajikistan, for example, it is suggested that much of the variation in spending by region can be attributed to the size of the revenue base rather than to social needs (Richter 1998). This permitted a region to build up and maintain a large publicly financed infrastructure and led to wide differences in funding within each country.

Once begun, these inequities were self-perpetuating. Since the overall budget was dominated by the hospital whose activity was largely supply driven, large hospitals led to more patients, in turn increasing the budget for non-staff items, and even justifying greater investment in infrastructure.

In recent years, the health care system has broken down in the face of a deteriorating macroeconomic situation and declining state revenues. According to World Bank estimates, real per person national income (as an unweighted average) declined by more than 40 per cent between 1991 and 1995 across central Asia (World Bank 1996), while government revenue declined by more than 60 per cent. In practice, the annual process of rigorously reworking budgets according to inputs and national norms has been supplanted by a system of adjustment according to the revenues available and the past pattern of inflation-adjusted expenditure. As a consequence, institutions at every level report underfunding of needs.

One advantage of the system was that almost everyone had access to a health care network. Although health care was undoubtedly more sophisticated in the urban areas, it was probably no more so than in other middle- and high-income countries. Another advantage was that strong financial control was maintained.

From an economic viewpoint, the disadvantages of the health care system are well known and documented (Ensor 1993; Preker and Feachem 1993). Some of the main disadvantages are discussed below: an absence of provider incentives, little local control over resources, the absence of positive provider incentives, and overspecialization and duplication of facilities.

Absence of provider incentives to economize on inputs

Because current allocations were determined by the capacity, as measured by beds and bed-days, there was little incentive to economize on factors of production. The line budgets ensured that excess capacity was quickly filled. The incentive to increase the number of patients treated was minimal, since it was always cheaper to treat one patient for 20 days than to treat four patients for 5 days each – the budget remaining the same in each situation. The result was crowded specialist hospitals, disproportionate finance for hospitals and lengthy stays. A study in North Kazakhstan, for example, found that the average length of stay for gastric ulcers was 23 days, compared to 7 days in the United Kingdom (Ensor and Thompson 1999). Similar differences were found for many other conditions. There was no incentive to update medical technology to the best international (Western) standards, since these called for reduced hospitalization and increased use of ambulatory care. Furthermore, clinical protocols based on outdated methods of patient management called for long stays in hospital.

Little local control over resources

Top-down normative planning meant there was little official room to vary the use of resources at the local level. There was no official way a hospital director could, for example, increase the amount spent on equipment and reduce the amount spent on staff. The facility had no bank account or powers to move funds between budget lines. In recent years, unofficial ways of varying expenditure have arisen, as a consequence of financial difficulties. Since all lines are under-funded, managers have some say over relative under-funding. They can, for example, choose not to fill certain posts, thus allowing increased funding for other items.

Few incentives for medical workers

The system had few positive financial incentives for medical workers. Medical workers were paid according to years of service and specialty. They were also paid for working in certain dangerous areas. For example, the area around the Aral Sea and sites of nuclear tests were considered dangerous, so justifying a higher salary. Most medical workers received a salary that was lower than the national average wage but were offered a job for life. In Soviet times, there were other non-financial incentives, particularly for Communist Party members. Public medical workers also had the possibility of adding to their income through unofficial payments. Although it is generally accepted that unofficial payment was a feature of the pre-transition Soviet Union, their nature and scale is unclear. Anecdotal evidence suggests that although unofficial payments existed, their scale is much greater now as a result of the decline in overall funding and greater possibilities for doctors to earn higher incomes in other occupations. It is probable that the Russian principle of *blat* (informal system of influence), together with the central Asian tradition of service gifts, meant that monetary and non-monetary unofficial payments were substantial well before the financial decline began (Thompson and Witter 2000).

Over-specialization

There was a culture of specialization. Individual practitioners were encouraged to place a high value on specialty qualifications. At the facility level, important health problems tended to be addressed by the creation of a plethora of specialist institutes. As a result, in most regions – apart from a general regional hospital and city and districts hospitals – there are also usually institutes for oncology, narcology, infections, tuberculosis and venereology. Their high status meant that they usually received a considerable proportion of available funds. In Almaty *oblast* in Kazakhstan, for example, it was estimated that more than 40 per cent of health service spending was on tuberculosis and infectious diseases (University of York 1998). In the current recession, it appears that these institutes survive by charging for services or by obtaining donations from foreign enterprises, whereas lower status general hospitals have little access to such resources.

Allocating resources: catalysts for change

One of the features of the Soviet system of financing was that resource allocation to geographic areas was indistinguishable from, and had similar incentives to, the reimbursement of providers. Aggregate inputs determined the pattern of finance at each level of the system, and it was in the interests of all administrators to ensure that capacity was maintained at a high level. This began to change after the break-up of the Soviet Union, as countries began to review their systems and to change the way health care was financed and provided. Change has been driven by a number of, sometimes conflicting, factors.

Introduction of health insurance

An important motivation behind changes in finance systems has been the introduction of health insurance. Health insurance has been introduced most comprehensively and quickly in Kazakhstan. After 2 years of debate and pilot projects in four *oblasts*, a law was passed in June 1995 and implemented at the beginning of 1996. The insurance fund obtains funding for the employed from enterprises, while funding for the socially protected is transferred from the state budget. In practice, most funding originated from the budget system. In 1996, for example, only 14 per cent was not derived from the budget, although this proportion has increased as insurance fund collections improved.

In Kyrgyzstan, an insurance law was passed in 1992, piloted in one area of the country, but not introduced nationally until 1998. In Turkmenistan, a voluntary system of insurance was introduced in 1996, covering drugs for ambulatory patients and prosthetics. Proposals are under consideration in Azerbaijan, Tajikistan and Uzbekistan.

The creation of an insurance fund has raised questions over how funding should be allocated to local branches and how a system of activity-based payment should be established. In the case of Kazakhstan, the fund initially was wholly separate from the health ministry and budget. In Kyrgyzstan, it was made subordinate to the ministry. In each case, one of the potential advantages of the fund is its ability to catalyse change through selective purchasing. In practice, this promise has yet to be realized.

Influence of international experts

The entire former Soviet Union, including central Asia, is now open to the influence and advice of foreign experts and international ideas. Much technical assistance has flowed into the region through such agencies as the European Union (TACIS, ACE, INTAS programs), the World Bank, the World Health Organization (WHO), the Asian Development Bank (ADB) and bilateral donors such as the US Agency for International Development (USAID), the Department for International Development (DFID) in the United Kingdom and the German Technical Cooperation Agency (GTZ). Most of these agencies have incorporated review and reform of provider payment mechanisms into projects examining health system finance.

The focus of many proposals has been the creation of payment systems that reward activity rather than the use of inputs. This has been applied in different ways, often according to the background of the advising consultants, and has often led to innovative and contrasting experiments. It has also led to insufficient consideration of local impediments to change.

Public expenditure review and reform

Alongside the many sector experiments and changes have been reviews of the entire public expenditure system. The Soviet system of finance applied to all sectors not just the health sector. The system was – and is – characterized by a high level of decentralization in budget formulation and in revenue generation. Although common in federal systems, this characteristic often is missed by foreign experts visiting from unitary states. In the United Kingdom, for example, it is possible to devise an allocation formula for the entire public health sector. In post-Soviet countries, this is complicated by the fact that local budgets are formulated across all sectors by each administrative body. Sector departments have control only over facilities at that level. Thus, the health ministry controls funding for national facilities, the *oblast* department for *oblast* facilities and the *rayon* for *rayon* facilities. To promote more equitable resource allocation across the system requires a fundamental change in the way in which resources are allocated for health – for example, by allocating the entire budget through the health ministry. Alternatively, the finance ministry may be involved in a more general review of public financing principles. Anything else is a partial solution and leads to fragmented funding.

Two changes in the system of resource allocation are important. The first is the way in which resources are allocated to regions and districts of the country. The second is the way in which medical institutions and individual practitioners are paid.

Allocation on a geographical basis

The normative basis for regional allocations hampers attempts at rationalizing the health sector, lest the budget be cut as a result. The need for a new formula is reinforced by significant and growing inequalities between regions, as a consequence of unequal economic development, and by the ability of most regions to retain much of the revenues raised. In Kyrgyzstan and Uzbekistan, the region with the highest allocation receives around 60 per cent more per person than the region with the lowest allocation (Ministry of Health of Kyrgyzstan 1996). In Tajikistan and Turkmenistan, the difference is threefold (Ministry of Health 1997; World Bank 1998).

Countries that have developed a geographic resource allocation formula have tended to base allocations on population size adjusted for key need factors, such as age, gender mix and proxies for morbidity (Bourne *et al.* 1990; Birch and Chambers 1993; Mays 1995). To aid transparency, minimize information requirements and reduce the possibility of double counting, experience suggests that the resulting formula should be kept as simple as possible. Most countries adjust population size by age and gender mix, and many also weight it by some simple proxy for morbidity, such as the standardized mortality rate. Some countries have also included factors that account for special national characteristics such as remoteness of population in certain areas (which tend to increase the cost of providing care to people living in these areas). But the overwhelming message is to keep the formula simple, while allowing for the possibility for future refinement (Gilbert *et al.* 1992; Mays 1995).

In central Asia, despite much debate, practical implementation has been hindered by the government deconcentration discussed earlier. In general, while the need to implement a population-based formula has been accepted, there has been a tendency to overcomplicate the need factor adjustment.

In Kazakhstan, various formulae have been proposed that attempt to adjust simple population-based allocation for other need factors. One proposal suggested the use of per person allocations adjusted for death rates and disability as proxies for need (WHO 1994). Although there is little discussion of why these proxies should be preferred to others, such as standardized mortality rates, the proposed formula was transparent and demand-driven.

In contrast, Zhughanov *et al.* (1994) proposed a statistical approach to allocation that used multiple regression to model expenditures per person as a function of a variety of demand and supply indicators. This formula had two disadvantages. First, it was difficult to understand and thus was not transparent. Arguably, this is not a fatal flaw. The refinement to the United Kingdom formula of 1994, for example, was based on complex statistical modelling that would not be understood by most policy-makers. Yet in a society where processes are endemically hidden from the public eye and also corrupt, greater openness is certainly desirable and, possibly, mandatory. More fundamentally, the formula failed to adjust for supply-led demand for services. In the United Kingdom, early attempts to refine an earlier population-based formula made the mistake of assuming that patterns of use reflected need rather than accepting that much use is induced by supply (Carr-Hill 1990). The standard statistical techniques for correcting for this problem were not used until a further revision of the formula in 1994 (Carr-Hill *et al.* 1994).

Some changes in resource allocation in Kazakhstan were promoted by the introduction of insurance in 1996, which established a dual system of funding, via the traditional budget system and the insurance fund (University of York 1998). Since most of the revenue collected by insurance funds remains within the *oblast* (20 per cent is remitted to the national fund for reallocation), it is clear that resource allocation of insurance funds is based primarily on ability to collect revenue rather than on health need.

The government intends to introduce a per person formula that bases the agreed budget allocation to *oblasts* on the population size, but also includes other supply indicators such as the number of doctors (Kulzhanov and Healy 1999). The formula was designed by the Scientific Centre of Medical and Economic Problems in Health Care and has received government approval. It is not yet clear how far it will advance a change in the distribution of resources.

Inequalities in resource allocation are a problem at the district as well as the *oblast* level. This is because consolidated district budgets are based on revenue collections by local administrations. *Oblasts* have limited power to control the extent of the redistribution. The insurance funds in the *oblasts* offer a means of redistributing funding between districts according to population size rather than economic capacity or level of infrastructure. In some *oblasts*, notably in Zhezkazgan and the Semipalatinsk area of East Kazakhstan, the funds began to allocate funding to *rayon* level facilities on a weighted capitation basis (Zdravreform 1999). This process has been hampered recently by the reorganization of the fund (as discussed later).

As with many other health system reform issues, discussions on resource allocation in Kyrgyzstan have been led by the MANAS master plan funded by the United Nations Development Programme (UNDP) and WHO (Ministry of Health of Kyrgyzstan 1996). The MANAS plan recommended that finance be allocated to the seven *oblasts* on the basis of population, adjusted for age distribution, standardized mortality rates and altitude. The latter proxy indicator recognizes that those with least access to health care and the worst health status are populations living in remote locations at higher altitudes. Since 1996, modified versions of similar formulae were proposed, but not implemented, often because discussions have not involved the Ministry of Finance.

Since 1997, the Ministry of Finance has developed a system of categorical grants for health care and pre-tertiary education. This has been progressively refined and is now based on age weights, an index of cost of providing services in remote and high-altitude areas and some other factors (Ministry of Finance 1999). The formula will be implemented over a period of 4 years and, if fully introduced, will lead to significant changes in resource allocation (regional increases or decreases of up to 20 per cent). The relatively simple method and transparent process is a significant advance on earlier formulae, which relied largely on patronage and the strength of local administrations.

In Turkmenistan, the WHO/Ministry of Health Lukman Program also recommended the development of a population-based formula (Ministry of Health/WHO 1997). If the explicit targets for mother and child health care were to be met, greater use of facilities was required by these groups, so that the allocations were adjusted by the proportion of children (0- to 4-year-olds) and women of reproductive age (15- to 49-year-olds).

In Tajikistan, population-based formulae have been suggested, but no attempt has been made to change the allocation of resources from the old normative basis (World Bank 1998).

Paying providers

There are three main methods of reimbursing health care institutions and workers. These are time-based, service-based and population-based payments. For a time-based payment, providers are paid according to the length of time spent providing the service, irrespective of the number served. For a service-based remuneration, payment depends on the number of services provided or patients treated. For a population-based remuneration, payment is according to the size of population served by the facility, irrespective of the number of patients actually attending. Most types of payment can be categorized under one of these groups (Table 9.2).

Table 9.2 Main types of provider payments

Base	Individual practitioner	Medical institution
Time-based	Salary	Fixed budget (usually based on historic allocations)
Service-based	Fee for service Fee for patient Target payments	Fee for service Fee for patient Budget based on case-mix/utilization
Population-based	Per person payment Territorial payment	Block contract

In the Soviet system, provider remuneration was mainly time- and population-based. Much of the budget of hospitals was based on the number of staff working in the facility during the course of the year. Clinics were expected to serve a given territory and were given a budget based on the size of this area (population-based). Most staff were paid a time-based salary that was fixed, irrespective of the amount of work or size of the population catchment area.

It is possible for both time- and population-based methods to be implemented in a way that encourages institutions and practitioners to provide high-quality services. Time-based remuneration can be linked to contracts that specify what is expected of a facility or employee. Population-based remuneration can vary according to the number of patients choosing to register with a particular practitioner or clinic (open enrolment). In the Soviet system, however, these refinements were not used. Time-based payments were not dependent on current work, but were dependent on past qualifications and years of experience. Polyclinic catchments were fixed by government. Patients were not permitted to change to other providers if the service was unsatisfactory. In each case, there were few positive financial incentives to provide high-volume or quality care. Since the transition to independence, even the non-financial incentives alluded to earlier have disappeared. Real salaries have fallen and medical workers have fewer formalized positive incentives. Coupled with this is the perverse incentive to fill hospital beds with patients to maximize payments obtained through the normative system of budgeting. Under these circumstances, it is not surprising that there is a desire to reorient the system of payment towards activities. This is reinforced by the experience of many health insurance systems in western Europe and North America that utilize service-based systems of payment.

There have been considerable attempts across the region to change the prevailing system of incentives through payment reform. These efforts began during the new economic mechanism in the Soviet era and continued throughout the 1990s. Political, administrative and organizational changes have, however, often slowed or reversed reform, as in Kazakhstan when many *oblasts* were merged in 1997 and reform attempts in one *oblast* were then reversed by the newly formed administration (Horst 1998).

Hospital payment systems

At the hospital level, there has been considerable interest in both case-based payment systems and global budgeting. These are sometimes seen as competing methods although, under the right circumstances, they can be complementary. A global budget based only on past expenditure adjusted for inflation has the advantage over a norm-based system that it does not encourage overuse of beds. But it could lead to a system where there is no incentive to deliver medical care. The opposite danger is the creation of an overly complex system that requires more information than is available and which is administratively costly to implement and maintain.

In general, the central Asian republics have avoided defining large numbers of disease groups as in parts of Russia. Kemerovo, Siberia, was an exception in introducing up to 50,000 groups (later abandoned). Significantly, fee-for-service systems, which led to problems of cost escalation in the Czech Republic and Baltic states, have not been introduced in any of the republics in central Asia.

In Kazakhstan, activity-based systems have been used in a variety of locations. Experiments in the early 1990s under the new economic mechanism mostly used modified fundholding (whereby primary care practices hold a budget to buy specialist services on behalf of those enrolled) and per diem systems. The demonstrations did little to push the technology of inpatient payment systems. Fundholders in a Zhezkazgan project used only a simple per diem payment system with administrative guidelines for admissions and discharges. Average lengths of stay did not drop and case mix did not appear to change over time.

When the insurance fund began operation in 1996, it decided to pay providers a fixed amount for each patient treated. This initially was an average across the hospital, but later case-mix adjustments were envisaged. Several issues have arisen. One is that, in the initial stages, the computation of the price per patient was based on the average cost per patient at each individual hospital. So high-cost hospitals got a higher payment and more efficient hospitals were penalized.

A second issue is hospitals usually being paid only a proportion of the computed average patient costs based on the expected salary, food and medicine costs. This occurred because the insurance fund was short of money and could not afford to fully finance hospitals. Although this had the side benefit of less incentive for a hospital to treat too many patients, it also led to confusion. In some hospitals – in Kokchetav, for example – doctors were given bonuses according to the number of patients treated, which increased activity. Hospitals later found that they could not afford the bonus payments because the fund reimbursement was reduced (Ensor and Thompson 1999).

A third issue is that a patient-based system was introduced alongside, rather than instead of, the budget system. The services financed by the state were divided up between the insurance fund and budget. The budget continued to be allocated along historic (norm-based) lines and facilities could receive funding from both sources. As a result, if a hospital cuts beds and length of stay to economize or increase the throughput of patients, it is penalized by the budget but rewarded by the insurance fund. This division in the package, and duality in payment systems, also occurred in Kyrgyzstan, although a unified system is now being introduced in each *oblast* (Savas *et al.* 1998).

An obvious weakness with the average-patient payment system is that it does not account for case mix. There are a number of case-mix initiatives. In Kazakhstan, the new insurance funds in regions such as Semipalatinsk and Zhezkazgan have successively moved from per diem payments in the mid-1990s, to simple one payment-level per case, to more sophisticated case-mix systems of 55 categories. The changes have coincided with other organizational and management reforms. In Zhezkazgan, hospitals were reduced from 55 to 22 between 1994 and 1997, with the number of beds decreasing from 6225 to 2919 in the same period (Horst 1998). The Almaty City Health Administration has expressed interest in developing a diagnosis-related group (DRG) system of payment for specialist outpatient services. One hospital in the city is now paid according to a DRG-type system.

At the beginning of 1999, the Government of Kazakhstan abolished the insurance fund, transforming it into a Centre for Health Purchasing, under the Ministry of Education, Health and Culture, with local *oblast* offices no longer under the control of the *oblast* health administrations. The centres are supposed to contract with health facilities for services for the population on an open-tender basis. This could, in theory, mean that the most efficient facilities gain through additional funding. The centres are no longer responsible for collecting contributions from enterprises and must rely on transfers from the *oblast* administrations. These transfers are often not made and so centres, just like the insurance funds that preceded them, often lack money to make effective purchasing decisions.

In Kyrgyzstan, the Fund has switched from the traditional 18 category line items to a system of 55 and later 154 patient diagnostic groups. Initially, the system was introduced for district hospitals and those targeted for closure were excluded. The Fund has not been able to pay full cost per case, but only for staff, drugs, supplies and food. The intent was to pay only for variable costs. Fixed costs in the health sector are complicated and need to be addressed simultaneously with rationalization and changes in the budget flow. Nevertheless, the funding supplements the provider, is visible and encourages reform. The Fund now has a database of over 300,000 cases available for analysis, which covers admissions to hospital, length of stay and other clinical indicators (O'Dougherty 1999).

Health insurance in Tajikistan is in its early stages. Initial proposals suggest a retrospective reimbursement system based on a fee for item of service (World Bank 1998). This is a classic recipe for cost escalation in a country that can ill afford to waste resources – the average salary of a doctor is less than US$3 a month.

There are two further issues that concern case-mix-adjusted systems. One is a discrepancy between sophisticated and lower-level hospitals. Although more sophisticated hospitals may have the management capability and computing power to support a case-mix payment system, hospitals at lower levels of the system often do not have this capability. The second and perhaps more fundamental issue is that, even if all hospitals can be given expertise, the reimbursement system will be unable to address, and may even distract attention from, the fundamental problems of the need to restructure the entire system (Henscher 1999). If hospitals are concerned primarily with billing for services (perhaps playing the system to ensure that higher value patients are treated), fundamental challenges such as treating more patients at the ambulatory level may not be addressed. Although higher payments for ambulatory care can help to encourage a shift in care patterns, the changes are likely to be marginal compared to planned shifts in the nature and size of facilities.

In Kyrgyzstan, policy-makers have attempted to incorporate restructuring prerequisites alongside new payment systems. To be eligible for a contract with the Fund, the facility must be accredited and have an adequate information system in place. Hospitals are also being encouraged to utilize a national drug formulary.

In Turkmenistan, there have been several attempts to introduce global hospital budgets. The intention is to permit hospitals to move expenditure between line items and also to establish a different basis for setting the budget, so that incentives are not dependent on capacity-led norms. Changes in hospitals in Ashgabat permit some expenditure flexibility. In the district of Tedzhen, the hospital has been given a global hospital budget as part of wider health system changes proposed under a World Bank loan (World Bank 1997). Because financial reports are currently typed by hand, it would be administratively costly to introduce a more complex payment system.

One of the complaints made in the initial stages of global budgets was that the administration saw it as a licence to defraud. This was based on the idea that a global budget implies handing all the money to the chief doctor and letting the hospital spend it as they wish. To respond to this complaint, and to ensure compliance with overall national health reform objectives, the global budget was to be based on a business plan mutually agreed on with the Ministry of Health (Ensor and Amannyazova 2000). This plan shows how the hospital will meet the main objectives for health in the district through planned activities, resource re-allocation and expenditure by line item. Expenditure will then be monitored on the basis of the approved budget, and restructuring objectives can be incorporated during the planning process.

It should be noted that none of these systems needs to compete with another; rather, they are complementary. As Barnum *et al.* (1998) have pointed out, most mature payment systems are mixed. Case-mix-adjusted payment can be thought of as a development of a global budget system with adjustments for levels of activity. Both a case-mix-adjusted payment and a global budget system require good financial control and overall restructuring goals that can be provided through multi-hospital regional and facility planning.

Primary care payment systems

At the primary level, alongside the interest in developing a system of general practitioner care (see Gedik, Oztek and Lewis, Chapter 11), there is also a desire to encourage competition for patients through a system of capitation payment for each patient registered. There are a growing number of experiments in paying primary care doctors (either trained general practitioners or a team comprising a paediatrician, therapist and gynaecologist) on the basis of capitation.

In Turkmenistan, primary care staff have been paid by a modified form of capitation payment since 1997 (WHO 1998). Doctors, nurses and feldshers are paid for every 100 people registered beyond a minimum of 1000. Average remuneration is significantly beyond what a hospital doctor can earn. Currently, while patients can choose between doctors, remuneration is based on the population in the territory, so that the incentive for doctors to improve practice as a result of competition is lost.

In Kazakhstan, several regions (notably Zhezkazgan and Semipalatinsk) have implemented enrolment schemes with general practitioners and capitation budgets for ambulatory centres. Similar schemes are being used in Kyrgyzstan in more than 600 group practices and in Uzbekistan, both with financial and technical assistance from a variety of donors. Bonus schemes within the centres provide the stimulus to improve care. These systems have been hampered by a lack of funding, so that most of the budget goes to pay basic staff salaries, with little left to develop services or pay bonuses. A second problem is getting the administration to accept new forms of self-management within the public sector. This has led to suggestions that the activities are illegal.

In common with many other western and eastern European countries, the region has also shown a strong interest in fundholding. The regions of Zhezkazgan in Kazakhstan and Kara Kul in Kyrgyzstan have pioneered this approach, and other regions have also adopted plans to develop fundholding. Following initial demonstrations in Zhezkazgan, other parts of the *oblast* now plan to introduce fundholding (Horst 1998). Through the use of fundholding, the Zhezkazgan pilot area (Langenbrunner *et al.* 1994) saw drops in admissions of 26 per cent and drops in beds by 32 per cent. Reforms have been hampered by questions about the legislative status of local management of state budgets. As in the West, changes also require a significant investment in technology and managerial expertise. This is often beyond the scope of the state budget, although foreign donors have assisted with financing in certain regions.

As in other countries in transition, the depressed and changing economic environment hampers the development of new payment systems and increases local financial control. For example, much current spending occurs not on a cash basis, but instead through a process of mutual debt settlement. A facility wishing to use part of its budget for, say, building maintenance must first find a contractor with an outstanding debt with the local administration or insurance fund (depending on the source of funding). This debt is then cancelled or reduced to an agreed value in return for repairs to the building. If a debtor cannot be found for the service or commodity required, a facility may be tempted to obtain some other commodity just to ensure that the budget is spent. The mutual debt settlement system helps to ensure that services can be provided even in cashless circumstances, but it does lead to suboptimal allocation decisions and is administratively costly to operate. This problem has hampered attempts to give facilities greater financial control.

Paying practitioners

Bonuses

Most of the reforms being undertaken in central Asia have concentrated on changing the way in which facilities are paid. The main exception is changes in the way primary providers are reimbursed leading to a direct system of capitation remuneration for practitioners, as occurs in Turkmenistan. In other countries, capitation remuneration is allocated to facilities rather than to individual practitioners.

Several systems for bonus payments have been designed by local experts. These tend to be overly complex and emphasize indicators that are either difficult to measure or ambiguous. In Almaty, Kazakhstan, for example, proposals to award bonuses to doctors included penalties for high levels of infant mortality. In contrast, some countries may provide doctors with more, not less, funds to improve infant mortality, even though this is only partly amenable to reduction through medical intervention. The Almaty proposals also penalized doctors for untreated morbidity among patients that had not visited a health facility. Such perverse incentives encourage false reporting or under-reporting and are a key area for future development. Policies must move on from micro-management based on individual penalties towards the use of aggregate indices based on clinical audit and quality assurance.

Unofficial payments

No discussion of provider payment mechanisms in eastern Europe would be complete without mentioning the phenomenon of unofficial payments. As both Falkingham (Chapter 4) and Kutzin and Cashin (Chapter 8) discuss, there is growing evidence that unofficial payments contribute significant revenue to the health sector in all eastern European countries and to those of central Asia (Thompson and Witter 2000). Unofficial payments could have a significant impact on the success of reforming the formal provider payment system. If unofficial payments make up a significant proportion of practitioners' salaries, then the effect of any reform in the way they are officially paid is diluted. In some cases, incentives may even contradict the goals intended. An incentive to reduce the length of a patient's stay through case (rather than daily) payments could fail to have the desired effect if practitioners find that they can derive greater unofficial fees by extending their patient's hospital stay. Insufficient attention to the phenomenon and effects of unofficial payments may mean that reforms do not achieve their desired impact. It could be dangerous, therefore, for governments and donors to ignore or play down their significance.

Conclusions

The pattern of change across the region has varied considerably. While countries such as Kazakhstan, Kyrgyzstan and, to a lesser extent, Turkmenistan have tested a number of resource allocation reforms, little change has occurred in Tajikistan or Uzbekistan. Changes in geographical resource allocation have moved fastest in those countries tackling the problem at the level of the finance ministry. The new formula in Kyrgyzstan appears to be the most advanced, introducing a transparent and relatively simple population formula for much of the health and education sector. Similar changes are being considered in Kazakhstan. In general, the region has stayed away from retrospective reimbursement, involving fee-for-service payment methods. A number of lessons are suggested from this experience.

New payment systems cannot be developed in isolation from other system reforms. In particular, quality assurance and aggregate monitoring of activity are just as important as ensuring a technically refined reimbursement system. The developing specialty-based system, in Kyrgyzstan in particular, places considerable emphasis on quality management to ensure that the system is not driven by financial considerations alone (O'Dougherty 1998). A simple reimbursement system that places little strain on administrative capabilities can be more effective than a more sophisticated system, provided it is supported by a plan for restructuring and a strategy for comparing the impact on aggregate process and outcome quality indicators.

Institutional impediments remain the most serious obstacle to fundamental change. Although the experience and impact of the extensive experiments in innovative payment mechanisms is poorly documented, the available evidence suggests that these experiments are often blocked or prevented from having maximal impact by legal or administrative impediments.

The way in which funding is allocated to regions remains a key administrative weakness. Significant benefits would accrue to all public services by changing public expenditure regional allocations to a population-based, rather than infrastructure-based, system. Significant vested interests, however, wish to preserve the current system. Another institutional weakness is the system of property rights, which often impedes a facility in gaining more autonomy over the use of funds.

The love affair with health insurance in transitional countries is also evident in central Asia. A major challenge for health reformers is to convert these funds into effective purchasers that can use new payment systems creatively to bring about change. Although there are interesting developments, such as the selective contracting of services now being implemented in Kazakhstan, the need to develop effective purchasing capacity remains.

A further challenge posed by the development of a health insurance fund is the creation of dual payment systems, which is the case in both Kazakhstan and Kyrgyzstan. This has led to confused signals for change and has placed an added burden on overly stretched management information systems. The creation of unified funding channels for health services remains a major challenge for health systems in the transitional economies that are developing insurance finance.

Finally, new payment methods are only effective if the facility is fully recompensed in a timely manner for the (effective) activities provided. Partial funding of health care, unofficial payments and the system of mutual debt settlement, all make the incentives introduced more virtual than real. It is difficult to see how payments can result in real change without one of the following three factors: the reduction of state guarantees to a more effective level, the growth of revenues within an improved macroeconomic climate, or the increase of patient co-payments.

References

Barnum, H., Kutzin, J. and Saxenian, H. (1998) *Incentive and Provider Payment Methods*: *Human Capital Development and Operations Policy*, Working Paper No. 51. Washington, DC: World Bank.

Birch, S. and Chambers, S. (1993) To each according to need: a community-based approach to allocating health care resources, *Canadian Medical Association Journal*, 149(5): 607–61.

Bourne, D., Pick, W., Taylor, S., McIntyre, D. and Klopper, J. (1990) A methodology for resource allocation in health care for South Africa: Part 3: A South African health resource allocation formula, *South African Medical Journal*, 77: 456–9.

Carr-Hill, R. (1990) RAWP is dead: long live RAWP, in A.J. Culyer, A.K. Maynard and J.W. Posnett (eds) *Competition in Health Care: Reforming the NHS*. London: Macmillan.

Carr-Hill, R., Hardman, G., Martin, S. *et al.* (1994) *A Formula for Distributing NHS Revenues Based on Small Area Use of Hospital Beds*. York: University of York.

Ensor, T. (1993) Health system reform in former Socialist countries of Europe, *International Journal of Health Planning and Management*, 8(3): 169–78.

Ensor, T. and Amannyazova, B. (2000) Using business planning to monitor global budgets in Turkmenistan, *Bulletin of the World Health Organization,* 78: 1045–53.

Ensor, T. and Thompson, R. (1999) Rationalising rural hospital services in Kazakhstan, *International Journal of Health Planning and Management*, 14: 155–67.

Gilbert, R., Gibberd, B. and Stewart, J. (1992) The New South Wales resource allocation formula: a method for equitable health funding, *Australian Health Review*, 15: 6–21.

Henscher, M. (1999) The rationalization and management of hospitals, in Z. Feachem, M. Henscher and L. Rose (eds) *Implementing Health Sector Reform in Central Asia*. Washington, DC: EDI Learning Resources, World Bank.

Horst, K. (1998) *Implementation of Health Care Reform in Central Asia: Concepts and Examples from the Experience of Dzheskasgan Oblast, Kazakstan*. Almaty: Abt Associates.

Kulzhanov, M. and Healy, J. (1999) *Health Care Systems in Transition: Kazakhstan*. Copenhagen: European Observatory on Health Care Systems.

Langenbrunner, J., Sheiman, I., Zaman, S. *et al.* (1994) *Evaluation of Health Insurance Demonstrations in Kazakhstan: Dzheskasgan and South Kazakhstan Oblasts*. Washington, DC: Health Financing and Sustainability Project.

Mays, N. (1995) Geographical resource allocation in the English National Health Service, 1971–1994: the tension between normative and empirical approaches, *International Journal of Epidemiology*, 24(suppl. 1): S96–S102.

Ministry of Finance (1999) *On the Order of Calculation of Categorical and Equalisation Grants for the 1999 Financial Year*. Bishkek: Ministry of Finance.

Ministry of Health (1997) *Administrative Order on Payment of General Practitioners*, Supplement 19. Ashgabat: Ministry of Health.

Ministry of Health of Kyrgyzstan (1996) *Manas National Programme on Health Care Reforms 1996–2006*. Ankara: WHO.

Ministry of Health/WHO (1997) *Realisation Plan for the Presidential Health Programme, Lukman Plan*. Ashgabat: Ministry of Health.

O'Dougherty, S. (1998) *Health Reform in Kyrgyzstan: Provider Payment Component*, Progress Report on the World Bank Project. Tashkent: Abt Associates.

O'Dougherty, S. (1999) *Health Financing Reforms in Kyrgyzstan*, Progress Report. Almaty: Abt Associates.

Preker, A.S. and Feachem, R.G.A. (1993) *Market Forces in the Health Sector: The Experience of the Former Socialist States, Central and Eastern Europe*, EDI Senior Policy Seminar, Beijing. Washington, DC: World Bank.

Richter, K. (1998) *The Social Sector in Tajikistan: Some Recent Developments*, Report to the World Bank. London: LSE.

Savas, S., Gedik, G., Kutzin, J., Coskun, B. and Imanbaev, A. (1998) *Report on the Implementation of Health Care Reforms in Kyrgyzstan for the Period: May–November 1997*, Document EUR/KGZ/CARE 07 01 01 (B). Copenhagen: WHO Regional Office for Europe.

Thompson, R. and Witter, S. (2000) Informal payments in transition economies: implications for health sector reform, *International Journal of Health Planning and Policy*, 15: 169–87.

University of York (1998) *Projection Preparation for the Kazakhstan Health Sector Project: Final Report*. York: Ministry of Education, Culture and Health and Fund for Compulsory Health Insurance.

WHO (1994) *Resource Allocation in the Context of Health Reform in Kazakhstan and the ESU*, CARNET Tashkent Meeting. Copenhagen: WHO Regional Office for Europe.

WHO (1998) *Lukman Health Program*, Document EUR/TKM/CARE 070508. Ashgabat: WHO.

World Bank (1996) *World Development Report*. Oxford: Oxford University Press.

World Bank (1997) *Project Appraisal Document on a Proposed Loan to Turkmenistan for a Health Project*. Washington, DC: World Bank.

World Bank (1998) *Tajikistan*, Health Sector Note. Washington, DC: World Bank.

Zdravreform (1999) *Policy Environment for Implementation of Health Reforms*, Paper for World Bank Supervision Mission. Almaty: Abt Associates.

Zhughanov, O.T., Vagner, A.V. and Zhuganov, N.O. (1994) *The System of Health Finance Allocation*. Almaty: Institute of Medical Sciences.

chapter ten

The health care workforce

Judith Healy

Introduction

Health care systems are labour-intensive enterprises that depend upon their staff to achieve cost-effective outcomes for patients. Any changes in policy, therefore, must take health care workers into account. Staff can be regarded as a resource, as a cost and as stakeholders in health-sector reform. This chapter examines these aspects of the health care workforce in the five central Asian republics.

Before their unexpected independence from the Soviet Union in 1991, their health care systems were run as branches from Moscow, albeit very distant branches (see Field, Chapter 6). The health care workforce (in terms of numbers, occupational groups, training and functions) followed the pattern set for all Soviet republics. The central Asian republics now are grappling with both the good and the bad features of this Soviet legacy. Despite very severe funding constraints, these republics until recently delayed the politically difficult and socially painful task of restructuring their large health care workforces. The following human resource issues are now on the health policy agenda:

- *Overstaffing.* These health care systems are characterized by large numbers of staff. A legacy of the Soviet period, staffing was based on generous quantitative norms, such as number of physicians per 1000 population, set by the Semashko All-Union Research Institute of Social Hygiene and Public Administration in Moscow. The number of physicians, in particular, was regarded as an indicator of a good health care system.
- *Deteriorating infrastructures.* Once built, health facilities were run as labour-intensive, rather than capital-intensive, enterprises. Over the last few decades, buildings have deteriorated (since shrinking government health budgets have allowed little capital investment), while technology is ever more obsolete, and pharmaceuticals and other medical supplies are less affordable.

- *Hospital-centred health systems.* In these hospital-dominated health care systems, hospitals consume most of the health budgets, monopolize the best trained staff, are a power base for physicians, and contain the most equipment and medical supplies. Also, hospitals admit many people who are kept for long periods, although many could be treated in an ambulatory setting.
- *Specialized physicians/low skills.* Medical education is highly specialized, with general practice only recently introduced. Medical training is outdated, so that, combined with specialization, patients are referred to hospitals for conditions that elsewhere would be treated by general practitioners. The health care workforce is weighted heavily towards physicians, while other groups, termed 'middle level personnel', are fewer, poorly trained and subordinate to doctors.
- *Low salaries.* The low and flat wage structure has kept the salary bill down. Under the Soviet model, the health sector was not regarded as productive – for example, compared with mining (Field, Chapter 6) – so that health workers earn little more than the workforce average. Low salaries are the price being paid for maintaining high workforce numbers. Patients also are paying the price in terms of informal (under-the-table) payments to health workers that supplement low salaries. Health care personnel are pressing for higher pay and better working conditions.
- *Few performance incentives.* There are few external incentives for staff to provide better quality care and to use scarce resources more efficiently. Efforts by health ministries to improve staff performance include supply-side levers (new payment mechanisms) and demand-side levers (encouraging behavioural change), and payment methods are moving from input funding towards performance funding. To bring about behavioural change requires setting clinical standards, retraining staff, strengthening emergent professional associations and allowing more autonomy to health care managers.

Identifying trends

This chapter seeks to identify broad trends, rather than discuss detailed findings, since workforce statistics must be treated with caution. First, personnel statistics are perennially problematic, given terminological tangles on how personnel are counted: whether as physical persons (PP), full-time equivalents (FTE) or active staff. Second, occupational categories in this region may differ from international usage; for example, a qualified nurse in the central Asian republics may be categorized as an assistant nurse or aide in most European Union (EU) countries. Third, health care statistics count only public-sector staff, although so far few health professionals in central Asia have moved into the private sector. Fourth, population statistics are based on inter-census estimates; since the last census (10 years ago in most countries), however, there have been substantial population movements, while the registration of births and deaths has broken down in some areas. The denominator for staff per 1000 population is thus not necessarily accurate. Finally, the data for Tajikistan are particularly problematic, given the large population movements during the civil war and its aftermath.

Staff as a resource

The central Asian republics have a substantial asset in their human capital – that is, their plentiful supply of trained health care staff. There are three main problems, however: first, this workforce, arguably, is too large; second, the skill mix is very limited; and third, health professionals need to upgrade their training. It should be noted that there is no international consensus on the correct level and mix of staffing, since this varies between countries – for historical and structural reasons.

Health workers are a large and increasing proportion of the total workforce. For example, the health sector employs 4–10 per cent of the workforce in the G7 industrialized countries (OECD 1999). Although the precise proportion is not known for most central Asian republics, their large health workforces must be put in the context of high public-sector employment. First, under the Soviet economic system, the state was the sole employer – and is still the major employer in most republics, which are moving very cautiously towards more market-oriented economies. Second, the Soviet Union social contract with its citizens guaranteed full employment accompanied by economic and social security, the trade-off being low wages. The dissolution of this contract (given the collapse of these political and economic systems) has brought about widespread impoverishment among central Asian populations (UNDP 2000). Third, medical education, although of lesser status than in western Europe, continues to attract many students.

Privatization in the health sector has been limited mainly to pharmacies and, to a lesser extent, dental practices. All five republics legalized private health care in the early 1990s, so that physicians can practise privately, but most do so only as an adjunct to public-sector jobs, reflecting the low purchasing power of the population. Private health insurance schemes, which have emerged in a few countries, such as Kazakhstan, remain embryonic.

The health care workforce can be divided into five categories: (1) physicians; (2) other graduate-level professionals, such as dentists, scientists, economists and managers; (3) nurses and midwives; (4) allied health professionals, such as physiotherapists and dieticians; and (5) support staff, such as clerks, cooks and cleaners. In high-income countries, these five categories cover a proliferation of occupational groups. The health care workforce in the former Soviet republics, however, is much less differentiated, being divided between physicians, middle-level personnel and lower-level staff. Physicians are the health care professionals and others, as the term 'middle level' suggests, are lesser occupational groups, mainly nurses, who assist physicians.

Physicians

Although inter-country comparisons help frame human resource issues, there is no agreement across European countries on the optimal number of physicians. Some countries have attempted to limit physician numbers but without much success. The number of physicians in relation to population has risen

Figure 10.1 Number of physicians per 100,000 population in regions of Europe

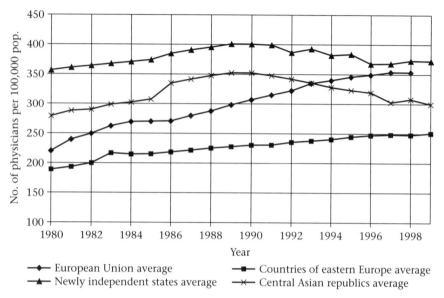

Source: WHO (2000a)

steadily in Europe, to a level previously only seen in the former Soviet republics (Figure 10.1).

The central Asian republics now have fewer physicians with 3.1 per 1000 population, than the 3.5 for the 15 countries of the EU (an average which masks considerable variation) and the 3.7 in the 15 countries of the former Soviet Union (NIS and Baltic states). The central Asian republics all have dropped from a peak around 1990. In 1998, there were 3.0 physicians per 1000 population in Turkmenistan, 3.5 per 1000 population in Kazakhstan, while Tajikistan remains the outlier with only 2.0 physicians per 1000 population (Figure 10.2). Although Tajikistan generally is regarded as having a smaller health care workforce for its population than the other countries (as noted earlier), the data are not necessarily reliable.

Examining the actual number of doctors (physical persons) gives a slightly different picture. The number of physicians dropped substantially in Kazakhstan by 20 per cent between 1990 and 1998, but much less, if at all, in the other countries (Table 10.1). Kazakhstan dropped from a very high level, and this country still has the most doctors for its population. The drop since independence is attributed to the out-migration of ethnic Russian doctors (and other non-Kazakhs) and to staff reductions, with fewer jobs due to closures of hospitals and beds (Kulzhanov and Healy 1999). In Tajikistan, the already low number of physicians dropped by 8 per cent between 1990 and 1998 due to out-migration after independence and the civil war. The state invests heavily in training physicians, so that out-migration of physicians means a loss of investment, as well as a loss of skilled people. The number of physicians in Turkmenistan and Uzbekistan, however, increased over that period.

Figure 10.2 Number of physicians per 100,000 population in central Asian republics

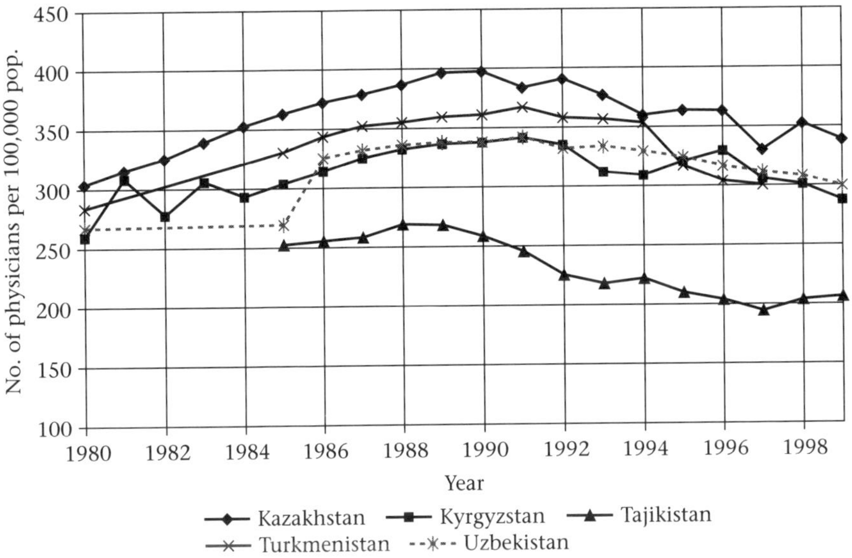

Source: WHO (2000a)

Table 10.1 Numbers of physicians and nurses, physical persons, per cent change

Country	Number of physicians, 1998	Physicians (% change 1990–98)	Number of nurses, 1998	Nurses (% change 1990–98)
Kazakhstan	53 181	−20.0	97 849	−34
Kyrgyzstan	14 048	−4.6	35 019	−11
Tajikistan	12 387	−8.4	29 846	−30
Turkmenistan[a]	1 396	+6.0	27 252	−12
Uzbekistan	73 903	+6.0	242 281	+13

[a] 1997 statistics

Source: WHO (2000a)

Physician training

In relation to their populations throughout the 1990s, the central Asian republics produced more doctors than other European regions before dropping to 14.2 graduates per 100,000 in 1998. This was still above the 10.3 graduates per 100,000 in the EU, which had dropped from a peak in the mid-1980s (WHO 2000a). From a trough around independence in 1990, medical graduates increased in most central Asian republics (except Uzbekistan), both in terms of numbers per population (Figure 10.3) and actual numbers (WHO 2000b). Kazakhstan and Uzbekistan have restricted admissions, as did Kyrgyzstan more recently. The effect of a changed admission policy does not become apparent until graduation about 6 years later, as in Uzbekistan, where a total of 4556 persons graduated in 1997 but only 2412 in 1998.

Figure 10.3 Numbers of physicians graduated per 100,000 population in central Asian republics

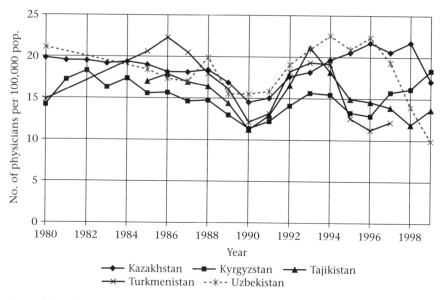

Source: WHO (2000a)

Medical students (based on the Soviet medical education system) enter separate faculties of general medicine, paediatrics, obstetrics, stomatology (dentistry), or sanitary-epidemiology medicine. Many specialize after graduation in around 100 listed specialities. Physician training has changed little for decades, using outdated Russian textbooks and didactic teaching methods with little direct experience in treating patients before graduation. Admission and progression each year is not necessarily based on competitive examinations. Kazakhstan, Kyrgyzstan and Tajikistan are in the process of combining undergraduate faculties of general medicine, paediatrics, and obstetrics and gynaecology. General practice or family medicine was introduced recently in the final year of the undergraduate course (in Kazakhstan, Turkmenistan and Uzbekistan) and as a postgraduate speciality (in Kyrgyzstan). An institute of advanced training in each country conducts postgraduate education.

Uzbekistan retains separate undergraduate faculties in its seven medical schools and awards a bachelor degree after 6 years (5 years for pharmacists, dentists and Sanepid physicians). General practice was introduced into the final year, with the first group of general practitioners graduating in 1999. A diploma in medicine follows a 2 year pre-registration period working in medical practice (Sultanov 1999).

General practice has been divided between therapeutists, obstetrician–gynaecologists and paediatricians. Some of these physicians are being retrained as family physicians in short courses of a few months in institutes of advanced training (see Gedik, Oztek and Lewis, Chapter 11). The lack of teachers and funds, however, means that these courses have become ever shorter and most

Figure 10.4 Number of nurses per 100,000 population in central Asian republics

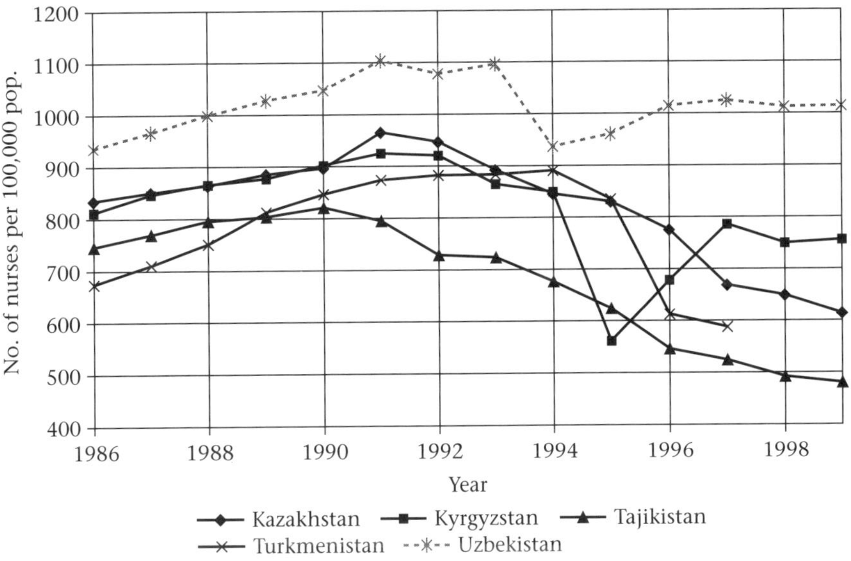

Year

—◆— Kazakhstan —■— Kyrgyzstan —▲— Tajikistan
—✕— Turkmenistan --✳-- Uzbekistan

Source: WHO (2000a)

physicians have to learn on the job, while in Turkmenistan specialists were re-labelled as family physicians by presidential decree (Mamedkuliev *et al.* 2000). At the current rate of progress, retraining doctors as family physicians will take many years.

Nurses and feldshers

Nurses are the largest occupational group in the health sector. Nurses in Soviet republics, however, never achieved full professional recognition, and nurse training and development stagnated for decades (Salvage and Heijnen 1997). Nurses are described as middle-level personnel along with other paraprofessionals. The definition of a nurse is problematic, since auxiliary and unqualified staff comprise over half of nursing personnel in former Soviet Union countries and are counted in statistics as nurses (Salvage and Heijnen 1997).

Uzbekistan has the most nurses in the region, with 10.2 per 1000 population; Tajikistan has the least, with 5.2 per 1000 population (Figure 10.4). The number of nurses, in terms of physical persons, dropped substantially between 1990 and 1998 in all countries, except Uzbekistan – for reasons that are unclear (see Table 10.1). Kazakhstan had the largest drop, with a 34 per cent reduction, followed by Tajikistan, where the health care system is in severe crisis (and data collection is not reliably maintained). The drops in these countries are generally attributed to nurses leaving a poorly paid occupation.

Feldshers are a distinctive occupation (but counted within nursing) in former Soviet Union countries, being described as 'doctor's assistants' with limited rights to prescribe drugs. They mostly work in rural areas, where doctors are difficult to recruit and retain, where they staff primary health care posts and emergency care posts. Given this history, feldshers are regarded as second-class physicians for the rural poor, but potentially offer a nurse-practitioner model, as promoted in industrialized countries. The future for feldshers is unclear, although Tajikistan with its physician shortage plans to upgrade training and increase their number (Rahminov *et al.* 2000).

Nurse training

Many students were streamed into vocational secondary schools in the former Soviet Union (Laporte and Schweizer 1994). After completing year 8, and as young as age 14 years, students entered vocational schools for a 2–3 year training course. Entry to nurse training now requires 10 years of education (in practice sometimes less), and the course is being upgraded gradually into post-secondary school nursing colleges. Most countries have introduced tertiary-level 2 or 3 year diploma courses in medical colleges, although nurses generally continue to be trained by doctors rather than nurses.

Other staff

The central Asian republics have a very limited range of other health professionals compared to high-income countries. For example, in 1998 there were 2.4 dentists (stomatologists) per 1000 population compared to a 6.8 per 1000 population EU average. There are also far fewer pharmacists, but the apparent rapid drop in the 1990s was due to the privatization of pharmacies, so that many pharmacists are no longer counted in public-sector statistics.

Traditional medicine providers were suppressed in the Soviet system and are not acknowledged in the central Asian republics, although traditional practices have survived among semi-nomadic peoples. Tajikistan, however, continued with herbal medicine and established a centre in 1997 to research the production of herbal-based pharmaceuticals (Rahminov *et al.* 2000).

Positions and people

The numbers of physicians and nurses (physical persons) have dropped in Kazakhstan, Kyrgyzstan and Tajikistan. The question is whether some of this reduction is on paper rather than in actuality. There is undoubtedly spare capacity on paper that managers can resort to when required to cut staff numbers. There are several reasons why official staff numbers are higher than active staff numbers.

First, it is in the budgetary interests of health facilities to maximize staff numbers. Health care facilities continue to be, as in Soviet times, mainly funded according to line item inputs, such as number of staff (Ensor and Langenbrunner, Chapter 9). The more staff, the larger the budget, and as yet there are few financial incentives to reduce staff. Second, staff may hold more than one position. The usual workforce pattern in high-income countries is for physical persons to outnumber positions, since many women, in particular,

Table 10.2 Physicians: full-time equivalent (FTE) persons compared to physical persons (PP)

Country	% FTE to PP, 1990	% FTE to PP, 1998
Kazakhstan	+12.2	+5.8
Kyrgyzstan	+27.1	+12.1
Tajikistan	+21.8	—
Turkmenistan	+10.5	+14.6[a]
Uzbekistan	+5.6	+10.5

[a] 1997

Source: WHO (2000a)

are part-time workers. The opposite is the case in the central Asian republics. People are appointed to more than one job as a way of supplementing low salaries. This is officially recognized; for example, in Turkmenistan, the Ministry of Health allows health care professionals to hold another half-time extra post (Mamedkuliev *et al.* 2000). Most countries had 10 per cent more physician positions than persons in 1990 and also in 1998, although this disparity was less in Kazakhstan and Kyrgyzstan in 1998 where staff positions had been cut (Table 10.2).

Third, persons on the payroll are not necessarily active workers, but may be disabled or retired. For budgetary purposes, these might be described as 'dead souls'. [In the Gogol novel *Dead Souls* published in 1842 (Gogol 1961), the businessman, Chichikov, purchased dead serfs or 'souls' whose names still appeared on the government census and who could, therefore, be mortgaged as property.] Furthermore, during the fiscal crises of the 1990s, many employers placed employees on leave without pay rather than make them redundant. Both employer and employee benefit from this practice. The employer maximizes the budget allocation, which is partly based upon staff positions, while the employee maintains access to social and health benefits and to the social status that largely derives from one's job. It is extremely important to people to keep their link to employment, however tenuous, for both social and economic reasons. The extent of this practice is unknown, but anecdotal evidence from hospital audits suggests that as many as 20 per cent of staff may be so-called inactive workers.

Stratification

These health care systems are highly stratified and, thus, inflexible in their ability to redeploy staff. There are horizontal divisions between levels of administration (national, regional, city and district) and vertical divisions between health services (such as different ministries), between closed and open health services (with better services for the elite), between specialities (such as adult medicine and paediatrics), between service types (such as general and speciality hospitals) and between separate programmes (such as primary care and family planning).

Some redistribution of staff should follow structural shifts within health care systems, but this is very difficult to achieve. Kazakhstan reduced the number of hospital beds by over 20 per cent between 1990 and 1997, followed by apparent drops in the numbers of physicians and nurses (Kulzhanov and Healy 1999). Kyrgyzstan reduced the number of hospital beds, but not hospitals, followed by only a small drop in the number of staff (Sargaldakova *et al.* 2000). Hospitals employ over 50 per cent of physicians and over 60 per cent of nurses (WHO 2000a). Governments are seeking to shift some resources from hospitals to primary care. Downsizing hospital systems, however, will not necessarily free staff for redeployment in ambulatory and primary care, given different employers and the difficulties of retraining hospital staff to work in the community.

Central Asian countries have many more doctors and nurses in urban areas than in rural areas, a common problem in many countries. For example, Kazakhstan has 3.5 physicians per 1000 population in urban *oblasts*, but only 1.6 physicians per 1000 population in rural *oblasts* (Kulzhanov and Healy 1999). Health care workers are no longer given compulsory postings (as in Soviet times), but few incentives have been put in place to encourage staff to go to rural areas.

Gender issues are very important, since most health workers are women. Over 80 per cent of physicians in the former Soviet Union were women, in large part because men went into occupations with higher status and pay, such as engineering (Kauppinen-Toropainen 1993). In Kazakhstan, the health and welfare sector is highly feminized, with 84 per cent female employees in 1995 (UNDP 1997: 84). In Kyrgyzstan, women constitute about 75 per cent of the health and welfare sector (UNDP 1998: 29) and 76 per cent of the physicians (International Labour Office and Public Services International 2000). There is also vertical stratification (men's work and women's work) within medicine; for example, men are more likely to be surgeons and be promoted as chief physicians of hospitals. The feminized nature of the health care workforce arguably has contributed to the low status of the health sector.

Skill mix

Human resource planning is about deciding on the appropriate staff to undertake the most cost-effective performance of necessary tasks when and where required (Armstrong 1991). International organizations argue that countries should weight the doctor-to-nurse ratio more towards nurses (World Bank 1993; WHO 1999). The physician-to-nurse ratio in the EU is around 1:4 versus only 1:2 in the central Asian republics (WHO 2000a), although it is much lower than that, since many nurses are not tertiary-level qualified nurses. Western European health systems are experimenting with skill mixes, such as substituting other staff to carry out tasks previously carried out by more expensive and more intensively trained staff. The main forms of substitution involve identifying tasks that qualified nurses could perform in place of doctors, and tasks that assistant nurses could perform in place of qualified nurses. Industrialized countries have paid particular attention to skill mix as part of re-engineering the hospital workforce, although the costs and benefits of sub-stitution continue to be debated (Walston and Kimberley 1997).

Skill mix has received little attention in central Asia, since physicians are not paid substantially more than nurses. Furthermore, there is a limited range of other health professionals. This explains why physicians perform many tasks that in other countries would be performed by nurses. Nurse training is being upgraded but physicians can be expected to oppose any loss of task domain and medical employment. These health care systems lack the skill-mix options for reassigning tasks currently carried out by physicians, for offering new health services (such as dietetics), or for developing new functions (such as health information systems). Also, the lack of training for health policy analysts and managers is a major gap, although health administration masters degree courses have begun in most countries, and a School of Public Health opened in Kazakhstan in 1997.

Productivity gains will become more important in these underfunded health care systems. The large numbers of staff are not reflected in the amount of work they perform, since health system utilization rates have been dropping in such areas as hospital admissions and outpatient contacts (WHO 2000b). For example, the anecdotal evidence on the workload of physicians (who may see only ten cases a day in polyclinics) suggests it is way below that in most industrialized countries.

Staff as a cost

By the mid-1990s, health sectors were surviving on barely a quarter to a third of their 1990 budgets (Kutzin and Cashin, Chapter 8). In these circumstances, the immediate priority of a health system may switch to maintaining staff rather than treating patients.

Salaries account for over half of health expenditures in the EU (WHO 2000a). The central Asian proportion is lower because salaries are lower, standing at 30 per cent in Kazakhstan, 36 per cent in Uzbekistan and 40 per cent in Kyrgyzstan (WHO 2000a). As the health budget contracted, salaries were allowed to erode, while other essential items, such as utilities (power and heating) and food, were maintained.

Wage payments by public-sector employers were delayed by months, parti-cularly during the worst of the government budgetary crises in the mid-1990s (International Labour Office and Public Services International 2000). This has contributed greatly to the income difficulties experienced by many health workers.

Low pay

Governments have kept a ceiling on salaries, although these have eroded with inflation and with the abolition of price subsidies for consumer goods. The real value of salaries for the total workforce dropped to about one-third their

Table 10.3   Real wages for total workforce (base year = 100)

Country	1990	1991	1992	1993	1994	1995	1996	1997	1998
Kazakhstan		100.0	64.8	49.1	32.9	33.4	34.4	36.6	38.7
Kyrgyzstan	100	70.7	59.4	49.6	42.0	43.5	44.5	49.1	54.1
Tajikistan				—	—	—	—	—	—
Turkmenistan				100.0	52.9	24.8	20.2	30.9	32.4
Uzbekistan				—	—	—	—	—	—

Source: UNICEF TransMONEE database (1999)

level in the early 1990s in some countries (Table 10.3). This fall has been particularly hard on health workers who traditionally have received low salaries. Many nurses receive below subsistence wages, while physicians receive lower salaries than other professionals with a comparable education. These very low salaries adversely affect recruitment, retention, morale, productivity and quality of services, and cause health professionals to seek gratuities from patients.

Public-sector workers in the central Asian republics, as in other former Soviet countries, are paid according to a national pay scale, drawn up on a grid plan by type of job and number of years of experience. In addition to this basic salary, they receive overtime payments and bonus payments in a number of situations, such as working at night and working under dangerous conditions. Many physicians regularly double their income through such bonus payments. Substantial in-kind remunerations are disappearing, however, such as subsidized rents, childcare, health services and spa treatments.

Nurses earn below the workforce average and even below the subsistence minimum (Kulzhanov and Healy 1999; Ilkhamov and Jakubowski 2000). In Kazakhstan, in 1999, the workforce monthly wage average was US$75, a physician earned US$115 and a nurse earned US$70 (International Labour Office and Public Services International 2000). The official salary of physicians in 1998 in Tajikistan, the poorest of these countries, was only US$2.80–3.50 per month; nurses received US$2.30 per month, while the workforce average was US$11 per month (Rahminov *et al.* 2000). These extraordinarily low amounts have higher purchasing power within the country, but are still below a household poverty line (Falkingham, Chapter 4). In terms of salary relativities, a physician's basic salary is perhaps one-third more than that of a nurse, compared to a four-fold difference in western European countries.

Physicians increase their official income through under-the-table payments (in-cash or in-kind) from patients. These payments have long been common in former Soviet republics, but most people now report paying health care staff for services that are officially free, and as a precondition of service, rather than as a gift in gratitude (Falkingham, Chapter 4). Hospital specialists have more such opportunities than other occupational groups. For example, patients may be required to pay two crates of vodka plus other gifts for a birth (Balfour 1999). Given the hidden nature of such payments, the amount they contribute to physicians' income is unknown. It is likely to be substantial, however, since the World Bank *Living Standards Measurement Surveys* suggest that informal payments (both official and unofficial) constitute one- to two-thirds of health sector revenue in the central Asian republics (Falkingham, Chapter 4). According to anecdotal evidence, many physicians at least double their income through such informal payments.

Employment status and conditions

More health responsibilities are being devolved to local government in Kazakhstan and Kyrgyzstan, while some hospitals are being transformed into autonomous public organizations with independent financial and legal status. The emergence of new employers, in place of the central state, makes it more difficult for unions to protect conditions of employment across a more complex health care field.

Health personnel come under a general employment law that covers conditions of employment, assumes an open-ended contract, and sets out remuneration and severance pay. Health professionals expect to have a job for life. In practice, therefore, employers have little say over staffing, either overall numbers or redeployment. General employment laws protect staff, so that few workers have been made redundant. The only option is not to fill posts left by retiring workers. Medical unemployment appears to be an issue so far only in Kazakhstan, where staff numbers are being reduced and the demand for new employees remains low (International Labour Office and Public Services International 2000).

Although most salaries are paid according to the national wage scale, organizations in some pilot programmes (for example, in Tajikistan) have begun to employ physicians on contract rather than permanent salaries. In Kyrgyzstan, the family practice pilot programmes are experimenting with new physician payment methods, such as patient capitation (Sargaldakova *et al.* 2000).

All central Asian republics have joined the International Labour Office and have ratified selected conventions. For example, Kazakhstan, Tajikistan and Uzbekistan have ratified conventions on the right to form associations. The extent of compliance with these conventions is unknown, since basic international labour standards on freedom of association and collective bargaining are restricted by national legislation in some countries, and some health services, such as hospitals, are considered to be essential services, with the right to strike by workers restricted or denied (International Labour Office and Public Services International 2000).

Staff as stakeholders

So far, the health workforce is not an important player in policy-making in central Asia for the following reasons. There is no tradition of a tripartite policy process involving government, employers and unions; in the Soviet era, these groups were not seen as separate entities with differing interests. The state remains the monopoly employer, with few alternative avenues of employment for dissenting staff. Health care professionals are not organized as pressure groups, although individual physicians, such as chief physicians of national hospitals, exert considerable influence. In contrast, in central Europe, physician associations have re-emerged as key pressure groups, especially given the power vacuum in health policy-making, but these associations had a pre-Soviet tradition.

International organizations are urging the transition countries to strengthen their civil societies, given the link between good governance and social and economic progress (World Bank 1999). Health-sector reform also requires the participation of such stakeholders as professional associations and unions (Asian Development Bank 1999). So far, the health policy process remains top-down rather than bottom-up, being driven by health ministries and *oblast* administrators in response to severe budgetary constraints. Many reforms, such as raising clinical standards, however, require behavioural change by staff within a more participatory culture, whereas the prevailing organizational culture stresses compliance with rules.

Professional associations and unions

The process of professionalization is driven by groups seeking to formalize control over their work jurisdictions (Friedson 1984). In the former Soviet countries, however, professional groups did not achieve significant power, since the employer (the state) controlled their work and set educational requirements. In the central Asian republics, from 1992 onwards, physicians and nurses have established professional associations, but these have no official status, are seldom represented on policy-making bodies and have yet to emerge as significant policy actors. The idea of non-governmental organizations that are independent from government is unfamiliar to both professionals and politicians.

In the Soviet era, a formal licensing procedure was not necessary, since the state both trained and employed physicians. There are as yet no independent statutory bodies, but new forms of registration and licensing are emerging. For example, the Ministry of Health in Kyrgyzstan has set up a certification committee with representatives from government, the medical schools and the professional associations.

New systems of industrial relations must be developed, and labour ministries are drawing up a range of workforce legislation. The function of unions has had to be redefined since the Soviet era, when health care workers belonged to a single union and membership in effect was compulsory. The main union function was to represent the state to the workers, rather than represent the workers to the state. These unions controlled significant union assets and allocated substantial benefits, such as holidays and spa treatments, to their members. Old unions have been discredited in central Europe, but in central Asia few alternative unions have emerged (Lines 1995). These unions now have statutory status and are slowly taking on new functions, but a single health-sector union in each country continues to cover most health care workers. For example, in Kazakhstan, the Health Workers Union claims to cover 95 per cent of health workers through 14 regional affiliates (Kulzhanov and Healy 1999).

Conclusions

Health-sector reform in these countries has been slow to address human resource planning issues. These issues are politically and socially difficult, given the large size of this workforce, the lack of alternative employment and the negative effect upon morale of redundancies. Some important steps are being taken. First, education and training are being addressed with efforts to upgrade standards, update the curriculum and restructure training (such as the introduction of general practice). Second, some countries have reduced their large numbers of physicians as a result of out-migration, through retirement and by restricting admission to medical schools. Other health care occupations are being developed to broaden the skill mix, especially since physicians will become more expensive if their claims for higher pay are met. Third, informal payments to health workers with low pay remain a big problem, since these payments reduce accountability to employers and greatly increase inequities for patients. Finally, higher pay for professionals will have to be matched by increases in productivity.

References

Armstrong, M. (1991) *A Handbook of Personnel Management*. London: Kogan Page.

Asian Development Bank (1999) *Health Sector Reform in Asia and the Pacific: Options for Developing Countries*. Manila: Asian Development Bank.

Balfour, F. (1999) Letter from Uzbekistan, *Guardian Weekly*.

Friedson, E. (1984) The changing nature of professional control, *Annual Review of Sociology*, 10: 1–20.

Gogol, N. (1961) *Dead Souls*. London: Penguin.

Ilkhamov, A. and Jakubowski, E. (2000) *Health Care Systems in Transition: Uzbekistan*. Copenhagen: European Observatory on Health Care Systems.

International Labour Office and Public Services International (2000) *Employment and Working Conditions in the Health Sector of Central Asian Countries*, ILO/PSI Conference, Almaty, Kazakhstan, 24–26 March 1999. Geneva: International Labour Office.

Kauppinen-Toropainen, K. (1993) Comparative study of women's work satisfaction and work commitment: research findings from Estonia, Moscow and Scandinavia, in V. Moghadam (ed.) *Democratic Reform and the Position of Women in Transitional Economies*. Oxford: Clarendon Press.

Kulzhanov, M. and Healy, J. (1999) *Health Care Systems in Transition: Kazakhstan*. Copenhagen: European Observatory on Health Care Systems.

Laporte, B. and Schweizer, J. (1994) Education and training, in N. Barr (ed.) *Labor Markets and Social Policy in Central and Eastern Europe: The Transition and Beyond*. New York: Oxford University Press.

Lines, T. (1995) *Public Services Trade Unions in Central Asia: Fact-finding Mission on Kazakhstan, Kyrgyzstan, Tajikistan, Turkmenistan and Uzbekistan*. Ferney Voltaire: Public Services International.

Mamedkuliev, C., Shevkun, E. and Hajioff, S. (2000) *Health Care Systems in Transition: Turkmenistan*. Copenhagen: European Observatory on Health Care Systems.

OECD (1999) *OECD Health Data 99: A Comparative Analysis of 29 Countries*. Paris: OECD.

Rahminov, R., Gedik, G. and Healy, J. (2000) *Health Care Systems in Transition: Tajikistan*. Copenhagen: European Observatory on Health Care Systems.

Salvage, J. and Heijnen, S. (1997) *Nursing in Europe: A Resource for Better Health*, WHO Regional Publications, European Series, No. 74. Copenhagen: WHO Regional Office for Europe.

Sargaldakova, A., Healy, J., Kutzin, J. and Gedik, G. (2000) *Health Care Systems in Transition: Kyrgyzstan*. Copenhagen: European Observatory on Health Care Systems.

Sultanov, R. (1999) *Health System Reform in Uzbekistan*. Washington, DC: World Bank.

UNDP (1997) *Human Development Report: Kazakstan 1997*. Almaty: UNDP.

UNDP (1998) *Kyrgyzstan: Human Development Report 1998*. Bishkek: UNDP.

UNDP (2000) *Human Development Report 2000*. New York, Oxford: Oxford University Press.

UNICEF (1999) *TransMONEE database*. www.unicef-icdc.org

Walston, S. and Kimberley, J. (1997) Re-engineering hospitals: experience and analysis from the field, *Hospital and Health Service Administration*, 42: 143–63.

WHO (1999) *The World Health Report 1999: Making a Difference*. Geneva: WHO.

WHO (2000a) *WHO European Health for all Database*. Copenhagen: WHO Regional Office for Europe.

WHO (2000b) *The World Health Report 2000. Health Systems: Improving Performance*. Geneva: World Health Organization.

World Bank (1993) *Investing in Health*. Washington, DC: World Bank.

World Bank (1999) *World Development Report*. Washington, DC: World Bank.

chapter eleven

Modernizing primary health care

Gülin Gedik, Zafer Oztek and
Antony Lewis

Introduction

In this chapter, we provide an overview of developments in primary health care in central Asia. The first part sets the scene and describes the problems that were common in all central Asian republics in the early 1990s and which led to reform. This is followed by a brief account of developments in each country and their implications. Finally, the challenges for the way forward are highlighted.

The need to modernize

Organization and management

Health care systems in the central Asian republics still exhibit many of the features of the inherited Soviet structure, as described by Field in Chapter 6. Primary health care, although in the process of change, still retains the same basic structure.

In urban areas, primary care is provided in polyclinics. People are assigned to physicians based on their area of residence. There were separate polyclinics for adults and for children, but after independence these were merged in many countries. Polyclinics typically are staffed by many specialists, including cardiologists, neurologists, gastroenterologists and surgeons.

Rural areas are served by feldsher-midwife posts (FAPs) and by rural out-patient clinics (SVAs). There are also a few maternity homes and health centres on collective farms. The FAPs are the most peripheral health units staffed by a feldsher or sometimes a feldsher-midwife. Feldshers manage minor diseases and sell some drugs, such as analgesics and antibiotics. The SVAs provide the outpatient services in rural areas and, usually, are staffed by the four core types of physicians (therapist, paediatrician, obstetrician and stomatologist/ dentist). Maternity homes located in collective farms have five or six beds and are staffed by a midwife whose main responsibility is to assist deliveries. Small rural hospitals (SUBs) have about 25–30 beds. These mainly admit individuals receiving courses of injections, reflecting the common use of injectable antibiotics. Most have very low occupancy rates (World Bank 1995).

Geographic coverage is very good, so that virtually the entire population has ready access to a health facility. Primary care in the central Asian republics, however, is weak in several important respects, and the quality of care provided is often deficient.

Primary health care is entirely government supported and highly bureaucratic. All staff are government employees and facilities are state owned. Decision-making is centralized and still depends on strict norms, most of which were established in Moscow during the Soviet era. They are, in general, out of date, limit the development of services and fail to anticipate changing population health needs. Rural primary health care facilities are administered by chief physicians of the local hospitals, who may have little interest in primary care.

A complex management information system exists, but it is very rigid and designed to send data upwards for central planning rather than to assist in decision-making at the local level. These decisions, in many instances, are not based on evidence, even at the central level.

Human resources in primary care

Human resource policies are characterized by over-specialization, inappropriate tasks, overlapping job descriptions, outdated undergraduate and postgraduate training, and pay little attention to motivating staff.

Primary care is provided by paediatricians, therapists (for adults), obstetricians/ gynaecologists, pharmacists, sanitary-epidemiological physicians (epidemiologists and hygienists) and stomatologists (dentists). Paediatricians and therapists specialize at the undergraduate level, but few have specialist postgraduate training (WHO 1999). In some central Asian republics, such as Kyrgyzstan and Turkmenistan, all newly graduated physicians are obliged to work for 2–3 years in the public sector, typically in remote areas, before undertaking further specialist training.

There are three main groups of so-called middle-level health care personnel: feldshers, nurses and midwives. In addition, there are two kinds of support staff: assistants and auxiliaries. Feldshers work in remote areas, mostly in FAPs (nurse posts) and manage some common diseases.

Viewed in terms of numbers, the central Asian republics have sufficient health staff, with most facilities being overstaffed. The challenges are to rationalize the skill mix, upgrade training and reduce specialization. Many existing training programmes need to be improved, but new programmes have little relevance to primary health care. Salary scales are highly compressed, and there are few incentives for better performance.

Financing primary health care

The sums allocated to health care have been declining in all central Asian republics since independence. Primary health care has always had low fiscal priority, receiving only 10–15 per cent of the health budget.

Primary care allocations to facilities are based on norms related to inputs (such as the number of employees), the services provided and some other indicators (see Ensor and Langenbrunner, Chapter 9). The salaries of health care workers are strictly controlled through a national salary schedule, with salaries mostly below the average for the public sector. The low salaries are exacerbated by late payments. In addition, there are shortages of all types of resources and much of the infrastructure is inadequate.

Primary care is still officially free of charge to the patient, although informal payments by patients are reported to be widespread (see Falkingham, Chapter 4). Drugs and supplies, however, are not free.

Utilization of primary health care

A prominent feature of health systems in the central Asian republics is the over-emphasis of the role of hospitals in health care. In contrast, primary care is used poorly. Although accessibility is good, quality of care is often poor and there is considerable inefficiency. Rates of referral to hospitals are very high due to the lack of diagnostic facilities and outdated treatment protocols, which require referral even in cases that can be treated at the primary care level.

Reform trends

Each country sees the strengthening of primary care as a major reform objective. Although some themes are similar, each country has worked in different ways and at a different pace. Besides attention to traditional priorities, such as mother and child health and control of communicable diseases, a common approach has been the introduction of family physicians to replace specialists in primary care settings. This has been accompanied by some restructuring and by changes in financing mechanisms.

Kazakhstan

In Kazakhstan, family group practices were established in pilot regions in Zhezkazgan and Semipalatinsk *oblasts*, and some financial incentives were introduced with the aim of improving the efficiency of primary health care workers. In Zhezkazgan *oblast*, a pilot project set up a non-profit organization funded by the state to allow family practice to be restructured. The family group practices contracted with the health insurance fund on the basis of the number of patients enrolled, but payment now flows through the health purchasing centres under the *oblast* health administration. (The health insurance fund was abolished at the beginning of 1998.) An initiative has been launched to retrain some specialists as family physicians. The Ministry of Health issued an order in 1998 to extend retraining to the whole country, but this has not been implemented widely.

Kyrgyzstan

In Kyrgyzstan, the strategy for primary health care was defined in the MANAS National Programme on Health Care Reforms, adopted in 1996 (details are given by Savas, Gedik and Craig, Chapter 7), and these strategies have been translated into action in pilot regions. Family group practices are being formed in Issyk-Kul and Chui *oblasts*, in the capital city, Bishkek, and are being ex- tended to other *oblasts*. Existing rural physician clinics and urban polyclinics served as the basis for the newly formed family group practices. These facilities are being renovated and supplied with basic equipment in the city of Bishkek and in Chui *oblast*. The plan is to cover the whole of the country in the next 5 years. Retraining of physicians is also emphasized. All physicians working in primary care in Chui and Bishkek have undertaken retraining lasting 12 weeks, spread over a 12 month period. This initiative is now being extended to the Issyk-Kul and Osh regions and is to be extended to the rest of the country by 2002.

The Kyrgyzstan Medical Academy is introducing a postgraduate residency programme for future family physicians. A programme for trainers of family physicians also has been established.

Tajikistan

In Tajikistan, primary health care was adversely affected by the civil unrest (WHO 1997a). Much of the physical infrastructure was destroyed, and there were major problems with lack of supplies and drugs. Efforts thus focused on maintenance of existing services, rather than on restructuring. Nevertheless, the Tajik Government has recently embarked on a comprehensive reform plan that includes primary health care. They have also begun to retrain specialists to work as generalists in primary care. A training centre for family physicians has been established, and the trainers have had 1 year of training abroad. The training of family physicians started in 1999, but due to limited capacity and resources only about 20–30 physicians can be trained each year. Family physi- cians have begun work in two polyclinics in the capital, Dushanbe. There are some prospects for the process to be accelerated with international support through soft loans, although these are in the planning stage.

Turkmenistan

In Turkmenistan, the Ministry of Health and Medical Industry issued an order in February 1996 that defined the functions and responsibilities of family physicians and nurses. The initial order envisaged one family physician per 600 population. After 1 year of experience with the order, it was revised to stipulate one family physician per 1000–1500 population. On average, each family physician is supported by two family nurses. Families are allocated family physicians according to their area of residence, and patients can choose a physician with the permission of the chief physician of the polyclinic. Some retraining programmes are provided by district hospitals, but they do not have common curricula. The department of family physicians in the Medical Institute is developing a 1 year postgraduate training programme. All physicians working in SVAs (rural physician clinics) or city polyclinics have been reclassified as family physicians, although most have not yet been retrained. The rural clinics and the FAPs have been renamed as *oba saglik oyu* (rural health houses) without any change in their functions. Management guidelines, including clinical protocols, have been produced in pilot primary care facilities in the Kara-Kala and Turkmenbashi regions.

Uzbekistan

Since the early years of independence, Uzbekistan has emphasized strengthening primary health care, especially in rural areas. In recent years, the focus has shifted to strengthening the emergency care network. Family physicians are to be introduced into rural physician outpatient clinics. Some short retraining programmes have begun. A pilot programme in three *oblasts* in Fergana aims to give more managerial and financial autonomy to primary care facilities.

Implications of reform trends
Restructuring

Restructuring generally has concentrated on the establishment of family group practices. Physicians with backgrounds in therapy, paediatrics and gynaecology have been redesignated (and some retrained) as family physicians. The aim is to widen the skill mix in primary care and to facilitate the cross-fertilization of ideas between professional groups. Family practice, however, differs in its implementation among the central Asian republics.

One strategy is to redefine the population of a family group practice. In Kazakhstan and Kyrgyzstan, this was based on the principle of free choice of physician. The intention was to introduce competition among primary care providers. In areas covered by a demonstration project, each citizen could choose the family practice in which to enrol. Although this process worked reasonably well in towns, there were problems in cities and in rural areas. In the Issyk-Kul *oblast* of Kyrgyzstan, people who enrolled in a family practice far away from their home faced difficulties in travelling to the service. Kyrgyzstan then revised the enrolment process, limiting the choice to within a defined catchment. Uzbekistan introduced a similar approach in pilot regions.

Turkmenistan continues to assign the population to physicians and clinics within a defined catchment. In Tajikistan, envisaged changes have not yet been implemented. There are plans to introduce an element of choice in urban areas, but to retain catchments in rural areas where facilities and staff are scarce and where there is, in reality, little choice.

Restructuring primary health care also requires improving the infrastructure, involving both building renovation and equipment. Lack of resources, however, has been the main problem. Renovation generally has been limited to projects funded by donors or has relied on loans.

In the central Asian republics, 45–70 per cent of the population lives in rural areas. This emphasizes the need for strengthening primary health care in rural areas, but in many reform programmes the focus is on restructuring urban facilities. Kazakhstan has drawn attention to the issue of rural health care in a Presidential decree (President of Kazakhstan 1997) and is in the process of strengthening nurse posts and other rural services.

The timeliness of legislation and decrees can be important. Delays in passing the necessary legislation can retard the implementation of reforms, especially in demonstration projects. In contrast, in Turkmenistan, decrees were issued before the plans were developed, resulting in a lack of clarity among those who had to implement them.

Human resources for primary health care

Although replacing specialists with generalists at the primary care level is a common strategy, it reflects an agenda promoted by the international community. There was widespread confusion about whether the term 'family physician' represented a health care model or a type of physician with particular knowledge and skills. So far, the main change has been in terminology, with therapists, paediatricians and obstetricians redesignated as family physicians. Inevitably, this had little impact on the services they provide. Some countries, such as Kazakhstan and Kyrgyzstan, followed a more systematic approach, with comprehensive training programmes. In Kyrgyzstan, a comprehensive cycle in selected *oblasts* has recently been completed, but the impact on clinical practice remains to be assessed.

The medical model dominates primary care with few roles being assigned to nurses. The process of reforming health care has brought the concept of the primary health care team onto the agenda, and attempts have been made to define the roles of each team member. A greater role for nurses in primary health care is being emphasized, and gradual improvement can be observed in some countries. Nurses now undertake new tasks, such as phlebotomy, health education, management of some chronic diseases and triage of simple illness. Kyrgyzstan and Tajikistan have started family nurse training programmes, but there is a long way to go in defining the skill mix among the members of the primary health care team, and the roles and responsibilities of each member.

The practice manager is another innovation, at least in Kazakhstan and Kyrgyzstan. Practice managers are expected to assume the administrative work, such as budgeting, reporting and maintenance of facilities, of family group practices (Meimanaliev and O'Dougherty 1997). After brief training, each manager takes on several practices, depending on the location and service capacity.

The roles and responsibilities of practice managers, however, are still unclear (Adams *et al.* 1998).

Financing

Primary health care remains underfunded. Allocation mechanisms need to be reoriented to increase funds for primary health care. This has not been achieved for several reasons. First, all central Asian republics have adopted strategies to increase the share of the public budget devoted to primary care. But there are difficulties in changing allocations without changing the budgetary system. Where the allocation to primary health care was increased (for example, by up to 30 per cent in the Zhezkazgan *oblast* of Kazakhstan), the impact of the increase was reduced because of a sharp decrease in gross domestic product and, consequently, in public expenditure (see Kutzin and Cashin, Chapter 8).

Other strategies have been to change the way that primary care providers are paid. The most common approach has been to move from salaries to capitation payments. This takes time, however. In Kyrgyzstan, the state budget continues to be allocated on the basis of norms related to infrastructure, number of outpatient visits and staff salaries. The health insurance fund initiated capitation payment, but only as a small part of a family group practice budget. It allowed salaries to be topped-up as well as the provision of some emergency drugs and purchase of some equipment. The existence of this fund has encouraged primary care providers to establish family group practices. In Kazakhstan, a new payment method in selected *oblasts* was tried to motivate health personnel. A new system of payment was also introduced in primary care in Turkmenistan, where family physicians receive a basic salary plus additional payments based on every 100 people over 1000 on their enrolled patient list.

Some very complicated methods, such as fundholding, were initially promoted in the central Asian republics (Ensor and Langenbrunner, Chapter 9). After almost a decade of experience, most proponents have stepped back, realizing the difficulties inherent in such approaches. Currently, there is no capacity for such a complicated mechanism, whether in terms of technical, managerial and negotiation skills or in terms of technological infrastructure. Such methods introduce a considerable administrative burden to an already unstable system. Some commentators have proposed a transitional solution of partial fundholding. Given the difficulties of introducing capitation payments without fundholding, the implementation of even partial fundholding seems premature. Furthermore, the concept of fundholding in the United Kingdom has now been abandoned, partly because of issues of equity, but not least because of high management costs. The best approach may be to concentrate on introducing capitation-based payment mechanisms (Savas and Gedik 1999).

Functions

Considerable attempts have been made to address some of the higher priority health problems. Mother and child health services have been strengthened through retraining and better medical supplies. New programmes have been introduced, such as DOTS (directly observed treatment short course) for the management of tuberculosis, which offers an active and supervised course of drugs on an outpatient basis (WHO 1997b). The expanded programme of immunization, with its shorter immunization schedule, has resulted in a more effective and less costly system. Such developments have brought identifiable benefits. These efforts have, however, been piecemeal and fragmented because of the vertical, specialist, single-issue approach and, as a result, a lack of sustainability.

Restructuring has not taken changes in services into account, while changes across different parts of the system have not been coordinated. For example, family practices were created mainly as a means of introducing new payment mechanisms, while their changed functions were left undefined. Likewise, specific problems were addressed through vertical programmes without taking into account developments elsewhere in the system.

Uncoordinated approaches to restructuring, as well as vertical programmes, resulted in missed opportunities and inefficient use of resources (Feilden *et al.* 1999). For example, retraining programmes for primary care physicians are not coordinated with other specialist retraining programmes in a way that would maximize scarce resources. Another problem is inconsistency in the selection of target groups for training. For example, in primary care settings, reproductive health programmes target obstetricians, while immunization programmes target paediatricians; the intention, however, was that all physicians in primary care settings should work together as family physicians.

Role of family practice associations

In Kazakhstan and Kyrgyzstan, family practice associations have been established as non-governmental organizations to support family group practices. Although autonomous, in principle, they initially worked very closely with the Ministry of Health, actually being part of the Ministry of Health in Kyrgyzstan. These family practice associations are actively involved in the design and implementation of primary health care reforms.

These associations are expected to gradually assume a greater role, but their viability will depend on the successful introduction of family group practices and the training of family physicians. Their role in representing family practices in the preparation and negotiation of contracts, in training and accreditation, and in the development of a performance assessment system is potentially large.

Communication strategies

The communication of health care reforms, within the health sector and to the general public, has been emphasized in Kyrgyzstan. A communication team was established at the Department of Reform Coordination and Implementation of the Ministry of Health. This has served as a two-way conduit between the Ministry of Health and the population. On the one hand, the team brought information to decision-makers about public perceptions and opinions about health care reform. On the other hand, it has actively marketed key aspects of health care reform, most notably encouraging the public to enrol in family group practices.

A wide variety of products has been developed and distributed. These include educational leaflets, billboards, posters, television documentaries, public service announcements, polyclinic stands and local authority meeting displays. The team also engaged in public health education and promotion in pilot districts. Media and population perception surveys were used to gauge public opinion and to develop better skills in communication, marketing and consumer research.

The interventions mainly dealt with general issues related to health care reform. These communication activities have not involved local people and thus have failed to gain their confidence and participation in policy decisions on primary health care. Primary care professionals do not yet have the necessary skills to disseminate the key messages to the public and to other professionals. So far, central Asia has little tradition of public participation in health policy decision-making.

Challenges ahead

Many challenges remain. Change has been welcomed by governments and by many (but not all) health workers, although the views of the public generally have not been sought. There is always the risk of introducing change for the sake of change. It is important to acknowledge that the previous system had considerable achievements as well as shortcomings. The main challenge is to maintain the positive aspects of the existing system, while overcoming its problems. Easy and free access by the public to primary health care services must be retained, as must the data collection and public health aspects of primary care.

Expectations were high that benefits would flow from restructuring primary care and from changing payment systems. This process, however, has taken longer than expected, because of inflexible state budgetary systems and because new payment mechanisms involved few fiscal incentives – given the sharp economic decline and limited resources. The focus now is moving towards improving the quality of services at the primary care level by changing clinical practices and by retraining staff.

Restructuring plans have not paid enough attention to defining the range of services that should be provided within primary care settings. Vertical structures have been maintained, but little has been done to ensure an integrated approach to health care at the primary level.

A concerted effort is needed by all governments to translate the rhetoric in their policy documents into action. This would mean reaffirming the sentiments expressed in Alma Ata 20 years ago: 'primary health care is essential health care based on practical, scientifically sound and socially acceptable methods and technology made universally accessible to individuals and families in the community'. Strengthening primary care requires a balancing act between primary and secondary health care, the needs of the population and the aspirations of professionals. Furthermore, primary health care must incorporate health promotion approaches, which are crucial for the sustainable development of healthy communities.

To achieve improvements in the health of populations in central Asia, the guiding principle must be health rather than illness. This is particularly relevant for primary health care. Health care professionals must also understand that good health care is a balance between excellent clinical practice and sound management. Health professionals must be able to work across disciplines and across sectors, and acknowledge that they are not always the appropriate people to lead health services. Only by working in a cooperative way can health services deliver quality care to improve the health of the population. Medical education at undergraduate and postgraduate levels must reflect this new philosophy, while other training courses must also be developed. The Kazakhstan School of Public Health has the potential to train public health professionals and health managers with a broader perspective on primary health care.

Health cannot be seen in isolation from other factors, such as nutrition, income and education. Health status will not be improved by health services alone, but requires investment in other areas. The translation of the holistic primary health care approach defined in the Alma Ata declaration requires leadership. The development of this leadership and securing access to the necessary resources remain a challenge for primary health care in the central Asian republics.

References

Adams, O., Apfel, F., Gedik, G. and Kuzin, J. (1998) *Report on the Implementation of Health Care Reforms in Kyrgyzstan for the Period May–November 1998*, Document EUR/KGZ/CARE 07 04 10 (B). Copenhagen: WHO Regional Office for Europe.

Feilden, R., Firsova, S., Gedik, G. *et al.* (1999) *Immunization and Health Sector Reform in the Kyrgyz Republic.* Report to ICCC.

Meimanaliev, T.S. and O'Dougherty, S. (1997) *Health Reform Project, Provider Payment Component: Project Start-up Report, January–June 1997.* Bishkek: Ministry of Health, Policy, Planning and Coordination Unit.

President of Kazakhstan (1997) *Kazakhstan 2030: Prosperity, Security and Welfare for All People of Kazakhstan.* Almaty: Office of the President.

Savas, S. and Gedik, G. (1999) Health care reforms in central Asia, in UNDP (ed.) *Central Asia 2010: Prospects for Human Development.* New York: UNDP Regional Bureau for Europe and the CIS.

WHO (1997a) *Tajikistan Country Paper Prepared for CARNET Cycle 4: The Role of General Practitioners in Primary Health Care.* Copenhagen: WHO Regional Office for Europe.

WHO (1997b) *Treatment of Tuberculosis: Guidelines for National Programmes*, WHO/TB/97.220. Geneva: World Health Organization.

WHO (1999) *Medical Education and the CARNET Countries.* Copenhagen: WHO Regional Office for Europe.

World Bank (1995) *Turkmenistan – Rationalizing the Health Sector.* Washington, DC: Human Resources Division, World Bank.

twelve

Rationalizing
hospital services

Johannes Vang and Steve Hajioff

Introduction

The central Asian republics face many difficulties exacerbated by the fundamental societal changes of the last decade. These changes have resulted in
failing economies and in the need to revise previously established structures,
values and ingrained models of behaviour in society at large and in health
care systems in particular. Health care system reform, therefore, is taking place
in an environment that is not always supportive and where the speed of
change is slow.

In this chapter, we examine the experiences of reforming the hospitals of
central Asia under these difficult circumstances. We draw on the deliberations
of a WHO meeting on hospital reform in the central Asian republics that took
place in Istanbul in December 1998 (CARNET 2000). We also draw on interviews with key informants who helped produce the *Health Care Systems in
Transition* country profiles published by the European Observatory on Health
Care Systems (www.observatory.dk).

The inherited hospital system

Health care systems in central Asia were based upon the Soviet Semashko model
(Field, Chapter 6), the starting point for hospital sector reforms since independence. According to this model, the hospital is dominant and is the key to
the delivery of health care, with primary care serving largely as a referral point.
The prevailing belief was (and is) that high-quality health care could (and can)
only be obtained in a hospital setting. Services were planned on the basis of
political need and health need, so that both funds and political kudos were
associated with large hospital infrastructures and high degrees of specialization.

Hospitals in the central Asian republics are organized hierarchically, corresponding to geographic/administrative levels: rural hospitals, central district hospitals, specialized hospitals, national hospitals and dispensaries. Hospitals also are run by separate administrative levels of government.

Rural hospitals

At the local level are the rural hospitals (SUBs). These small units, with less than 50 beds, offer simple nursing and maternity services and some basic medical care. Buildings are generally poorly maintained and are often unheated. They also often lack equipment and even basic sanitary facilities. There were many such small hospitals. In Uzbekistan, for example, a third of the hospitals contain only 10 per cent of all hospital beds (CARNET 2000). Many of the beds in rural hospitals have historically been unoccupied and may have been notional beds (existing on paper to enhance local funding), rather than actual beds.

Across the central Asian republics, many small hospitals have been closed or converted to outpatient units. Uzbekistan plans to retain small hospitals only in remote or mountainous communities (Ilkhamov and Jakubowski 2000). Between 1994 and 1997, Kazakhstan closed about 70 per cent of village hospitals, although some continue to function on an outpatient basis. Tajikistan has a programme of bed closure in village hospitals (except in remote areas), combined with better links to primary care. Between 1995 and 1996, Turkmenistan reduced rural hospitals by 30 per cent. In Kyrgyzstan, service rationalization has concentrated more on bed closures than on hospital closures.

Central district hospitals

A central district hospital is located in the largest town of each district (*rayon* or *etrap*). Each has around 200–500 beds, provides a range of basic specialist services and often houses a separately staffed polyclinic. The chief physician of these hospitals also manages primary care services within the district. In all these republics, reform processes emphasize district hospitals, while reducing village hospitals. Nevertheless, some district hospitals have been closed, with a 30 per cent reduction in Kazakhstan between 1994 and 1997; Turkmenistan, however, saw a 25 per cent reduction in these hospital beds between 1995 and 1996 (but did not close hospitals).

City hospitals

City hospitals are located in larger urban centres and provide more advanced secondary care. These hospitals are run by the municipalities and are generally better equipped and better maintained than the smaller hospitals.

Oblast *hospitals*

Oblast hospitals are administered by the regional (*oblast* or *velayat*) level of government. With between 600 and 1000 beds, these provide a broad range of specialist secondary care. They usually contain outpatient units, which, in addition to ambulatory secondary care, also deliver primary care services to urban populations. These hospitals have not been closed but have experienced some bed reductions in recent years. Approximately 40 per cent of hospital beds are provided in city and *oblast* hospitals.

Specialized hospitals

Specialized hospitals are very numerous at the district, regional and national levels. Many disease categories and care groups are treated in separate hospitals, such as children's hospitals, and cardiology, psychiatric, neurology, maternity and emergency hospitals. Emergency hospitals are an interesting case. Accident and emergency care is not a feature of general hospitals, as is the case in western Europe, but is provided by specialist emergency hospitals, usually separate from secondary care general hospitals. Specialized advanced hospital care in the major cities does not necessarily equate with tertiary care: first, these hospitals often lack up-to-date skills and equipment and, second, they also provide basic care for the local population, in many cases without referral from primary or secondary care units.

Dispensaries

Specialist long-term care is also provided in dispensaries as both inpatient and outpatient care. These single-speciality institutions cover tuberculosis, dermatology and genitourinary medicine, oncology, endocrinology, psychiatry and addiction services. The various specialist hospitals and dispensaries are seen as an essential part of this hospital system, so that mergers with general hospitals are difficult to achieve.

National (republican) hospitals

National hospitals provide advanced care and usually are teaching hospitals, while research institutes provide advanced care and undertake clinical research. In the Soviet era, highly specialized tertiary care was carried out in Moscow or Leningrad. In Kyrgyzstan, 88 per cent of patients are admitted to these hospitals without referral and many do not need the specialized facilities provided at the tertiary level. In practice, tertiary level services in Bishkek are used mostly by citizens from the capital and the neighbouring Chui *oblast* (CARNET 2000). This situation is replicated in the other central Asian republics. In recent years, there has been an increase in the number of beds in tertiary centres and an accompanying decrease in the proportion of care delivered to residents of more rural districts.

Hospital management

In this section, we highlight some of the key issues and controversies. It should be noted that, while some controversies are quite active theoretically, in practice management has changed little since Soviet times. This is exemplified by the debate about the optimal educational background for a hospital director. Three different views can be discerned. One favours someone with a background in economics (although this is often interpreted as accountancy), one favours individuals with a medical background and one considers background less important than attitudes and skills. These different approaches, however, are of less importance than the general organizational culture – one of administration rather than management, with hospital hierarchies and funding systems that militate against innovation and responsive service delivery. A second key factor is the lack of basic management skills and of the infrastructure for the enhancement of the managerial skill base.

The organizational culture in each republic has begun to diverge slightly from the Soviet model. In the central Asian republics, the medical director (chief physician) manages the hospital and is subordinate to the head of the government administration or to the Ministry of Health (depending on the administrative–territorial position of the hospital). The medical director's deputies are responsible for the medical, administrative and support functions of the various departments of the hospital and also for staffing issues, in collaboration with the nursing director (head nurse) of the hospital (where such a post exists). The head physician appoints the heads of all departments, who are responsible for the quality of medical services and the management of clinical staff. The staff can influence administrative decisions through medical councils. This is regulated by legislation.

Physicians occupy the key administrative posts in all hospitals in Turkmenistan (Mamedkuliev *et al.* 2000), which have a fairly uniform organizational structure at the higher levels. The director is responsible for the medical functions of the hospital and for the management of finance and personnel. Apart from these responsibilities, the director of an *etrap* (district) hospital is also responsible for the delivery of primary health care. The administrative structure of *etrap* hospitals is different from that of city, *velayat* (regional) and national hospitals. Although it is customary that hospital directors are doctors, the existing legislation allows the appointment of specialists in management to this position. In the future, it is planned that specially trained managers will replace physicians.

In Uzbekistan, hospitals are also managed by physicians, who distribute the annual budget according to the previous year's production and the expected workload for the coming year (Ilkhamov and Jakubowski 2000). Managers in Bishkek, Kyrgyzstan, have some discretion in defining the pattern of services provided within their allocated budget. These are pilot programmes, and hospitals in other regions continue to be managed by physicians not well acquainted with issues of planning and management (Sargaldakova *et al.* 2000).

The shortage of trained personnel is a major obstacle to the development of health care administration and management. In Kazakhstan, the School of Public Health is addressing this skill shortage by offering retraining courses to clinical personnel (Kulzhanov and Healy 1999).

Basic hospital utilization and activity data are measured and monitored in a similar way in all the republics. In Uzbekistan, for instance, each hospital has a department of statistics, which prepares statistical data and presents them annually to a Regional Statistics, Information and Prognosis Bureau, to the Department of Statistics at the Ministry of Health and to the National Calculation Centre. Variables such as average length of stay, bed occupancy rate and data on specific areas of activity are all collected, and the raw statistical data are published annually. More detailed analysis and comparative studies are performed by specialist staff in health ministries and in local health administrations, to inform the management and commissioning processes. Although the results of these studies are available to the public, they are rarely shared with staff or publicized.

The fragmentation of the hospital system is another factor that militates against hospital rationalization, since hospitals are administered by four different levels of government: district, municipal, regional and national. In addition, there are large numbers of specialized hospitals. This fragmentation makes it difficult for policy-makers and hospital administrators to collaborate across hospitals, to transfer resources or to merge hospitals.

The challenge for hospital reform

There is almost universal agreement on the areas that require reform. These include an outdated and excessive hospital infrastructure, a fragmented hospital system, an over-reliance on hospital care, underdeveloped primary health care services, an organizational culture that administers rather than manages, and ineffective regulatory and budgetary practices that militate against service efficiency and necessary rationalization. The broader context, such as civil war in Tajikistan, mass migrations and struggling national economies, further exacerbate the situation. These problems contribute to the belief among central Asian health care workers that the problems of the health care system stem mainly from underfunding. The following sections will examine the disposition and utilization of hospital resources, the organization and management of hospital care, and the issues that relate to attempts to strengthen ambulatory and social care.

Patterns of hospital utilization

Because the norm-based funding system called for large numbers of hospital beds and doctors, the central Asian republics inherited hospital systems with excessive beds and doctors for their populations. Because supply created demand

and because fiscal incentives and clinical traditions called for admitting patients for long periods, average stays were long, bed occupancy rates were low and population admission rates were high. The legislation and the financial incentives in place in the Soviet era favoured the development of large hospitals with many beds. As is apparent from the utilization data below on average length of stay, admission rates and hospital and bed numbers, little attention was paid to the cost-effectiveness of hospitals and the rational utilization of beds.

Average length of stay

The years since independence in 1991 have seen some fluctuations in average length of stay in all hospitals (long-term and acute care), but with a downward trend since the mid-1990s. The average length of stay changed very little in acute care hospitals in the central Asian republics, however, until about the late 1990s, except in Kyrgyzstan (Figure 12.1). (Data on acute hospitals in Uzbekistan are unavailable.) These averages for length of stay remain high relative to western Europe. In 1996, the most recent comparable year, the average length of stay in acute beds for the central Asian republics was 13.8 days, which is close to the average of 13.9 days for the former Soviet Union countries, but considerably longer than the average of 9.7 days for the countries of central and eastern Europe. Averages for length of stay in the European Union (EU) are lower still, with a mean of 8.6 days. Difficulties with the

Figure 12.1 Average length of stay (days) in acute hospitals in the central Asian republics, 1991–98

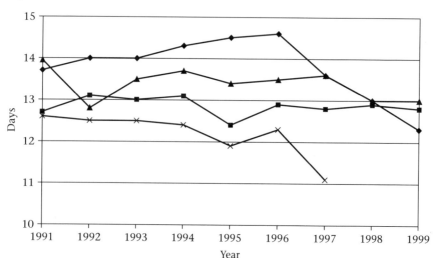

Source: WHO (2000)

internal organization of hospitals, such as long delays before patients receive treatment, have been reported. It was reported that, on average, patients in Kyrgyzstan wait in hospital for more than a week (range 1–23 days) for an operation. Shortages of certain types of equipment, drugs and disposables add to the difficulties. Together, these factors suggest that there could be a significant reduction in hospital capacity through changes in physician behaviour and patient expectations, the introduction of more effective technology and better collaboration with primary health care.

Admission rates

Before independence, admission rates were extremely high for several reasons, not the least of which was inadequate service provision at the primary care level. In the early 1990s, nearly a quarter of the populations of the central Asian republics were being hospitalized annually, as opposed to about 15 per cent in the EU. In the intervening decade, admission rates have decreased markedly, down to 10–15 per cent of the population admitted annually (Figure 12.2). Development of the primary care sector, however, has been limited, and only a small secondary to primary care task reallocation has occurred. Meanwhile, the incentives to keep people in hospitals remain – for example, the presence of co-payments for pharmaceuticals in ambulatory care. For this reason, it is probable that much of the reduction in admission rates may be due not to better care targeting, but to a growing unmet need.

Figure 12.2 Admissions to acute care beds per 100 population in the central Asian republics, 1991–98

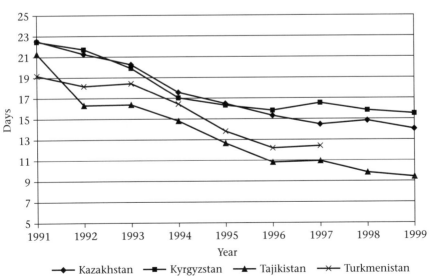

Source: WHO (2000)

Figure 12.3 Acute care beds per 100,000 population in the central Asian republics, 1991–98

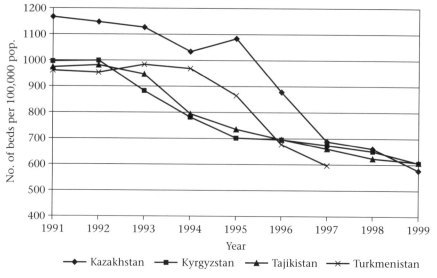

Source: WHO (2000)

Table 12.1 Acute care beds per 100,000 population in the central Asian republics, 1991–98

Country	1991	1992	1993	1994	1995	1996	1997	1998	% change 1991–98
Kazakhstan	1167	1147	1126	1033	1085	877	689	662	–43
Kyrgyzstan	996	1000	882	782	702	695	752	670	–33
Tajikistan	974	981	946	795	735	697	661	615	–37
Turkmenistan	962	953	984	968	865	678	597	—	–38

Source: WHO (2000)

Hospital and bed numbers

The nature and disposition of the existing hospital infrastructure are as much issues as the ways in which hospitals are used, given the excessive provision of hospitals and of beds, and the poor provision of supplies and basic facilities. Between 1991 and 1997, acute care bed numbers per 100,000 population declined across central Asia from about 1100 to 600 beds (Figure 12.3). Table 12.1 shows reductions of between 33 and 43 per cent in acute care beds per person between 1991 and 1998. As noted earlier, these data are not available for Uzbekistan; however, during the same period, the total number of beds per 100,000 population declined by 49 per cent, a slightly greater overall reduction than in the other republics.

Table 12.2 Total number of hospitals in the central Asian republics, 1991–98

Country	1991	1992	1993	1994	1995	1996	1997	1998	% change 1991–98
Kazakhstan	1796	1821	1812	1649	1518	1245	963	991	–45
Kyrgyzstan	323	332	335	341	341	335	342	345	7
Tajikistan	374	386	389	408	412	416	411	420	12
Turkmenistan	368	381	398	399	295	351	331	—	–10
Uzbekistan	1370	1344	1339	1334	1328	1275	1199	1071	–22

Source: WHO (2000)

Table 12.3 Acute care hospitals per 100,000 population in the central Asian republics, 1991–98

Country	1991	1992	1993	1994	1995	1996	1997	1998	% change 1991–98
Kazakhstan	9.52	9.6	9.56	8.78	8.22	6.91	5.26	5.73	–40
Kyrgyzstan	6.22	6.37	6.4	6.53	6.43	6.21	6.65	6.58	6
Tajikistan	6.7	6.64	6.7	6.86	6.9	6.84	6.55	6.43	–4
Turkmenistan	8.49	8.53	8.71	8.53	5.36	6.57	6.03	—	–29

Source: WHO (2000)

Table 12.2 shows that hospital numbers have fluctuated across central Asia between 1991 and 1998, varying from a 45 per cent reduction in Kazakhstan to a 12 per cent increase in Tajikistan (although the latter figure must be treated with some caution). Similarly, with regard to acute care and short stay hospitals, there was a 6 per cent increase in hospitals per 100,000 population in Kyrgyzstan and a 40 per cent reduction in Kazakhstan (Table 12.3). Because 'ghost beds' (maintained only on paper) were included in figures reported by hospitals to attract financing under the previous funding system, the accuracy of the bed closures reported, particularly those in the smaller rural hospitals, is unclear. The relatively stable workforce structure (Healy, Chapter 10) suggests the use of this deceptive practice.

Hospital closures have mainly involved the smallest rural hospitals, many of which were barely functioning. In Kazakhstan, for example, the number of central district hospitals fell from 215 to 157 and rural hospitals fell from 830 to 208. Both Uzbekistan (through its development of emergency hospitals) and Turkmenistan (with its new specialist hospitals) have increased specialized hospitals in recent years.

Alternatives to hospital care

Hospitals and other types of health and social care are interdependent. As a Kazakh commentator noted at the Istanbul meeting, reforming the hospital service is impossible without reforming the entire health care system and, in particular, the primary health care service (CARNET 2000). This is a particular concern in rural areas, where the closure of small rural hospitals left only inadequate primary care services. The delivery of primary care in the central Asian republics is dealt with elsewhere in this book (see Gedik, Oztek and Lewis, Chapter 11).

The referral system has deteriorated since 1991 and is seen as a cause for concern in all republics. The absence of the highly structured health care monopoly of Soviet times has disrupted previous referral patterns and led to a greater variation in physician referrals. Furthermore, the high cost of drugs with co-payments required for pharmaceuticals bought outside the hospitals may make hospital treatment more attractive to patients. In contrast, freeing up the system has made innovation easier and, in Uzbekistan, improved management of the primary–secondary care interface is believed to have contributed to a reduction in length of stay from 14.2 days in 1995 to 13.8 days in 1997.

Another issue requiring attention is the way in which hospitals compensate for failures in other areas, such as social services and support of the elderly, the chronically ill and the dying. Social care apart from the family is often rudimentary in central Asia and, thus, a significant reliance is placed upon hospital services in the provision of intermediate or pure social care. Some steps have been taken to address this problem.

Some medical institutions have started to provide medical and nursing services to outpatients, for example in Tajikistan. In 1998, eight outpatient surgery centres were in operation. In 1997, 36,348 patients were treated and 277 received surgery in the outpatient and clinical surgery centre in Dushanbe. This shift towards ambulatory service delivery is a theme in all the countries of central Asia. Kazakhstan has identified the optimization of the hospital system as a principal goal, and some resources released by hospital closures have been used to develop ambulatory care services. By the end of 1997, 428 polyclinics and 94 hospitals offered day-care services, which is believed to have contributed to a 30 per cent reduction in the rate of hospitalization.

Policy development and legal framework

Each country has adopted a programme of reform. Although there are common themes, since each country inherited the same legacy, a distinctive approach is being taken by each one. The following sections identify the emphasis in hospital sector reform for each country.

Kazakhstan

From 1992 to 1997, the Kazakh health services tested reform ideas in pilot projects. In recent years, organization, management and financing reforms have been introduced. The Ili region pilot project aimed to improve technology and enhance the quality of medical care. New methods of management led to some changes in the structure of hospitals and to a reduction in bed numbers, coupled with the development of primary and ambulatory care. Also, there has been an extensive programme of closure of rural hospitals (Kulzhanov and Healy 1999). Overall, the number of hospitals in Kazakhstan has declined by 45 per cent between 1991 and 1998, the largest decrease among the central Asian republics. Of these, acute care hospitals per 100,000 population have declined by 40 per cent and hospital beds by 43 per cent (Tables 12.1–12.3).

Kyrgyzstan

In Kyrgyzstan, the current laws 'On people's health protection in the Republic of Kyrgyzstan' and 'On medical insurance of citizens in the Republic of Kyrgyzstan' do not specifically regulate activities of hospitals. These still are regulated according to the Soviet era directives, with financing and staff numbers related to the number of beds. Changes are being introduced in the city of Bishkek and in Chui *oblast* pilot regions. Since January 1999, hospitals in these regions are financed according to the number of patients treated.

Kyrgyzstan is in the process of developing the legal framework for a revised national health policy. A detailed analysis of the costs of Bishkek hospitals concluded that there is room for a substantial reduction in the smaller hospitals. Between 1992 and 1998, the number of beds in city hospitals fell by 50 per cent. Unfortunately, any potential savings were almost completely absorbed by significant increases in the price of drugs, equipment, disposables and electricity. Further proposals called for hospital closures, for reducing the capacity and average length of stay, and for the introduction of stringent criteria for hospitalization (Sargaldakova *et al.* 2000).

Following implementation of these proposals, some resources were released and invested in areas of particular need, such as the Children's Clinical Hospital and the Bishkek Perinatal Centre. In the Children's Clinical Hospital, for example, a 30 bed-day surgery unit was opened, with a bed-day in this unit in 1997 estimated to cost 26 som compared with 57.6 som in an inpatient bed (CARNET 2000).

Other resources released were invested in primary care, particularly in city polyclinics. Further closure of hospitals is not foreseen. Further rationalization will be undertaken by restructuring existing units, changing types of service available in hospitals and by improving clinical effectiveness. Although there are reports of hospital reductions and financial savings in Kyrgyzstan, the closure of acute care hospital beds has been the most modest of the republics, with a 33 per cent decrease in the number of beds between 1991 and 1998 (Table 12.1). In the same period, there was a modest increase in the total number of hospitals (Table 12.2) and, unlike the other republics, an increase in the number of acute care hospital beds per 100,000 population (Table 12.3).

Tajikistan

After the civil war, Tajikistan was finally able to develop a programme of reform. In 1994, a Presidential decree outlined its main directions. In 1995, the programme of economic reforms, including health care, was approved. On that basis, the Ministry of Health adopted a programme of reforms in 1996.

Up to this point, the health care system of Tajikistan was entirely state owned. The Ministry of Health controlled all the medical institutions, from primary care and rural hospitals to hospitals in regional and national centres, as well as medical educational and research institutions. The recent 'Law on Health Protection', however, envisages launching a parallel private health care system (CARNET 2000).

As in the other republics, there is a planned shift from secondary to primary care and a planned programme of rationalization of rural hospitals. The legislation 'On Measures on Reorganization of the Healthcare System of the Republic of Tajikistan' instructed the Ministry of Finance to use resources freed from hospital rationalization to strengthen primary health care. Unfortunately, this did not happen due to budget deficits (Rahminov *et al.* 2000). The hospital closure programme has been less marked than in the other republics, in part because of the civil war.

Turkmenistan

Turkmenistan followed a gradual approach, as set out in the Presidential state health programme (Turkmenbasi 1995). This defined a policy framework, which was to be followed by a detailed plan for its realization (Turkmenbasi 1997), but *ad hoc* decisions continue to be taken, sometimes conflicting with the state health programme.

The 1995 programme envisaged a shift of focus from hospitals to prevention and primary care. By the year 2000, the country intends to reduce the number of hospital beds by 40–45 per cent (compared to 1995). It is envisaged that the target will be reached by increasing efficiency by 95 per cent and by decreasing hospitalization rates and the length of stays. Between 1991 and 1997, the hospital and bed closure programmes showed significant progress, with acute care beds and acute care hospitals being reduced by 38 per cent and 29 per cent, respectively (Tables 12.1 and 12.3), and the total number of hospitals being reduced by 10 per cent (Table 12.2).

The autonomy of hospitals is expected to be enhanced in such areas as personnel management, use of financial resources, and the scope and range of services provided, as a step towards the creation of fully autonomous hospitals. The management capacities of hospitals are to be strengthened to prepare them for increased autonomy, and hospitals are to be permitted to outsource some of their support services. Clinical practice in hospitals is expected to be improved by the introduction of clinical guidelines, a clinical audit system, education and training, and by involving patients in quality evaluations (Mamedkuliev *et al.* 2000).

Uzbekistan

The Ministry of Health drew up proposals for reform in 1992, which included the rationalization of hospital organization and structure. Efforts were made to increase the productivity of each institution, and over 40 per cent of hospital beds were closed between 1991 and 1997. To compensate for reduced inpatient facilities, a range of day-care services was developed, such as day-care patient facilities, home-care services, outpatient surgery centres and special 24 hour outpatient treatment centres (Ilkhamov and Jakubowski 2000).

The November 1998 Presidential decree 'State Programme of the Republic of Uzbekistan on Health Protection System Reform' established the National Emergency Hospital in Tashkent with branches planned for the Republic of Karakalpakstan and for the regions. Other emergency service and ambulance services are also planned (CARNET 2000).

Conclusions

Hospitals in this region are undergoing reform. This process, however, has proceeded at a different pace in each country, reflecting diverging economic and political contexts. Although it is relatively easy to describe the quantitative aspects of change, such as the reported reduction in hospital beds, it is more difficult to know whether these changes have led to better and more appropriate medical care, or whether they simply reflect the unplanned closure of large numbers of small facilities that, in other parts of the world, would barely be recognizable as hospitals. One of the major problems facing those undertaking reform is the dearth of evidence on its implementation and results so far.

Aside from this problem, four issues stand out. The first is the challenge of how to manage a smooth transfer from a state monopolistic health service to a more pluralistic system. This requires the development of explicit policies on quality of services and the implementation of effective management systems that focus on outcomes, not structures. The second issue is staff development – especially the need to strengthen knowledge and professional competence within the field of management and administration – and revised roles for different professionals, particularly nurses. The third issue is the development of primary care and supportive social services as a means of making more rational and economic use of hospitals and other highly specialized institutions. Finally, there is a need to develop a medico-industrial infrastructure that can support the technical function of the hospitals.

References

CARNET (2000) *Improving Hospital Services in CARNET Countries, Central Asian Republics' Network for Health Care Reforms*, Istanbul, December 1998, CARNET Series No. 3, Document AMS 501 68 88. Copenhagen: WHO Regional Office for Europe.

Ilkhamov, A. and Jakubowski, E. (2000) *Health Care Systems in Transition: Uzbekistan*. Copenhagen: European Observatory on Health Care Systems.

Kulzhanov, M. and Healy, J. (1999) *Health Care Systems in Transition: Kazakhstan*. Copenhagen: European Observatory on Health Care Systems.

Mamedkuliev, C., Shevkun, E. and Hajioff, S. (2000) *Health Care Systems in Transition: Turkmenistan*. Copenhagen: European Observatory on Health Care Systems.

Rahminov, R., Gedik, G. and Healy, J. (2000) *Health Care Systems in Transition: Tajikistan.* Copenhagen: European Observatory on Health Care Systems.

Sargaldakova, A., Healy, J., Kutzin, J. and Gedik, G. (2000) *Health Care Systems in Transition: Kyrgyzstan.* Copenhagen: European Observatory on Health Care Systems.

Turkmenbasi, S. (1995) *Presidential State Programme of Turkmenistan.* Ashgabat: Ministry of Health and Medical Industry.

Turkmenbasi, S. (1997) *Realization Plan for the Presidential Health Programme,* First draft for discussion. Ashgabat: Ministry of Health and Medical Industry.

WHO (2000) *WHO European Health for All Database.* Copenhagen: WHO Regional Office for Europe.

chapter thirteen

Restructuring public health services

Ian MacArthur and Elena Shevkun

Introduction

Public health services, also known as the sanitary-epidemiological service, the Sanepid service or just SES, have always been a core element of health care systems in the central Asian republics, with a strong network of stations throughout their territories. Their role in preventing ill health and, thereby, reducing the burden on curative health services is seen as fundamental to the health care system.

A classic product of the Soviet era, Sanepid services are found throughout the former Soviet Union and the transition economies of central and eastern Europe (CEE countries). While in some countries the Sanepid service has undergone major reform, it has changed little in central Asia since the republics became independent. Nevertheless, there is a realization that changes are necessary to build professional capacity, to improve effectiveness and to ensure that the Sanepid service is included in health care reforms. This chapter focuses on the Sanepid services and their plans and aspirations for reform.

What are public health services?

In writing about the formal health care system, McKee and Bojan (1998: 136) proposed a pragmatic definition of what constitutes a public health service: 'It is taken to mean those roles in which individuals with formal public health training are employed with the objective of improving the health of the population'. This definition limits a public health service to people with specialist professional credentials and so reflects the traditional view; it excludes sectors, such as the environmental, municipal and sanitary engineering sectors, that deal with public health issues because they are staffed by people not formally trained in public health. These excluded sectors are key players in public health improvement and, increasingly, are cited as part of a more integrated approach to addressing the key determinants of health (Blane *et al.* 1996). In a sense, it is this realization that lies at the heart of the desire to reform the Sanepid services in the central Asian region.

Since independence in 1991, environmental health problems in the central Asian republics have received considerable attention. The profligate exploitation of natural resources and past failures to recognize the full costs of environmental degradation can clearly be seen in the Aral Sea disaster. This increased awareness has led to the creation of new agencies, and the strengthening of environmental or ecological ministries and their executive networks, with responsibility for issues such as air quality, water standards, radiation and soil pollution. Municipalities are responsible for the water and sewerage infrastructure and for waste collection and disposal. Health care systems also are being urged to shift from a curative ill-health orientation towards a more holistic approach to health and health promotion, which means that the role of primary health care in addressing environmental health needs should be reassessed (WHO 1999).

As a result, the health, environment and economic sectors must cooperate to minimize health risks (Staines 1999). Existing legislation that sets out the precise relationship between the Saniped service and other relevant ministries gives the service a lead role in coordinating the field of environmental health. In any society, many different agencies may work on the same or similar issues. In such circumstances, it is important to recognize each partner's function and to set up procedures to ensure coordination and the exchange of information. It is from this perspective that many of the proposed reforms in environmental health are suggested. The need for a more effective system as a whole has primacy over the individual parts.

Sanepid: independent agency or poor relation?

The overall structure of health systems in all central Asian republics is similar, since they developed as a unified system under the former Soviet Union (Field, Chapter 6). The operational part of a health system consists of two main blocks. The Sanepid service is responsible for health protection at the population level and is charged with maintaining the sanitary and epidemiological well-being of the population; primary health care and hospital services are responsible for the health of individuals. The Sanepid system carries out surveillance of environmental conditions, including vector control, occupational health safety and health education. These health systems continue to have a curative orientation and a population-based approach has been neglected. As a result, the Sanepid service has been neglected, as has its potentially crucial role in achieving better health outcome for the population.

Health ministries manage the health systems, while governmental administrative levels (central government, regions, districts and municipalities) provide a framework. Sanepid services and curative health services, however, have parallel vertical structures with poor linkages at the regional and district levels.

Sanepid services can be found at different levels throughout the hierarchical government structures in central Asia (Green 1998). The Sanepid services are characterized by vertically organized structures at central, regional and district levels, plus a vertical reporting and information system (Savas and Gedik 1999). The Sanepid services are managed by a chief state sanitary physician, who is also a deputy minister of health. Regional Sanepid departments are independent of regional health authorities and have full juridical rights. This vertically established service has proven to be successful in the past in controlling epidemics (MacArthur and Bonnefoy 1997).

Sanepid services operate mainly at the regional and district level, including cities with district status. For example, Kyrgyzstan in 1993 had one republican level Sanepid department, six offices at the *oblast* level, ten at the city level and 41 *rayon* Sanepid stations (Ministry of Health and Ministry of Environmental Protection of the Kyrgyz Republic 1997).

During the Soviet period, Sanepid services had regulatory powers, which permitted relationships with other sectors on the basis of authoritarian supervision. The Sanepid service controlled sanitary norms and standards in most institutions and facilities. In case of infringements, it could invoke penalties and was, in theory, able to close institutions, although this was not easy due to the bureaucratic procedures involved.

Step by step, in the mentality of the service itself and in society in general, the control function became more important than the service function. The latter included health education, occupational health, school hygiene and other areas. The scale of an issue also influenced the effectiveness of the service. For instance, the Sanepid service could have a far greater impact on sanitary conditions within a food outlet or a medical facility than on environmental pollution from major industrial complexes. In a recent review of environmental health services in Europe, MacArthur and Bonnefoy (1997) argued that the effectiveness and efficiency of the services under former regimes were extremely limited. The system in which they had to operate constrained their activities to such an extent that they were unable to prevent large-scale environmental pollution.

The Sanepid service is an inheritance from a time when industry was state owned and of primary importance to the economic survival of countries. Costly environmental improvements were not viewed as a priority, and the Sanepid service had a limited capacity to enforce improvements. As a result, most of its work consisted of monitoring how far pollution exceeded the norms. In this closed economy, any fines would, in effect, redistribute state funds from one area to another, and so were not an effective deterrent against pollution (WHO European Centre for Environment and Health 1995). This system is common in the countries of the former Soviet Union and the CEE countries. At the time, authorities were responsible for monitoring pollution that emanated from industrial processes, and these results were compared against a national standard – normally set at a level comparable to those in the West. For every percentage point above the standard, the authority would impose a tax, levy or fine. On average, 30 per cent of this money would be retained by the inspection service and 70 per cent would be sent to the national authorities. As a result, it was not in the interests of local inspectorates to encourage industries to pollute less, as clearly their income budget would also be reduced. Furthermore, since the enterprises were state owned, the net effect was to keep public finances flowing rather than to address pollution levels.

The spread of corruption during the last years of the Soviet era, coupled with inefficient organization and management, meant that the Sanepid service was even further discredited. Eventually, in spite of many positive aspects of its activities, the Sanepid service was not viewed as a public protector, but as an additional burden upon the state. This reputation has been difficult to erase.

Other current problems facing the Sanepid service include insufficient training of personnel and a lack of research. These are compounded by the poor access that staff have to research on environmental health, epidemiology, health promotion, public health and health system development. For several decades, staff have been cut off from the considerable advances in knowledge and technology in these areas.

The Sanepid service, in common with other public services, has experienced extreme budgetary difficulties since the final years of the former Soviet Union. The net result is that the Sanepid service, despite its former achievements in controlling communicable disease, is losing its position and reputation. For example, *Plasmodium vivax* malaria epidemics have recurred in Tajikistan, as well as the more serious *Plasmodium falciparum* epidemics. These epidemics also affect the malaria situation in neighbouring countries, and the number of cases reported in Kazakhstan, Kyrgyzstan, Turkmenistan and Uzbekistan has increased considerably in the past 4 years (WHO 1999).

What can be done to strengthen the Sanepid service, so that it can voice, tackle and coordinate health-related issues at a multi-sectoral level? The Sanepid service should not be seen as a poor relation of the Ministry of Health, but rather as a full partner.

Reform processes

As the central Asian republics come to terms with their new-found independence and embark on a road of economic transition, they must also reform their institutional and governance structures. Various health care reforms have been initiated, triggered by external and internal factors (Savas 1998). During the first years of health care reforms, however, the Sanepid service was not the main focus, despite some legislative and organizational changes.

Recognizing that greater progress on common problems could be achieved through concerted action among neighbouring countries, a Central Asian Republics' Network on Health Care Reforms (CARNET) was established in 1994 with the support of the WHO Regional Office for Europe (CARNET 1997). The network aims to exchange experience and information among the central Asian republics on health system reforms.

A similar approach was adopted in the field of environmental health. Environment and health ministers held a conference at Lake Issyk-Kul, Kyrgyzstan in June 1996. They met to work out the principal practical actions to be taken on environment and health in the sub-region and adopted the Issyk-Kul Resolution.

This resolution recognizes reform of the Sanepid services as a high priority, in line with developing and implementing national environmental health action plans (NEHAPs) in each country (Ministers of Environment and Health 1996).

Against this background, a new joint CARNET/NEHAP cycle was undertaken in 1998 and 1999 with the aim of developing principles for improving Sanepid services in the region.

Mission

The 1996 Lake Issyk-Kyl conference concluded that the mission of the Sanepid service did not need to change significantly. First, the Sanepid service should be responsible for the health protection of the population. Second, it should coordinate the different agencies involved in public health. Third, it should continue to have a normative, standard-setting role. Fourth, it should operate in a more open and supportive way for health, concentrating more on health outcomes than technical interventions. Finally, legislative enforcement and penalties should be used as a last resort. These conclusions are broadly in line with modern thinking on public health services. Educational and promotional approaches are now generally accepted as more sustainable than legislative enforcement, although clearly recourse to statutory functions is necessary when all else fails.

Ownership

There was overwhelming agreement at the 1998 and 1999 CARNET/NEHAP meetings that the Sanepid service should remain under state control. This includes technical support functions within the services, such as laboratories and transport. While this opinion is not surprising, the issue of privatization remains on the policy agenda. One proposal is that laboratories should be accredited according to strict standards, which would reduce the excessive number of substandard public laboratories, allowing the private sector to undertake some of this work.

Legal framework

After independence, all central Asian republics revised their sanitary laws: Kyrgyzstan, Turkmenistan and Uzbekistan in 1992, Tajikistan in 1993 and Kazakhstan in 1994. The revised laws mostly mirrored the Sanitary Law of the former Soviet Union, but since this legislative framework was incomplete, *ad hoc* legislative revisions have continued in all countries.

Examples of these laws or regulations include (CARNET/NEHAP 1999): Kyrgyzstan passed laws on drinking water, food safety, radiation safety and immunoprevention in 1999. The Ministry of Health and Medical Industry of Turkmenistan issued orders on the control of infectious diseases (such as diphtheria, poliomyelitis and malaria) and on the sanitary certification of manufacturing. It also helped draw up laws on radiation safety, transportation of dangerous goods and preservation of air quality, and is a participant in a special commission on the water supply.

Most knowledgeable observers agree that the legal basis on which the Sanepid service operates needs to be strengthened, since it can only act where there is specific legislation. If it wishes to innovate or deviate from the legislation, it would be operating *ultra vires* and would need new legislation. Broader enabling legislation would encourage a less prescriptive approach. In particular, new legal provisions are required to provide greater clarity among different sectors within the health system, and between the health and the environmental sectors.

Organizational structure

Rationalization of the Sanepid service infrastructure has begun in all countries (CARNET/NEHAP 1999). In Kyrgyzstan, the Department of State Sanitary-Epidemiological Surveillance was established by merging the Republican Sanepid Services and the Sanitary-Epidemiological Department of the Ministry of Health. In Turkmenistan, the Sanepid service was reorganized in 1998 into the State Sanitary Epidemiology Inspectorate and took on hygiene certification as an additional function. To do this, the centre responsible for standards and certification of food products was transferred from the Ministry of Trade to the Sanitary Epidemiology Inspectorate. A central hygiene and epidemiology laboratory was established, reporting to the Sanitary Epidemiology Inspectorate (President of Turkmenistan 1999). Where activities were duplicated, some institutions have amalgamated, such as some regional and city Sanepid services in Kyrgyzstan and Turkmenistan.

The central Asian republics have continued to establish new vertical infrastructures, separate from the Sanepid services. For example, following the President's 1997 message 'Kazakhstan 2030' (President of Kazakhstan 1997), which emphasized the importance of public health and health promotion, the National Centre for Healthy Lifestyle was established with its own vertical structure. An intersectoral health promotion council also was set up. In Uzbekistan, a republican AIDS Centre for the prevention and treatment of HIV/AIDS was established in 1998 in Tashkent, with branches in each region.

The vertical top–down approach, a classic feature of the Sanepid organizational structure, has been called 'bureaucratic and obsolete' by some commentators (Vienonen and Springett 1998–99). Although the current structure is acknowledged as a little top heavy, those managing the system still see virtues in a command-and-control management structure. This underlines the need for a steady path towards reform. Ultimately, a more autonomous service may be possible, but stakeholders must be ready for such changes. A new system will not work if its staff are not equipped with new knowledge, skills and attitudes. On the other hand, a new system will not emerge until the staff and management are ready to create it. This symbiotic relationship between form and function is often overlooked in the rush to impose solutions and structures from above.

Nevertheless, there is a growing view that middle managers need more autonomy, which requires the devolution of some power. Furthermore, a strengthened institutional structure is needed, particularly for rural areas.

Functions

The functions of a Sanepid service must be clearly defined before the structure of the system can be adjusted. A clear split of responsibilities among the multi-sectoral parties must therefore be clarified. The CARNET/NEHAP meetings on improving the SES facilitated such discussions among representatives from the Sanepid services, health care delivery system and environmental services. The current Sanepid service functions, which are very similar across the countries (with few changes since the Soviet period), are as follows:

- surveillance of sanitary norms and standards;
- surveillance of planning and construction;
- surveillance of production, storage, transportation and use of health-related products;
- data collection, monitoring and assessment of the impact of environmental conditions on health;
- prevention of communicable, food-related and occupational diseases;
- data collection, monitoring and assessment of communicable and occupational diseases;
- procurement, storage, transportation and distribution of vaccines and serums; and
- health education of the population.

The Sanepid service has sole responsibility for most of the above functions, but greater efficiency could be achieved if primary health care was involved more closely in some functions. The network of primary health care facilities is better organized than that of the Sanepid service, especially in rural areas, and primary health care personnel have more opportunities to intervene on individual and community levels.

Immunization is an example of effective joint work between the Sanepid service and primary health care, where services work closely together and their job descriptions clearly identify their responsibilities. As a result, immunization coverage is high in the central Asian republics. Such joint approaches could be extended to other functions of the Sanepid service, such as the maintenance and control of sanitary norms, disease prevention and health promotion. The advantage of collaboration is that primary health care personnel have better access to the population and know their catchment: its people, territory and problems.

The Sanepid service is also involved in health education, but does not have the resources to develop a holistic approach. Currently, health promotion comes under the curative and preventive departments of a health ministry. Health promotion should be a priority in the region due to changing epidemiological patterns and increasing rates of non-communicable diseases, and the Sanepid service could play a more active role.

Sanepid service functions and staffing are not currently geared to non-communicable diseases, but in the future could contribute by offering a population perspective, by helping to develop policies and by carrying out monitoring and evaluation. Sanepid services need to cooperate with other sectors to ensure that services are provided in accordance with national health policies and standards. There is a consensus that the functions and responsibilities of the Sanepid service should be revised, particularly in light of its involvement in communicable and non-communicable diseases. The Sanepid service also believes that it needs better cooperation from the environment sector as well as the broader health sector.

Financing

The low funding remains a serious problem. The Uzbekistan Sanepid service receives about 4 per cent of the shrinking health budget. The Turkmenistan Sanepid service received only 3 per cent of the total health budget in 1997, with almost all funds used for salaries. The Kyrgyzstan Sanepid service did better, with 6.8 per cent of the health budget in 1998 (Sargaldakova *et al.* 2000), while Kazakhstan received 4.5 per cent in 1994. In Tajikistan in 1998, the service received only 3.9 per cent of the very small state health budget. In addition, Sanepid funding varies considerably across regions in each country.

Each country is considering ways to raise more revenue, such as charging fees for consultations, certificates and development approvals, and seeking funds from insurance schemes. Some central Asian republics charge fees for services, such as disinfections, although Kazakhstan stopped this practice in 1998. In other countries, fees comprise a very small part of Sanepid service revenue. The Turkmenistan Sanepid service has asked the Ministry of Finance to allow charges for some services. Kazakhstan and Kyrgyzstan plan to use health insurance funds to help finance laboratory services and some prevention activities. A separate ecological fund has been set up in Kazakhstan, and a special fund has been set up in Tajikistan to respond to epidemics. The CARNET/NEHAP workshop participants believed that extra sources of finance could help fund Sanepid services, but that most resources should come from the state budget. Sanepid budget allocations are based on historical line items, but per person resource allocation formulae that take population size into account are being discussed. Fines and taxes supplement core funding, but this can bias work activities, and it was agreed that these should be collected outside the Sanepid service.

Multi-sectorality

Coordination among sectors was viewed as a key element of reform. The workshop participants believed that the Sanepid service should be strengthened by setting up coordination committees at central, regional and district levels, with an appropriate legal base and with involvement of relevant institutions.

Sanepid services have plans for joint activities with the ministries of environment. Better coordination is needed on environmental health issues that involve joint analysis, planning, evaluation and monitoring. The problem of drinking water in Uzbekistan is an example of an area of considerable common concern, involving the environment and agriculture ministries, as well as the health ministry (Reynolds 1996).

Information exchange, plus joint laboratories and projects, could strengthen collaboration. Local plans could be formulated by the Sanepid service with other partners, including municipalities. For example, Bishkek recently participated in an international programme to develop a local environmental health action plan. Working with other partners, including the Sanepid service, the city developed a multi-sectoral plan that highlighted the major environmental health issues facing the city and that identified the key stakeholders responsible for remedial and preventative action.

Another suggestion was that Ministry of Health staff from the Sanepid service, the health care delivery system and the Ministry of Environment should exchange jobs on a short-term basis, to learn more about one another's work and systems.

Staffing and training

The central Asian republics employ specialist sanitary physicians and sanitary feldshers. Turkmenistan employed 835 sanitary physicians and 3529 middle-level medical personnel (such as feldshers and nurses) in 1996. Kyrgyzstan employed 621 sanitary physicians and 2050 middle-level medical personnel, including technicians, in 1998. There is a greater awareness that non-medical personnel are required in the Sanepid services and that a new professional staffing profile should be considered. The CARNET/NEHAP participants strongly recommended that Sanepid services should employ economists, lawyers, engineers, chemists, physicists, computer programmers and managers.

Most external analysts believe that the Sanepid service is overstaffed. Over the last decade, however, medical posts have been reduced in most central Asian republics (see Healy, Chapter 10). Sanepid personnel were also reduced in some countries; for example, in Tajikistan between 1990 and 1998, the number of sanitary physicians fell by 31 per cent and middle-level personnel by 64 per cent. Currently, the staffing of Sanepid stations is quite low compared to official staffing norms. There is a high turnover of personnel in some countries; for example, over 70 per cent of Sanepid personnel have left their positions in Tajikistan.

Salaries within the Sanepid services are very low. For instance, the monthly salary of a Sanepid physician in 1997 was between US$3 and US$5 in Tajikistan and between US$63 and US$85 in Kazakhstan. Diminishing wage levels in the public sector only serve to encourage petty corruption, unproductive staff or worse, while many good staff choose to leave the sector in search of better-paid employment. Appropriate remuneration is a prerequisite for effective services. Pay scales should reflect the appropriate level of qualification, as well as the work done by professionals other than medical doctors.

Sanepid staff recognize that if they are to move to new ways of working, they need retraining. For example, Sanepid staff have no background in economics, modern management techniques and law. Sanitary physicians graduate after a 5 year course in a sanitary-hygiene faculty of a medical institute. Middle-level personnel are trained in medical schools. Sanepid staff, therefore, have high-level academic credentials, but the appropriateness of this education needs review. Also, the knowledge and skills of Sanepid personnel have decreased since the unravelling of the Soviet Union. The enormous changes in the region over the past decade require environmental health professionals to respond to these new situations (Fitzpatrick and Bonnefoy 1998). The quality and availability of postgraduate training has declined significantly and left countries with shortages of teachers and training materials. Professional development is needed through distance learning courses and joint seminars with colleagues from the environment ministry. Postgraduate programmes are needed in health policy, management and economics. The Kazakhstan School of Public Health offers the potential to improve postgraduate training in Kazakhstan and the central Asian region.

Finally, the emergence of professional associations is critical in strengthening skills and knowledge. State authorities should support such associations and create a suitable legal and financial framework. Following a WHO/Chartered Institute of Environmental Health (UK) collaboration on the production of guidance for the formation of professional associations, the Kazhak Association of Sanepid Doctors was formed, with support from the Ministry of Health. The Kazakh Association recently has been accepted as a member of the International Federation of Environmental Health Officers Association of Eire.

Information

The Sanepid service is renowned for collecting vast quantities of data. It has better information systems than other health and environment agencies, given its experience with communicable diseases and emergencies. The challenges are to turn the data collected into information, to agree on common data sets between the partner organizations, to agree to exchange information and to prevent duplication of effort. For example, many agencies hold similar data on air and drinking water quality. In Kazakhstan, the Sanepid information system was modernized with international support and could act as the basis for such a collaborative effort. A common set of indicators should be developed across the range of mutual activities.

To facilitate fast and reliable information between agencies, improved information technology is needed. This is particularly useful if emergencies arise and information must be sent quickly to many people.

Infrastructure and supply

Sanepid services suffer from a serious lack of infrastructure and logistical supply. In Turkmenistan in 1996, 91 per cent of establishments were located in substandard buildings and 85 per cent of equipment was obsolete. There are significant problems with the lack of chemicals, biological reagents and laboratory supplies across central Asia. For instance, Tajikistan claimed in 1999 that most laboratory equipment and tools were obsolete, since 20 per cent needed repair and 30 per cent did not function at all. Of the 122 work vehicles, 65 were out of order, and 54 of the 97 disinfectant automobiles did not work.

These logistical issues reflect the external and internal problems of these countries, including financial, organizational and managerial problems. In parallel with financial support in renovation and provision of equipment, the countries need technical advice on the structural reorganization of the Sanepid services.

Principles of reform

In any reform process, there is a tendency to overhaul and radically change systems. This temptation needs to be guarded against, as rarely is a system designed from scratch, and there is the danger of throwing away the good points with the bad. In this sense, the restructuring of public health services in the central Asian republics should be looked upon as an *evolutionary* process and not as a *revolutionary* process. Although the Sanepid service has many detractors, it does perform core functions that are required in any new health care system. No-one believes that Sanepid service reform is easy. Whichever path is taken, any change of institutional structures inevitably calls for hard decisions. Since these affect individuals directly, many actions will meet resistance.

The following five principles, developed by the Chartered Institute of Environmental Health and presented at an early CARNET meeting, were offered as guidelines for formulating new policies.

Principle 1: leadership/commitment

Experience has shown that any reform process (be it in the private or public sector) will succeed only when there is clear and unambiguous commitment and leadership from the highest political authority within the organization. No matter how hard they try, people on or near the front line are in no position to launch or sustain the process of Sanepid service reform. Although participants in the whole reform process need to understand and accommodate the bottom-up concept, a grass roots approach must operate within a framework founded upon serious political commitment. At the end of the day, the process must produce something practical.

The act of making a political commitment will mark the beginning of the reform process. This commitment can be demonstrated in several ways, but it needs to be clear and unequivocal in its message, and it needs to be sustained consistently throughout the process.

Principle 2: equity

The concept of equity, a core value of WHO, is an implicit principle that any reform process must recognize. It is of particular importance for public health.

Disadvantaged groups within a country are often those who live and work in the worst environments: the worst housing with poor sanitation and water supplies, the most dangerous occupations, and limited access to a wholesome food supply.

Although the main factors contributing to ill health may stem from health-endangering behaviour, such as an inappropriate diet or excessive consumption of alcohol, the search for the root causes of such behaviour will require examination of the associated social conditions.

Lack of access to adequate education, the inability to obtain sufficient and balanced nutrition, poor housing conditions, unemployment and a physical environment that offers stresses at many different levels will undoubtedly have a major impact on health and quality of life. Remedying these conditions will require clean water, sanitation, adequate housing, safe and fulfilling employment, safe and nutritious food supplies, essential health care, educational services and welfare in times of need.

Equity is a (possibly *the*) fundamental principle of the reform process. The aim of a Sanepid service, to improve the living environment for current and future generations, requires an ability to recognize the needs of all of society. The equity principle signals a new way of approaching practical problems. It requires thought and effort to be directed to the source of the problem in policy terms and not merely to the adverse physical conditions that the original policy creates. Finally, it must ensure that services and support are directed towards those who most need them.

Principle 3: policy integration/inter-sectoral action

Put simply, this principle recognizes that improvements in the health of a population rely on many sectors working together. Not only must service sectors work with economic sectors, they must also recognize the issues with which the other sectors have to deal. The knowledge gained from this integrated approach would inform institutions, decision-making bodies and professional education and training programmes.

Improvements in health and quality of life rely on changes in social, economic and environmental conditions. A reformed Sanepid service can contribute to identifying and pursuing the issues that arise where these factors impact on one another. The interface between social and environmental factors, between environmental and economic factors, and between economic and social factors will hold the key to many of the more difficult problems that face the Sanepid service today. Complex and integrated solutions are needed for complex and integrated problems.

Principle 4: subsidiarity

The subsidiarity principle calls for decisions to be made and action to be taken at the level closest and most appropriate to the population affected. This normally means delegation of responsibility from the central level to the regional or local level. It may also mean looking outside the established institutional structure for new and more appropriate partners, such as local municipalities and non-governmental organizations.

Principle 5: democracy – accountability and public participation

This principle will require a fundamental change of attitude in many areas of the Sanepid service. Modern services, which address the environmental health and sustainable development agendas, recognize both the need to be accountable politically and the benefits of involving the public directly in decision-making.

The Convention on Public Participation in Environmental Decision-making, agreed in Åarhus, Denmark, in June 1998, is highly relevant (United Nations Economic Commission for Europe Committee on Environmental Policy 1998). Many services throughout Europe already are accountable politically to their local populations, and they engage representatives of the local community in the decision-making process in an equal and open partnership. Their experience has shown that this type of approach to decision-making and service delivery has greatly improved the nature and effect of the service provided.

Not only does public participation allow people to understand the issues, but it also gives them an opportunity to promote social change through their own actions. Public interest in environment and health issues has increased greatly in recent years. Sanepid services, in designing their strategies, should nurture, develop and manage public participation. Stating its value is not enough – Sanepid services must actively communicate with the public to encourage their participation.

Conclusions

As the speed of transition to a market economy gathers pace and as pressures for institutional reform grow, decision-makers in the central Asian republics increasingly look for advice and for models of public health systems, particularly from the West. We should all remember, however, that there are no ready-made solutions for the challenges facing the central Asian republics. No country in western Europe has found the perfect public health model that meets all aspirations; there are only a few signposts along the road of reform. What can be offered is soundly grounded principles, such as addressing inequity, recognizing subsidiarity and realizing the political power of public participation. We lose sight of these beacons at our peril.

At the time this chapter was drafted, the joint CARNET/NEHAP process was incomplete. From the evidence gathered already and laid out here, we can begin to see steps in the direction of evolutionary reforms. With strong support from the international community and with solidarity among the central Asian republics, there is both the foundation and the commitment to work tirelessly to improve public services for the good of the public's health.

References

Blane, D., Brunner, E. and Wilkinson, R. (1996) *Health and Social Organization: Towards a Health Policy for the Twenty-First Century*. London: Routledge.

CARNET (1997) *Central Asian Republics' Network on Health Care Reforms*, Document EUR/ICP CARE060301. Copenhagen: WHO Regional Office for Europe.

CARNET/NEHAP (1999) *National CARNET/NEHAP Workshop: Process on Improving Sanitary Epidemiology Services*. Bishkek: WHO Regional Office for Europe.

Fitzpatrick, M. and Bonnefoy, X. (1998) *Environmental Health Services in Europe 3: Professional Profiles*, WHO Regional Publications, European Series, No. 82. Copenhagen: WHO Regional Office for Europe.

Green, G. (1998) *Health and Governance in European Cities*. London: European Hospital Management Journal Ltd on behalf of WHO Regional Office for Europe.

MacArthur, I. and Bonnefoy, X. (1997) *Environmental Health Services in Europe 1: An Overview of Practice in the 1990s*, WHO Regional Publications, European Series, No. 76. Copenhagen: WHO Regional Office for Europe.

McKee, M. and Bojan, F. (1998) Reforming public health services, in R.B. Saltman, J. Figueras and C. Sakellarides (eds) *Critical Challenges for Health Care Reform in Europe*. Buckingham: Open University Press.

Ministers of Environment and Health (1996) *On Actions for Environment and Health Protection in the Central Asian Republics*, Issyk-Kul Meeting. Issyk-Kul: WHO Regional Office for Europe.

Ministry of Health and Ministry of Environmental Protection of the Kyrgyz Republic (1997) *Sanitary-Epidemiological Health of the Population of the Kyrgyz Republic, and the Regulations on State Sanitary-Epidemiological Surveillance*. Bishkek: Ministry of Health and Ministry of Environmental Protection of the Kyrgyz Republic.

President of Kazakhstan (1997) *Kazakhstan 2030: Prosperity, Security and Welfare for All People of Kazakhstan*. Almaty: Office of the President.

President of Turkmenistan (1999) *Plan for the Realization of the State Health Programme of the President of Turkmenistan*. Ashgabat: Office of the President.

Reynolds, S.J. (1996) Occupational and environmental health in Turkmenistan and Uzbekistan, *American Industrial Hygiene Association Journal*, 57: 1096–1102.

Sargaldakova, A., Healy, J., Kutzin, J. and Gedik, G. (2000) *Health Care Systems in Transition: Kyrgyzstan*. Copenhagen: European Observatory on Health Care Systems.

Savas, S. (1998) Health care reforms in central Asia: managing the change, *Eurohealth*, 4(6): 66–8.

Savas, S. and Gedik, G. (1999) Health care reforms in central Asia, in UNDP (eds) *Central Asia 2010: Prospects for Human Development*. New York: UNDP Regional Bureau for Europe and the CIS.

Staines, V. (1999) *A Health Sector Strategy for the Europe and Central Asia Region*, Health, Nutrition and Population Series. Washington, DC: World Bank.

United Nations Economic Commission for Europe Committee on Environmental Policy (1998) *Convention on Access to Information, Public Participation in Decision-making and Access to Justice in Environmental Matters*, Report on the Fourth Ministerial Conference 'Environment for Europe', Åarhus, Denmark, 23–25 June 1998, Document ECE/CEP/43. New York: United Nations.

Vienonen, M.A. and Springett, J. (1998–99) Public health, primary health care and health insurance, *Eurohealth*, 4(6): 17–20.

WHO (1999) *HEALTH21: The Health for All Policy Framework for the WHO European Region*, European Health for All Series No. 6. Copenhagen: WHO Regional Office for Europe.

WHO European Centre for Environment and Health (1995) *Concern for Europe's Tomorrow: Health and the Environment in the WHO European Region*. Stuttgart: Wissenschaftliche Verlagsgesellschaft.

chapter fourteen

Health care systems
in transition

*Judith Healy, Jane Falkingham and
Martin McKee*

Introduction

Health care systems across the central Asian republics are in transition from a
centralized command-and-control model to more decentralized and pluralistic
models. In the early 1990s, these health care systems fitted the description
of 'the bureaucratic model of direct service delivery so widely criticised as
monopolistic, over-centralised, hierarchical and unresponsive to users' (Russell
et al. 1999: 767). In many countries in western and eastern Europe (Saltman
et al. 1998), as well as in the countries of Asia (Peabody *et al.* 1999), ongoing
health care reforms are attempting to address such structural problems. The
central Asian republics inherited particularly inflexible health care systems,
which were no longer meeting the health needs of their populations, and
have faced the enormous challenge of implementing sustainable reforms despite
drastically shrinking public-sector revenues. Part one of this book has set out
the political, economic and social background against which reform is taking
place, while Part two has described the plans being developed. This conclud-
ing chapter examines what has been achieved since independence.

Field (Chapter 6) has described the health care systems inherited from the
Soviet Union. In marked contrast to many other regions at a similar level of
economic development, health care was widely available and generally free at
the point of use. But even before independence, these systems showed signs
of strain, symptomatic of the more deep-seated fault lines in the Soviet system that led Gorbachev to advocate a broad-based restructuring, or *perestroika*
(Gorbachev 1988). The economic collapse that followed independence pro-
pelled health services into crisis. As Akiner (Chapter 2) and Pomfret (Chapter
3) have shown, the integrated internal market in the Soviet Union left those

regions that were primarily responsible for producing raw materials especially vulnerable to the disruption of trading links. After independence, markets disappeared, means of exchange broke down and the supply of spare parts dried up. These events brought about a dramatic fall in government revenues, even allowing for the considerable uncertainties of the new accounting systems in a period of rapid change.

Rapid inflation led to a substantial fall in real wages. New currencies were introduced in the early 1990s. Kazakhstan and Kyrgyzstan, both facing serious balance of payment problems, soon introduced austerity programmes. Uzbekistan, which is somewhat better endowed with natural resources, pursued a more gradual programme of stabilization. Tajikistan, beset by civil war for most of this period, was for several years unable to tackle its serious financial problems effectively. Turkmenistan has been reluctant to make radical changes to its existing systems.

The reduction in output was exacerbated by a failure to recover tax from increasingly large informal economies. Tax revenues dried up, so that health budgets in the late 1990s amounted to a third or less of their pre-1991 amounts. Income inequalities have increased, with around a third more of the populations of the republics living in poverty (applying a US$4.30 per day poverty line), particularly in Kyrgyzstan and Tajikistan, where there are fewer primary and secondary economic resources (Falkingham, Chapter 4).

These macroeconomic changes rendered the Soviet era health care systems unsustainable. By the mid-1990s, all the central Asian republics were beginning to restructure their systems. In this they were not alone, since European countries, particularly in eastern Europe (Saltman *et al.* 1998) and in Asia (Asian Development Bank 1999; Peabody *et al.* 1999), were all in the process of making changes to their health care systems. Savas *et al.* (Chapter 7) described how most central Asian republics drew up national plans for health care and discussed the substantial barriers encountered in implementing these plans. The reform agenda, while driven primarily by drastic cuts in health care budgets, was also influenced by a belated recognition of the decline in the health of their populations (McKee and Chenet, Chapter 5). Finally, some, but by no means all, reformers wished to break with the Communist past.

Health-sector reform has not been easy, in part reflecting the lack of institutional capacity. Under the Soviet system, many important decisions were made in Moscow, giving republican health ministries a very limited role. This, when combined with the rigidity of the Soviet system and the limited scope for innovation, meant that the central Asian republics did not develop a critical mass of individuals skilled in policy development or implementation. In some republics, the pool of skilled health professionals was reduced further by emigration following independence. Although their roles have now changed dramatically, most health ministries remain very small and are frequently seen as relatively low in the hierarchy of ministries. Symbolically, the Ministry of Health in Uzbekistan is the only ministry outside the main complex of government buildings.

Primary health care has been a focus for much health reform activity in several countries, with professionals being reorganized to deliver primary health care from family group practices, rather than from separate locations and by separate types of physicians (Gedik, Oztek and Lewis, Chapter 11). Few extra resources, however, have been transferred to primary health care, while retraining health care professionals to enable them to treat rather than merely refer patients is a slow process. MacArthur and Shevkun (Chapter 13) discussed recent steps to improve public health and pointed out that the potential role of the Sanepid services in improving population health, like primary care, has been neglected. Reorienting primary care and the Sanepid services to fulfil their potential requires a considerable investment in retraining staff. Healy (Chapter 10) considered the problems and progress in the area of human resources, where the central Asian republics have large health care workforces, but very limited funds to invest in retraining, while staff considered excess to requirements do not have access to alternative jobs or to adequate retirement pensions. Human resource issues, as well as funding issues, are crucial to enabling these extensive health care systems to reorganize and to improve their performance.

As in many developed countries, the focus of health system reform has been on finding new ways to finance health systems, on allocating funds more efficiently and on paying health care providers in ways that reward more efficient and effective performance. Despite the severe financial constraints and institutional inertia, microeconomic reforms of the health systems in central Asia, albeit limited, *have* taken place. Several countries are reorganizing their financing systems. Kutzin and Cashin (Chapter 8) examined mechanisms for collecting funds, but concluded that securing extra resources through insurance schemes has failed and that the emphasis in future should be on making the existing system more efficient. Ensor and Langenbrunner (Chapter 9) concluded that new payment systems must be backed by reforms to the whole public-sector budgetary process. This highlights an important point: to be implemented successfully, any change to one part of the health care system must take into account the ramifications for the system as a whole.

The central Asian republic health care systems have thus engaged in lively debates on health care reform. As a result, their health care policies have been overhauled, limited administrative powers have been devolved, some health care services have been reorganized, pilot projects have been set up to test new ways of delivering services, and a series of changes have been introduced to health-service financing and delivery.

Given this considerable activity, what then has *actually* been achieved in terms of health system changes and outcomes during the transition years of the 1990s? This chapter puts the debate into context by examining how the central Asian republics fare on health system performance according to international indicators. Next, we analyse the two structural changes: the introduction of new sources of financing and the restructuring of hospital systems. We choose these areas for analysis for several reasons: they have been the focus of most health care reform in the region, they can be expected to affect population health and the available data indicate extensive changes. Finally, the challenges of implementing reform in the future are discussed.

Overall health system performance

How do the health systems in the central Asian republics perform when compared to those in other countries? *The World Health Report 2000* (WHO 2000b:
xi) argues that a country's health system should aim to achieve three goals:
good health, responsiveness to the expectations of the population and fairness
in financial contributions. The WHO measure of overall health system performance is a composite index of five measures adjusted for national wealth and
education level: health attainment on average for the population, its distribution within the population, responsiveness to patients, health attainment distribution within the population and fairness of financial contributions (WHO
2000b: 39). Limitations in data availability from the central Asian republics
mean that their ranking among world health systems must be regarded with
caution, and the precise order between the five countries is questionable.

On these measures of attainment, however, the central Asian republics rank
quite low, among the third quartile of countries in the world (out of 191
countries). Kazakhstan ranked higher than the other four central Asian republics
and Tajikistan ranked the lowest. These rankings are higher than many other
poor countries, such as those in Africa ravaged by disease and civil strife. This
relatively low level of achievement is disappointing, however, given that the
central Asian republics inherited an extensive health system infrastructure, a
large health care workforce and an ideological commitment to access and equity.

The UNDP human development index (HDI) allows us to track trends through
the 1990s. This index, intended to counter the international preoccupation
with economic indicators, contains three measures: life expectancy at birth,
adult literacy and per person income in US$ PPP. Given that life expectancy

Figure 14.1 Human development index, world rank order, for the central Asian
republics, 1990–98

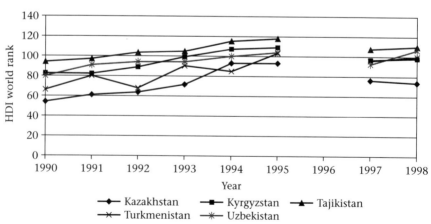

Sources: UNDP, 1993 through 2000: UNDP (1993, 1994, 1995, 1996, 1997, 1998, 1999,
2000)

declined in the central Asian republics (McKee and Chenet, Chapter 5), as did per person income (Falkingham, Chapter 4), one would expect the index to show a downward trend. On the other hand, these countries continue to report high rates of literacy and falling school enrolments, which make the validity of the data questionable.

The performance of the central Asian republics relative to the rest of the world may be gauged by looking at trends in rank order on the HDI (Figure 14.1). (The highest country is ranked 1 and the lowest 174.) There was a downward trend between 1991 and 1995, when all countries slipped several places down the rankings, but there was some improvement in 1997 and 1998. (No HDI figures were produced for 1996.) In 1998, in terms of rank order, the central Asian republics ranked mainly in the third quartile of countries in the world (as for the WHO health system performance index), with Kazakhstan ranking the highest among the five countries and Tajikistan ranking the lowest.

The next part of this chapter addresses progress in specific areas of health-sector reform.

Health system reforms

Much of the impetus for health system reform in the central Asian republics has come from government efforts to find more secure sources of public revenue and to reduce health system costs. Market model solutions, including privatization, were seen by many as the new way forward. The first priority was to halt the drop in revenue for the health budget. Some countries saw a health insurance scheme as the solution to securing guaranteed funding, but given their failing economies and difficulties in collecting payroll taxes, insurance contributions have proved to be only a small and complementary source of revenue. These countries, therefore, have increasingly resorted to charging fees to health care users, which in part have been justified under a market model rationale. The second thrust was to seek microeconomic reform, since it was increasingly clear that the health care system had to do better with fewer resources. Since the hospital system accounted for around 70 per cent of the health budget, and by most measures contained considerable excess capacity, the policy aim was to reduce both the number of hospitals and the number of beds.

What have been the successes and failures in these two areas? Table 14.1 suggests that the changes have been greatest in Kazakhstan, Kyrgyzstan and Uzbekistan, and least in Tajikistan and Turkmenistan. We now discuss how these policies have been implemented in the five countries.

New sources of finance

Each of the central Asian governments is struggling to establish new revenue collection systems to replace the revenue that previously came from state enterprises and from Moscow. Public-sector revenue declined by over 60 per cent in most countries in the first half of the 1990s, resulting in budget

Table 14.1 Policy changes, in selected areas, in the central Asian republics

Selected area	Kazakhstan	Kyrgyzstan	Tajikistan	Turkmenistan	Uzbekistan
Health insurance	Mandatory fund set up in 1996, but now state-funded	Mandatory fund set up in 1997; < 5% of 1999 state health budget	No state or private insurance funds	Voluntary state insurance set up in 1996; < 2% of 1998 state health budget	No state insurance fund
User charges	Legalized in 1995; 10% of Almaty *oblast* revenue in 1996	Legalized in 1991; 8.4% of state revenue in 1998	Partially legalized; wide charges	Partially legalized; 1% of state revenue in 1998	Partially legalized; 7% of state revenue in 1999
Change in hospital system, 1990–97	Hospitals: –46%; acute beds: –40%	Hospitals: +13%; acute beds: –24%	Hospitals: +15%; acute beds: –29%	Hospitals: –5%; acute beds: –37%	Hospitals: –21%; all beds: –48%
Hospital % of total health budget, latest available year	About 74%	65%	79%	63%	About 43%

Source: European Observatory on Health Care Systems, *Health Care Systems in Transition* series, selected countries and years

deficits, with severe cuts in health expenditure, down to a quarter or a third of their 1991 amounts (Kutzin and Cashin, Chapter 8).

Health insurance

Compulsory insurance schemes were introduced in Kazakhstan and Kyrgyzstan, with a voluntary state-run scheme in Turkmenistan. Tajikistan and Uzbekistan have retained tax-funded health care systems (Table 14.1). Insurance accounts for only a small proportion of health system revenue, however, since the same problems that limit the collection of taxation also limit the collection of payroll-based health insurance. The advantage was that insurance revenue went into a separate fund outside the traditional budgetary system, which allowed the introduction of new ways of paying health care providers. In the long run, however, this only postponed the need to reform the whole government budgetary process.

The success of these insurance schemes can be assessed in several ways, but a key indicator is the proportion of total health care expenditure raised. Insurance has contributed far less to public revenue than expected and has proved difficult to collect in the context of rising unemployment and the impoverishment of these populations. Insurance was expected to tap extra revenue, or at least secure earmarked funds for health, but its introduction has not averted the continuing decline in health budgets.

Kazakhstan introduced mandatory health insurance in 1996, but the scheme was short-lived, with contributions from a hypothecated payroll tax now replaced by transfers from the public budget, with the fund transformed into a government department for purchasing health services in early 1999. When it was functioning, perhaps 20 per cent of the state health budget was raised from insurance contributions, but public spending on health continued to decline (Kulzhanov and Healy 1999). Kyrgyzstan introduced mandatory health insurance in 1997, administered by the government and collected from a payroll tax. Population insurance coverage is being phased in, with about a third covered in 1999. Insurance currently contributes less than 5 per cent to the state health care budget (Sargaldakova et al. 2000). In Tajikistan, the health system is publicly funded from state taxes collected mainly by the national government, although the introduction of health insurance is on the policy agenda (Rahminov et al. 2000). Turkmenistan introduced a voluntary government health insurance scheme in 1996; it contributed about 7 per cent to the state health budget in 1997, but dropped to below 2 per cent in 1998, for reasons that are unclear (Mamedkuliev et al. 2000). Uzbekistan has retained a state health care system financed from taxes and state enterprises. A voluntary state health insurance scheme was considered, but did not proceed, while private insurance funds remain very small (Ilkhamov and Jakubowski 2000).

Kutzin and Cashin (Chapter 8) argue that, since there is little prospect of increasing the health budget from either insurance or taxes, the central Asian republics should concentrate on making their health care systems more cost-effective. The reasons for choosing social insurance as a financing system, however, included a drive for transparency and a desire to break with the past. Reformers within these countries argue that the process of implementing health insurance has catalysed change in the health system in other ways, such as new provider payment methods, selective purchasing and the monitoring of standards (Ensor and Langenbrunner, Chapter 9). The establishment of insurance funds that could contract with service providers, therefore, was partly a back-door way of introducing payment incentives to make health care services more efficient and effective.

Out-of-pocket payments

Although social insurance is less equitable than general taxation as a means of funding health care, any form of prepaid financing is fairer than widespread user fees (Van Doorslaer *et al.* 1993). Out-of-pocket payments by patients have, however, become a major source of funds for the health care system. They are now estimated to account for more than half of total health expenditure in Kazakhstan and Kyrgyzstan (Chapter 8) and perhaps 70 per cent of health expenditure in Tajikistan (Falkingham, in press). Less is known about Turkmenistan and Uzbekistan. Falkingham (Chapter 4) reviews household surveys from the central Asian republics, which typically report that over half of respondents indicated that they had paid, either officially or unofficially, for health care.

Three categories of out-of-pocket payments can be defined, although these are difficult both to separate and to estimate, especially since some payments can be in cash or in-kind. First, health providers (government or private) charge official fees. Second, semi-official charges are made for consumables, such as drugs and medical supplies. Third, patients make under-the-table payments to health care providers, either as a so-called gift or increasingly as a precondition for service.

Under-the-table payments are not considered here, since governments (at least officially) regard these as counter to their public policy. Informal payment was discussed in detail in Chapter 4 and is documented extensively elsewhere (Falkingham, in press; Lewis 2002). The semi-official charges levied on consumables, although less well documented, are also very common. Public-sector health facilities faced with serious shortages now require patients to bring or buy their own consumables. This mainly applies to hospitals – not just to hotel aspects but also to health aspects. For example, hospital inpatients in Kyrgyzstan mostly supply their own food, launder their own sheets and towels and buy their own medicines (Blomquist 1997). In Uzbekistan, patients are given a list of medical supplies to bring with them to the hospital (Ilkhamov and Jakubowski 2000), as is also the case in Kazakhstan (Kulzhanov and Healy 1999); there are similar stories from the other central Asian republics. This practice suggests that many hospitals are functioning only with direct financial support from patients.

User charges

Three main arguments are advanced for introducing official user charges. The first is that user charges discourage inappropriate demand (the problem of moral hazard). Given the very high level of health need in this region and the poor state of facilities, moral hazard (assuming it applies to those seeking health care anywhere, which is questionable) is unlikely to be an issue in this region. The second argument is that user charges tap an additional source of revenue for the health system. The third argument is that the opportunity for some self-financing encourages public-sector organizations, especially state-owned enterprises, to operate in a more business-like way in terms of producing more effective and efficient services.

The consensus in western Europe, however, is that user charges secure little extra revenue, are inequitable, deter sick as well as healthy people, have adverse consequences on health outcomes and are rarely well accepted by the public (Mossialos and Le Grand 1999).

Unfortunately, in central Asia, the search for sufficient or alternative sources of public funding has been unsuccessful; consequently, wages are not paid and hospitals run out of essential supplies. Under these circumstances, user charges may be inevitable. The consequences for equity are recognized and vulnerable groups (such as pensioners) are exempted, at least in theory. Systematic data on the extent of user charges are not available, but the following information has been gleaned from published material and interviews with key informants.

Kazakhstan legalized limited user charges in 1995. *Oblast* administrations decide the level and extent of fees and have drawn up price lists. These include full payment for 'non-essential' treatment, drugs and other medical supplies for outpatients, and a range of charges for diagnostic and treatment procedures. Almaty *oblast*, in 1996, for example, raised 10 per cent of its revenue from such charges, but this is likely to be less in rural *oblasts* (Kulzhanov and Healy 1999).

Kyrgyzstan legalized selected user fees in 1991. A Department of Non-Budgetary Activity, set up within the Ministry of Health in 1993, makes policy, regulates fees and approves the price list of republican facilities, while *oblast* finance departments approve *oblast*-level charges. Co-payments are now very extensive: patients pay for laboratory tests and drugs, for hospital admission fees, for 17 separate items while in hospital and for the initial ambulatory care consultation (primary care or specialist). These sources accounted for 8.4 per cent of government revenue in 1998. Health facilities originally transferred 20 per cent to the Treasury, but this was reduced in 1996 to a 2.3 per cent tax. Revenue from fees is now factored into budget allocations (Sargaldakova *et al.* 2000).

Tajikistan legalized user charges in the early 1990s. Some republican organizations, such as the National Diagnostic Centre, are expected to raise a significant portion of their revenue from this source. Hospitals and clinics charge for many goods and services, according to a price list approved by the Ministry of Health. For example, an X-ray costs the equivalent of 60 per cent of average weekly income. Official charges are estimated to contribute around 1 per cent to total health revenue, but this is an underestimate (Rahminov *et al.* 2000).

Turkmenistan has introduced official user charges gradually. The Ministry of Health approves the list of services and prices. Outpatients previously paid only for pharmaceuticals, but the list was extended in 1998 to include many diagnostic and treatment procedures. Health care providers keep 70 per cent of the money raised and transfer the rest into a state fund for health development, established in 1998 under government control. User fees are estimated to contribute less than 1 per cent to the health budget, but the basis for this estimate is unclear (Mamedkuliev *et al.* 2000).

Uzbekistan allows public-sector health providers to charge for goods and services, and these charges were estimated at 7 per cent of state health revenue in 1999. Full payments are made for 'non-essential' services and co-payments are made for laboratory tests, food and drugs (Ilkhamov and Jakubowski 2000).

All the central Asian republics, therefore, have implemented cost-sharing policies with patients. Official estimates suggest that these user charges contribute less than 10 per cent of revenue, but this is certainly an underestimate. The state aims to make these payments transparent by approving lists of items and associated charges. This is thought to be more acceptable to the public than under-the-table payments, but there is no evidence to date that official charges have replaced the unofficial charges levied by health care staff. The combined impact of user charges and continuing informal payments on service utilization by the population and on health outcomes appears to be negative, with many poor people being deterred from seeking health care (Chapter 4).

In summary, health care financing reform has not been very successful in any of the countries. Health insurance has failed to increase the revenues available for health care. User fees can at best be regarded as a temporary solution that must give way to a sustainable system of prepaid financing most reliably based upon taxation.

Restructuring hospital systems

The central Asian republics inherited very large Soviet model hospital systems, which took around 70 per cent of total health expenditure. Much of the hospital budget goes to paying utility costs and staff wages, with very little left for maintaining capital assets or for buying drugs and equipment – in other words, for treating patients. With the collapse of health budgets in the 1990s, all of the central Asian republics have been forced to reduce their hospital capacity, a process that has proceeded more rapidly than elsewhere in the former Soviet Union. The policy in all countries was to reduce their excessive hospital systems in order to contain costs and to transfer resources to ambulatory health services.

Hospital beds (long-term and acute-care) dropped sharply in all countries after 1992, from over 1100 beds per 100,000 population to 800 beds or fewer by 1998 (Figure 14.2). This is below the former Soviet Union average, but still above the European Union average of 700 beds per 100,000. Although some of this drop may be a paper reduction – since hospitals were funded in Soviet times partly on the number of beds, thus providing an incentive to maximize their count – the consensus is that there have been significant closures.

The drop from the former very high level of hospital capacity has largely been due to closures of small rural hospitals. This is evident in particular in Kazakhstan, where acute-care hospital beds were reduced by a massive 40 per cent between 1990 and 1997, and where the number of village 'hospitals' fell from 684 in 1994 to 208 in 1997. The Ministry of Health, backed by presidential

Figure 14.2 Number of hospital beds per 100,000 population in the central Asian republics, 1980–98

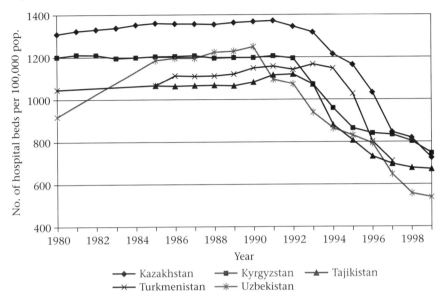

Source: WHO (2000a)

decrees, set national standards for hospitals (which village hospitals could not meet), while *oblast* administrations had insufficient funds to keep these small hospitals functioning (Kulzhanov and Healy 1999).

The rationalization of larger hospitals, typically concentrated in the capital cities, however, has proved very difficult. For example, a plan for hospital services in Bishkek, Kyrgyzstan, was developed but only partially implemented (Sargaldakova *et al.* 2000). Countries everywhere find it extremely difficult to close or to merge hospitals, but this is particularly so in the central Asian republics where hospitals are administered by different levels of government.

Although the hospital system has been downsized, mainly by closing small village hospitals and by reducing the number of beds in larger hospitals, this has not freed up substantial resources. Significant cost savings cannot be achieved through bed closures rather than hospital closures, since substantial hospital costs are associated with buildings and other fixed costs (Mossialos and Le Grand 1999). The reduction in the official number of hospital beds, therefore, does not necessarily indicate cost savings and budgetary transfers. Trends within health system funds are difficult to track, since these countries do not use programme budgeting systems. There is, however, little evidence that funds have been transferred to primary health care, which obtains less than around 10 per cent of the health budget (Chapter 11).

Utilization indicators for the acute-care hospital system (as well as the re-duction in bed numbers) also suggest a drop in hospital capacity (Chapter 12). Admissions dropped by a third or more in all countries between 1990 and 1998. Primary health care and specialist ambulatory health care services are also struggling, and the number of ambulatory care consultations has dropped, so that the drop in hospital admissions is not because alternative care is available. Instead, hospitals do not have the means to offer effective treatment, and patients do not have the means to pay for hospital services.

Another issue is that hospitals continue to manage patients in the traditional time-intensive way. Hospital utilization figures show little change over the decade in terms of patient management. Average occupancy in acute-care hospitals remains at over 80 per cent, while average length of stay remains at around 12–13 days. Financial incentives for hospitals and staff, outdated treatment protocols, and weak alternative ambulatory and social care options, all combine to keep patients in hospital for long periods. Hospitals in the central Asian republics thus manage patients differently, and serve different functions (such as social care), than acute care hospitals in western Europe.

Where to now?

Those responsible for health-sector reform in the central Asian republics face a daunting task. Reform is clearly necessary, as the existing systems are unsustainable and the scale of the health crisis is such that it will act as a brake on general economic development. Change must be implemented against a background of adverse political and economic circumstances, and where few health-sector staff are trained in modern public health care and management. If policies are to be sustainable, health policy-makers must identify who is responsible for policy implementation, how the process will be managed, what resources (both financial and human) are needed, how they will be obtained and whether the intended time scale is realistic in the circumstances that prevail.

Of the many challenges, we have selected four as especially important. The first is the difficulty of creating systems that can raise adequate resources to pay for services. A system based on solidarity is necessary, not only on grounds of equity, but also on grounds of ensuring sustainability of services. The attempts so far to implement health insurance have had very limited success and, as we have discussed, the population is increasingly forced to pay out-of-pocket for health care services, which they can ill afford.

A second major problem is how to implement effective decentralization that will ensure that local services reflect local needs. This is complicated by the strong, highly centralized system of presidential government in each country. Also, the presence of many informal ties can favour one area over another, with preferment based on connections rather than merit, while it is especially difficult to make certain decisions, such as those involving closure of regional and national hospitals.

The third major challenge is the pressure for privatization. Although privatization is featured as an important strategy in several programmes, it has been difficult to implement. The advantages claimed for privatization are: first, that the introduction of market incentives improves managerial performance and, second, that it can attract much needed private capital into the health care sector. In practice, these claimed advantages are outweighed by the disadvantages, such as market segmentation that leads to the abandonment of the needs of vulnerable groups (Saltman and van Otter 1987), the high cost of private capital compared with that raised publicly and the scope for opportunistic behaviour.

On the last point, the experience in some Western countries has highlighted the danger of state assets being disposed of at well below market value to political or personal supporters. This is especially worrying in the central Asian region, given the apparently high levels of corruption. For example, in an international survey of 99 countries undertaken by Transparency International, a non-governmental organization devoted to exposing illegal practices, Kazakhstan, Kyrgyzstan and Uzbekistan ranked among the 15 countries with the most problems with illegal practices (Transparency International 2000). Given the uncertainty of obtaining net benefits and the complexity of the process in countries where the financial systems are still poorly developed, it seems wise to argue against undue haste to privatize health system assets.

Finally, although there is an urgent need to restructure facilities, both to dispose of excess capacity and to renovate obsolete facilities, this conflicts with policies designed to ensure full employment. This is especially problematic as health services traditionally are seen (not just in this region) as a means of creating jobs. There are no easy solutions to these problems, especially in the absence of alternative jobs or adequate retirement pensions.

In comparison with CEE countries, external input to health sector reform has been limited in central Asia. WHO has established a network of central Asian republics (CARNET) that has facilitated the exchange of experience, and the World Bank and the Asian Development Bank are playing an important role in financing reform in several countries. External assistance will certainly continue to influence health reform in central Asia, but it must be effectively targeted and appropriate. In the first instance, external donors should seek to develop a sustainable infrastructure, including the creation of a cohort of trained staff with access to relevant information. They should also complement implementation with research. External advice is unlikely to achieve optimal results until much more is known about the economic, political and cultural circumstances. In particular, policy implementation requires a programme of research that will identify the conditions that facilitate change – the extent to which societal values conflict with or support policy objectives – and that will identify the interests of key stakeholders (Walt and Gilson 1994).

The literature on health-sector reform is conflicting on the subject of whether it is better to move gradually, with piloting and evaluation, or to adopt what has been described as a 'big-bang' approach (Klein 1995). Both approaches have been used successfully to introduce reform in western Europe. The former is undoubtedly slower and may be blown off course by opposition that has time to consolidate. The latter is more rapid, but may give rise to unintended adverse features, such as high reform costs (Stewart-Brown *et al.* 1996) and rapid and unsustainable inflation (McKee *et al.* 1994). On balance, however, given the scale of the task in the central Asian republics and given the lack of information on, for example, attitudes and affordability, it seems wise to counsel caution and to advocate pilot schemes that can be evaluated with results disseminated to those responsible for implementing change. Obviously, it is important to avoid paralysis by analysis, but a policy that applies models developed elsewhere without sufficient regard for local circumstances is doomed to failure.

Ultimately, the success or failure of health reform depends on the national context within which it takes place, most notably the macroeconomic situation and the political and social environment. Although some reform has been achieved, progress will remain slow in the absence of strong economic growth and wider political participation.

References

Asian Development Bank (1999) *Health Sector Reform in Asia and the Pacific: Options for Developing Countries*. Manila: Asian Development Bank.

Blomquist, J. (1997) *Results and Recommendations from the Social Services Household Survey of Jalal-Abad and Osh Oblasts, Kyrgyz Republic*, Report prepared for the Asian Development Bank. Bethesda, MD: Asian Development Bank.

Falkingham, J. (in press) Poverty, out-of-pocket payments and inequality in access to health care: evidence from Tajikistan, *Social Science and Medicine*.

Gorbachev, M.S. (1988) *Perestroika: New Thinking for Our Country and the World*. London: Fontana.

Ilkhamov, F. and Jakubowski, E. (2000) *Health Care Systems in Transition: Uzbekistan*. Copenhagen: European Observatory on Health Care Systems.

Klein, R. (1995) Big Bang health reform – does it work? The case of Britain's 19991 National Health Service reforms, *Millbank Quarterly*, 73: 299–337.

Kulzhanov, M. and Healy, J. (1999) *Health Care Systems in Transition: Kazakhstan*. Copenhagen: European Observatory on Health Care Systems.

Lewis, M. (2002) Informal health payments in eastern Europe and central Asia: issues, trends and policy implications, in E. Mossialos, A. Dixon, J. Figueras and J. Kutzin (eds) *Funding Health Care: Options for Europe*. Buckingham: Open University Press.

Mamedkuliev, C., Shevkun, E. and Hajioff, S. (2000) *Health Care Systems in Transition: Turkmenistan*. Copenhagen: European Observatory on Health Care Systems.

McKee, M., Bobak, M., Kalina, K., Bojan, F. and Enachescu, D. (1994) Health sector reform in the Czech Republic, Hungary and Romania, *Croatian Medical Journal*, 35: 238–44.

Mossialos, E. and Le Grand, J. (1999) Cost containment in the EU: an overview, in E. Mossialos and J. Le Grand (eds) *Health Care and Cost Containment in the European Union*. Aldershot: Ashgate.

Peabody, J.W., Rahman, M.O., Gertler, P. *et al.* (eds) (1999) *Policy and Health: Implications for Development in Asia*. Cambridge: Cambridge University Press.

Rahminov, R., Gedik, G. and Healy, J. (2000) *Health Care Systems in Transition: Tajikistan*. Copenhagen: European Observatory on Health Care Systems.

Russell, S., Bennett, S. and Mills, A. (1999) Reforming the health sector: towards a healthy new public management, *Journal of International Development*, 11: 767–75.

Saltman, R.B. and van Otter, C. (1987) Re-vitalising public health care systems: a proposal for public competition in Sweden, *Health Policy*, 7: 21–40.

Saltman, R.B., Figueras, J. and Sakellarides, C. (eds) (1998) *Critical Challenges for Health Care Reform in Europe*. Buckingham: Open University Press.

Sargaldakova, A., Healy, J., Kutzin, J. and Gedik, G. (2000) *Health Care Systems in Transition: Kyrgyzstan*. Copenhagen: European Observatory on Health Care Systems.

Stewart-Brown, S., Gillam, S. and Jewell, T. (1996) The problems of fundholding, *British Medical Journal*, 312: 1311–12.

Transparency International (2000) *Annual Report 2000*. Berlin: Transparency International.

UNDP (1993) *Human Development Report 1993*. New York: Oxford University Press.

UNDP (1994) *Human Development Report 1994*. New York: Oxford University Press.

UNDP (1995) *Human Development Report 1995*. New York: Oxford University Press.

UNDP (1996) *Human Development Report 1996*. New York: Oxford University Press.

UNDP (1997) *Human Development Report 1997*. New York: Oxford University Press.

UNDP (1998) *Human Development Report 1998*. New York: Oxford University Press.

UNDP (1999) *Human Development Report 1999*. New York: Oxford University Press.

UNDP (2000) *Human Development Report 2000*. New York: Oxford University Press.

Van Doorslaer, E., Wagstaff, A. and Rutten, F. (1993) *Equity in the Finance and Delivery of Health Care: An International Perspective*. Oxford: Oxford University Press.

Walt, G. and Gilson, L. (1994) Reforming the health sector in developing countries: the central role of policy analysis, *Health Policy Planning*, 9: 353–70.

WHO (2000a) *WHO European Health for All Database*. Copenhagen: WHO Regional Office for Europe.

WHO (2000b) *The World Health Report 2000: Health Systems – Improving Performance*. Geneva: World Health Organization.

part three

The countries

chapter fifteen

Profiles of country health care systems

This chapter provides an overview of the health care systems in each of the five central Asian republics. These summaries are based on the *Health Care Systems in Transition* country profiles published by the European Observatory on Health Care Systems (www.observatory.dk), which provide more detailed information on each country. These overviews are intended to complement the more thematic approach taken in other chapters. A map of each country is presented and each of the health care systems is summarized under five headings: background, health care finance and expenditure, organizational structure of the health care system, health care delivery system, and health care reforms.[1]

Kazakhstan

Maksut Kulzhanov and Judith Healy

Background

Kazakhstan has the largest land area of the five central Asian republics (about the size of the European Union). The terrain stretches across steppes and deserts to the high mountains in the south-east. It has a long border with the Russian Federation to the north, and borders with China to the east and its neighbouring republics to the south (see map of Kazakhstan, Figure 15.1). The government capital moved from Almaty to Astana in December 1998.

Figure 15.1   Kazakhstan

The population (now around 16.7 million) has an older structure than the other republics, with 8 per cent aged 65 years and over and with low or negative population growth. The population decrease during the 1990s was due mainly to the out-migration of ethnic Russians and other groups, many of which had settled (or been deported) to the New Lands in the 1950s and 1960s. Kazakhs again account for most of the population (over 52 per cent).

The country has substantial natural resources with large deposits of petroleum, natural gas and other minerals. The government hopes to exploit the hydrocarbon reserves and build new pipelines in partnership with multinational companies. Kazakhstan was a major grain producer in Soviet times and has a large agricultural sector. The country's traditional heavy industry products have suffered since the break-up of the Soviet Union.

Kazakhstan was the last Soviet republic to declare its independence, in December 1991. The dissolution of the Soviet Union came as a shock to the country, given its long ties with Russia and its large Russian population. Kazakhstan is a unitary state with a presidential form of government, under Nursultan Nazarbayev since 1991. A post-Soviet constitution was adopted in 1993 and amended in 1995. The President and the regional councils appoint members to the upper house of Parliament, while in the lower house (Majlis) seats are filled by popular election in 67 electorates. The country is divided into 14 administrative divisions (*oblasts*) and 14 municipalities plus the capital. The *oblasts* are subdivided further into about 200 districts (*rayons*). The President appoints the *oblast* governors (*akims*). The *oblasts* collect the majority of government revenue, transferring most to the central state, but keeping a significant proportion.

Health care finance and expenditure

Public expenditure on health dropped to 2.0 per cent of gross domestic product (GDP) in 1994 and 1995, before recovering somewhat to 3.5 per cent in 1998. In 1994, real expenditure on health had dropped to below 40 per cent of its pre-independence level. The health budget remains substantially below the funds needed to maintain the current infrastructure. In 1998, about 55 per cent of official revenue came from state taxes and about 40 per cent from payroll tax contributions (compulsory insurance). This, however, underestimates the substantial informal payments made by patients, which by some estimates account for about one-third of all health expenditures.

The first challenge after independence was to establish the health care system on a financially viable basis. A mandatory health insurance scheme, established in 1996, quickly ran into deficit; this was attributed to lower than expected insurance contributions based on payroll taxes, given high unemployment and problems with insurance and tax collections, as well as allegations of misappropriation. A new government authority (the Medical Service Payment Centre), set up in 1999, will purchase much of the country's health services, using funds allocated from general revenue. In effect, the country has reverted to a tax-funded health care system. There is a dual-payer system, however, since some national health services are funded directly by the state, while health enterprises (self-governing organizations with financial and legal autonomy) are funded partly through contracts with the Medical Service Payment Centre.

The budgetary process is changing. Population-based allocation methods to the *oblasts* are being debated, and funding to some health organizations has shifted to activity-based payments under contract to the new government payment centre. Pilot projects on new payment methods, including case-mix funding, are underway.

Organizational structure of the health care system

The Agency on Health (formerly Ministry of Health) formulates policy and runs republic-level institutes and hospitals. Given the large size of the country, the 14 *oblast* administrations (and the 14 *oblast* cities) run most health care services according to centrally set rules. The state still owns most health facilities. The Agency on Health administers national-level facilities, such as university hospitals, research institutes and specialist centres for cancer, infectious diseases and tuberculosis, and also runs blood services. The remainder, previously administered by the *oblasts* and cities, are being converted into state-owned health enterprises. Private health care services were permitted in 1991; however, given the low purchasing power of the population, so far they mainly involve pharmacies and public physicians with additional private practices.

Management reforms aim to decentralize management, to introduce more budgetary autonomy and self-management for health organizations, and to introduce market-like practices, such as contracts between purchasers and providers.

Health care delivery system

The primary care rural network of feldsher/midwife posts (FAPs) and physician clinics (SVAs) has deteriorated badly and is starved of funds. Primary care is in the process of being reorganized, family medicine has been introduced into the medical curriculum and family group practices are being set up, with patients having more choice of physician. Some pilot group practices are funded through patient capitation.

Polyclinics are being reorganized by amalgamating the separate clinics for adults, women's reproductive health and children, and by drawing a clearer distinction between primary and secondary care.

The policy on optimizing health care facilities has seen dramatic reductions in hospitals and beds (previously one of the highest rates of hospital capacity for its population in the world). In large part, these changes were budget-driven, since hospitals were taking nearly 75 per cent of the shrinking health budget. Between 1990 and 1997, the number of acute-care hospital beds was reduced by 44 per cent, and the number of all hospitals was reduced to nearly half, mainly through the closure of rural district hospitals. These small hospitals of less than 30 beds had little equipment or drugs and had low occupancy rates. Kazakhstan, however, still retains large numbers of single-speciality hospitals at the town, regional and national level.

The Sanepid service remains separate from the rest of the health care system, with its own administrative hierarchy. Its facilities and equipment are in poor repair and are ill-equipped to face current serious problems, such as rising rates of tuberculosis and HIV/AIDs. Environmental health issues remain neglected in terms of an inter-sectoral approach, although the government has declared three areas as ecological disasters: the Aral Sea region, the Semipalatinsk former nuclear region and heavily polluted industrial east Kazakhstan.

The health care workforce is being reduced in number mainly through attrition, while the undergraduate medical curriculum and continuing education is being upgraded. General practice has been introduced into the final year of the course.

Health care reforms

Programmes directed at population health have received more attention since the President's 1997 message *Kazakstan 2030*, a 1998 decree on the Health of the Nation Programme, and the establishment of a National Centre for Healthy Lifestyles.

Several inequities emerged during the 1990s – some associated with the budget crisis. As the government health budget shrank, people increasingly had to pay for services and drugs; rural areas have suffered most from funding cuts and hospital closures, and there are variations in health status and resources across the *oblasts*. Efficiency gains are not yet evident and pressure on expenditures will rise as health workers demand salaries commensurate with

their skills and responsibility. Health gains are not yet evident on broad measures, such as life expectancy and maternal mortality, since such gains must be
made against the impoverishment of the population.

Current policy developments include a recently drafted law on compulsory
health insurance, and the Agency on Health has set up a task force to draw up
a 10 year plan for health-sector development for Kazakhstan.

Kazakhstan looks to the future for improvements, given the substantial
natural and human resources of the country, and given its ongoing efforts to
reform its extensive health care system.

Source: Kulzhanov and Healy (1999).

Kyrgyzstan

*Acelle Sargaldakova, Judith Healy, Joe Kutzin and
Gülin Gedik*

Background

Kyrgyzstan gained its independence from the former Soviet Union in August
1991. Its 4.6 million population lives mainly in the fertile highland valleys.
The capital, Bishkek, surrounded by high mountains, is close to the border with
Kazakhstan (see Figure 15.2). The main ethnic groups are the Kyrgyz (about 60
per cent), followed by Russians, Uzbeks and others. The main religion is Sunni
Muslim, with minorities of Russian Orthodox and Roman Catholic. The country

Figure 15.2 Kyrgyzstan

has a young population with over a third under the age of 15 years, although the fertility rate is decreasing.

The country is small and poor, with a predominantly agricultural economy (45 per cent of GDP in 1997). The Kyrgyz economy suffered badly after the collapse of the Soviet Union, on whom the country depended for its export market and for substantial budget subsidies, but production began to recover in the late 1990s. The country has significant mineral deposits, as well as potential hydroelectric resources, which it hopes to develop. Poverty and income inequalities have increased substantially since independence.

Askar Akayev (first elected in October 1990) continues as President of the new republic. A new constitution and government structure was adopted by parliament in 1993. In its first two years of independence, Kyrgyzstan began to dismantle its Soviet structures, laid the foundation for a civil society and began to shift towards a market economy. In 1995, Akayev was re-elected for another 5 year term, and a referendum in 1996 significantly expanded the power of the President and consolidated a presidential style of government. In October 2000, Akayev was re-elected to another 5 year term. The upper house is partly appointed, while the lower house of 45 members is elected. The country is divided administratively into seven *oblasts*, each with its main city, plus the capital, and further subdivided into about 45 *rayons*. The President appoints the *oblast* governors (*akims*).

Health care finance and expenditure

Health care expenditure is around 3 per cent of GDP. The health care share of the government budget has dropped slightly, to below 12 per cent. Real per person expenditure has dropped from US$13.1 in 1995 to US$12.4 in 1998. Capital investment in health facilities and equipment has fallen drastically, particularly in *oblast* and district health services. Most medical equipment is outdated or not functioning.

The Mandatory Health Insurance Fund commenced activities in January 1997, funded by insurance contributions paid by employers (2 per cent of payroll) and by transfers from the Social Fund for coverage of pensioners and registered unemployed persons. Beginning in 2000, the republican budget directly transferred funds to cover all children (under age 16 years) to the Mandatory Health Insurance Fund. Currently, about 70 per cent of the population are insured. This coverage, however, is very limited, given the low level of revenue available to the Fund. In 1998, for example, insurance accounted for only about 4.3 per cent of the state health budget. Of necessity, the Fund is not fully responsible for the costs of care for covered persons, but instead supplements the state budget. Due to the overall low level of revenue from these two public sources, out-of-pocket payments by patients continue to be a major source of revenue for the health care system, perhaps half or more of total health care expenditure.

Organizational structure of the health care system

The health care system remains state-owned and administered. The Ministry of Health has a policy-making role and administers republic-level institutes and hospitals. The *oblast* and city administrations fund and run most health services. Several important structural and procedural changes are underway at the *oblast* level, as follows. *Oblast*-level hospitals are being merged under single administrations that merge general and specialized *oblast* hospitals into a single budgetary unit, thereby offering the opportunity to reorganize and an incentive to save on fixed costs. The *oblast*-level health insurance funds will become single payers that will disburse pooled health care funds from both budgetary and payroll-tax sources. The *oblast* health departments are being abolished; the *oblast* administrations will take over some of their administrative functions, but will retain an expert adviser on health issues. These new functions are in the process of being clarified.

Health care delivery system

Primary health care is being reorganized, and staff retrained, with specialized polyclinics (for adults and children) and maternity consultations being integrated in urban areas into multi-profile polyclinics. From the initial pilot project in Issyk-Kul Oblast in 1995, the family group practice model is spreading throughout the country. The family group practices will involve polyclinics in urban areas and medical centres (SVAs) in rural areas, as well as the feldsher/midwife posts (FAPs). The three basic types of physicians (therapists, paediatricians and obstetricians) are being retrained and urged to work more cooperatively. A Family Group Practice Association has formed to advocate and strengthen these new practices. The long-term intention is to separate primary care and secondary care, which currently are offered both by primary health care providers and by specialists in polyclinics and in hospital outpatient departments.

Hospital expenditure has remained high, accounting for over 70 per cent of the health budget, despite many (mostly unsuccessful) attempts to reduce excess capacity. Although about 26 per cent of hospital beds were closed between 1990 and 1996, the number of hospitals increased, so that few detectable savings were made in fixed costs. Some incentives (or penalties) are being introduced by the Mandatory Health Insurance Fund to encourage more cost-effective care. In primary care, for example, providers are to be partially funded through patient capitation.

The Sanepid services run their own separate vertical programme, but physical resources are inadequate and staff are ill-equipped and ill-trained to handle the requirements of a modern public health programme, involving surveillance of health, control of infectious diseases, monitoring of air, water and food standards, collection of data and promotion of health. There are considerable environmental health problems, with contaminated water supplies and increasing salinity. The move to a broader view of public health was signalled in the Healthy Nation national programme that aims to improve health status in several priority areas.

Health care reforms

The Ministry of Health embarked on ambitious reform plans (the MANAS programme) from the mid-1990s with assistance from international donors.

Many changes were introduced as pilot projects and are being gradually introduced to the rest of the country.

Concerns about equity are growing, however, as people increasingly have to pay for previously free services and drugs or must make under-the-table payments to physicians. More survey-based evidence on the extent of these practices is needed.

Kyrgyzstan has substantial natural and human resources, including strong cultural traditions, and remains optimistic about its capacity to reform its extensive health care system, bringing it in line with the needs of its population and the constraints of its revenue base.

Source: Sargaldakova *et al.* (2000).

Tajikistan

Rahmin Rahminov, Gülin Gedik and Judith Healy

Background

Tajikistan declared its independence in September 1991 after the break-up of the Soviet Union. It is a primarily mountainous country with the high Pamir Mountain range in the south and lowland plains in the west. The country is divided by mountain ranges and, during winter, many roads are impassable. Its post-independence development has been badly affected by 6 years of civil conflict, by interruptions to inter-republic trade and by its location in a politically volatile region, with continuing rebel incursions over its long border with Afghanistan (see map of Tajikistan, Figure 15.3). Russian Federation-led peacekeeping troops are based throughout the country and along the border with Afghanistan.

The population is estimated at 6.1 million, of whom nearly three-quarters live in rural areas. The country has the youngest population structure in the region due to a high fertility rate. The composition of the population changed after independence and during the civil war, when perhaps half the ethnic Russian population left the country. In addition, many other people died or fled the country. The population remains ethnically diverse: two-thirds Tajik and one-quarter Uzbek. Tajik (related to the Persian or Farsi language group) is the official state language, but Russian remains the main language of business. The main religion is Islam, mostly Sunni, but many in the Pamir Mountain region belong to the Shia branch.

Tajikistan supplied mainly agricultural and mineral primary products to the Soviet Union and was always the poorest of the Soviet republics. Its economy collapsed after independence, with the loss of its markets and its subsidies from Moscow, and given the enormous disruptions of the civil war. Agriculture is the main sector and has begun some recovery (accounting for 37 per cent of GDP in 1997), even though only 7 per cent of the land is arable. Tajikistan's population has been impoverished and living standards have plummeted. For example, the average monthly salary in 1998 was only US$11, while a monthly minimum 'food basket' provision for an adult was estimated

Figure 15.3 Tajikistan

© Copyright 1999 Lonely Planet Publications

at US$28. Over 80 per cent of the population, therefore, are estimated to live below the poverty line. Real GDP fell to 40 per cent of its 1990 level in 1996 before beginning to recover in 1997.

Widespread violence began in 1992 and continued intermittently until a peace agreement between rival factions was signed in 1997 (see Akiner, Chapter 2). The toll from the brutal civil war includes perhaps 60,000 killed, and much population displacement and destruction. Several opposition political parties were legalized in the peace agreement and are participating in elections. In November 1994, Emomali Rahmonov was elected President for a 5 year term and was re-elected in November 1999. The Committee for National Reconciliation has proposed a new two-chamber parliament.

The country is divided into five administrative units plus Dushanbe (the capital). The Gorno-Badakshan *oblast*, previously controlled by opponents of the government, is geographically often inaccessible and operates more autonomously.

Health care finance and expenditure

Given the collapse of the economy and state budget, health expenditure has fallen to below 2 per cent of GDP. The state budget consists of taxes collected by the national government and redistributed to local authorities. Average per person public expenditure on health has fallen precipitously from US$69 in 1990 to US$2.50 in 1998. The population increasingly is forced to pay out-of-pocket for health care. Private payments are now thought to be about two-thirds of health spending. External donors are crucial, accounting for perhaps a third of the government health budget in 1997.

Central government health budget funds from the Ministry of Finance go to *oblast* administrations (*hukomats*), to be managed by their finance departments on behalf of health facilities. The senior health system managers are based mostly in hospitals.

Organizational structure of the health care system

The state remains the main funder and provider of health care services. The Ministry of Health runs national-level institutes and hospitals, while local administrations run other health services. The system thus still runs as a centralized Soviet model health care system, although various changes have been discussed.

Health care delivery system

The intention is to strengthen primary care by retraining the existing staff as family physicians. The feldsher/midwife posts (FAPs) and rural physician clinics (SVAs) have been renamed 'medical houses'. Polyclinics in urban areas continue to specialize in adult health, children's health or women's reproductive health. The hospital system has been cut by 30 per cent of its beds, although few hospitals have closed.

Tajikistan lost many skilled staff during the civil war (particularly ethnic Russians who left the country) and retraining remains a priority. In particular, there is a shortage of skilled nurses. The state medical school now has introduced training in general practice.

Infectious disease has returned as a major threat to the Tajikistan population. It is fostered by damage to the water supply and sewerage infrastructure and by a breakdown in public health measures, such as mosquito control and immunization. These programmes are being restored with the help of international donors. Environmental health problems include soil salinity, high concentrations of chemicals in the soil from agriculture, and uncontrolled industrial pollution, such as emptying industrial waste into rivers.

Health care reforms

Health care reform was not high on the public agenda given the disastrous civil war and severe economic problems. The Somoni Project within the Ministry of Health was initiated in 1999 to develop a national plan for the health sector. The reform proposals so far include strengthening primary health care, reducing excess hospital capacity, developing human resources and introducing a reliable health information system. Tajikistan received substantial external funds during the emergency so that future assistance must be directed at establishing a sustainable health system. Tajikistan has proceeded slowly with health sector reform and wishes to retain the positive features of its health care system.

Source: Rahminov *et al.* (2000).

Figure 15.4   Turkmenistan

© Copyright 1999 Lonely Planet Publications

Turkmenistan

Chary Mamedkuliev, Elena Shevkun and Steve Hajioff

Background

Turkmenistan borders the Caspian Sea to the west, Kazakhstan and Uzbekistan to the north and east, and Afghanistan and Iran to the south. The Karakum Desert spreads over 80 per cent of the country, with the Kopet Mountains separating Turkmenistan from the Islamic Republic of Iran (see map of Turkmenistan, Figure 15.4). Natural resources are key to the Turkmenistan economy; the country has large reserves of natural gas and of oil, although the means to exploit these resources are limited. Turkmenistan is also one of the world's leading cotton producers. In the early years of independence, the economy of Turkmenistan faced a number of challenges. In particular, the collapse in the global cotton market, the closure of gas pipelines and non-payments for gas exports weighed heavily on an already fragile economy.

Turkmenistan has a young population structure, with nearly 40 per cent of the 4.9 million inhabitants under the age of 15 years. There is a high fertility rate, with 3.8 births per woman (1995) and a life expectancy of 66.4 years (1999). Life expectancy is 10 years lower in rural areas than in the capital, Ashgabat, and has worsened through the 1990s. Approximately 77 per cent of the population are ethnic Turkmens, with the largest minority groups being Uzbeks and Russians.

Turkmenistan declared its independence in October 1991, after the collapse of the Soviet Union. In December 1995, the United Nations General Assembly unanimously approved the country's neutral status. The Constitution, adopted in May 1992, established a President as head of state (controlling legislative, judicial and executive branches), an elected parliament (the Majlis) and a cabinet of ministers (appointed by the President). The People's Council (Khalk Maslakhaty), the supreme body, brings together the President, members of parliament, the cabinet, senior law officers and representatives of local government. There are five administrative regions (*velayats*), which are subdivided into 48 districts (*etraps*). The President directly appoints the regional governors (*velayat hakim*). President Saparmurat Niyazov has been in office since independence.

Health care finance and expenditure

Health sector spending fell from 3.2 per cent of GDP in 1991 to 0.8 per cent in 1994, increasing to 1.5 per cent in 1995 and 4.6 per cent in 1997, as the performance of the economy improved. The government health system remains largely financed by the central state budget (about 90 per cent). A voluntary medical insurance scheme introduced in 1996 produced about 8 per cent of total health expenditures in 1999. About 2 per cent of revenues are derived from user fees, but this does not take into account significant informal payments to physicians. In addition to the budgeted allocation, the President may allocate extra resources to the health sector, usually for pharmaceuticals and medical equipment and for hospital construction and renovation.

Funds other than those from the central government are collected and disbursed through the State Fund for Health Development, which is under the control of the President and the Health Minister. Budgets are distributed to the *velayat* administrations as part of their overall budget. The health ministry directly funds some central and tertiary institutions. Health care facilities continue to be paid according to line item budgets. Salaries are paid according to detailed tariffs that have been revised in recent years, with some capitation-based adjustments and target payments to primary care physicians.

Organizational structure of the health care system

The President and the Cabinet of Ministers develop policy with advice from the Ministry of Health and Medical Industry, which is responsible for the operation of all health services and also manages national institutions. Local health services are administratively accountable to the *velayat* or *etrap* administrations, and to the Ministry of Health and Medical Industry on technical and organizational issues. Most facilities are state-owned with limited voluntary-sector or community involvement.

There are very few private-sector providers of health services but the number is growing. One private hospital opened in 1999 and several self-financing units at public hospitals provide care outside the national basic benefits package.

Catering has been privatized and contracting out is being discussed for some ancillary and laboratory services.

Health services are administered, rather than managed, but management skills and information systems are being developed. For example, the intention is to move from line item to programme budgeting. The development of clinical guidelines is also envisaged.

Health care delivery system

Both buildings and equipment are badly in need of renovation and replacement. Considerable effort has gone into reforming primary health care. There are three types of primary care units. Rural health centres (*oba saglyk oyu*) are subdivided into levels one and two: level one units are the most numerous centres and are staffed by nurses, feldshers and midwives; level two units are staffed by physicians. Urban health centres (*sakher saglyk oyu*) remain similar to the polyclinics of Soviet times. Physicians are being retrained to practice family medicine from these units.

Turkmenistan has reduced its very large number of hospital beds since independence, but admission rates and bed occupancy rates remain low and the average length of stay remains high.

The State Sanitary and Epidemiology Inspectorate is based on the Sanepid model inherited from the Soviet system and is organizationally distinct from the remaining health services. It has concentrated upon the control of communicable disease and now also provides certification of environmental health and food standards.

The health care workforce has been relatively stable through the 1990s. Most physicians continue to work in hospitals (64 per cent in 1997), but the intention is to increase the proportion of the medical workforce engaged in community-based primary care. General practice now has been introduced into the undergraduate curriculum and postgraduate training in family medicine is being developed.

Health care reforms

The adoption of the Presidential State Health Programme has facilitated a more systematic approach to health sector reform. The President's strategy until the year 2010, ratified by the People's Council, includes health care reform plans. These include the continued rationalization of hospital services and the strengthening of primary care. Public health programmes are being promoted and recent presidential decrees have announced bans on smoking in public places and the naming of a national health day. Laws are being planned on public health, health promotion, disease prevention, medical insurance and pharmaceuticals. Primary care is a key area of health reform in relation to infrastructure and staff training. With a growing economy, significant mineral wealth and the will to reform, Turkmenistan believes that it can achieve an appropriate and responsive health care system.

Source: Mamedkuliev *et al.* (2000).

Figure 15.5 Uzbekistan

Uzbekistan

Farkhad A. Ilkhamov, Elke Jakubowski and Steve Hajioff

Background

Uzbekistan declared independence in August 1991, following the collapse of the Soviet Union. A landlocked country, it borders Kazakhstan to the north and west, Krgyzstan and Tajikistan to the east, and Turkmenistan and Afghanistan to the south (see map of Uzbekistan, Figure 15.5). Uzbekistan is the most populous of the central Asian republics, with 24.1 million inhabitants at the last estimate (1999). Eighty per cent of the population are ethnic Uzbeks. The government is a presidential model, with the President as head of the executive, legislative and judicial branches of government. President Islom Karimov has been in office since independence. Consensus is maintained within government through the presidential committee for state control. There is a unicameral parliament, headed by the Prime Minister (a presidential appointee), which consists of 250 deputies elected from regional constituencies. The President appoints the regional governors, who run the regional administrations (*khokiamats*). There are 12 regions (*velayats*), a municipal authority in the capital city, Tashkent, as well as the autonomous republic of Karakalpakstan. These regions are further subdivided into districts (*etraps*).

Uzbekistan has rich, under-exploited resources, such as natural gas, gold, uranium and other heavy metals. The country's cotton production accounts for 6 per cent of the world cotton market, in spite of conditions poorly suited to the cultivation of cotton. Fluctuations in this market have hit the Uzbek economy hard, but the hyperinflation that characterized the mid-1990s has been brought under some control.

The population has been steadily increasing for many decades and has a young structure, with 46 per cent of inhabitants under 18 years and only 4.2 per cent over 65 years. A decreasing birth rate, net outward migration and an increasing crude death rate have changed the demographic profile since the early 1990s, resulting in slowing population growth. Life expectancy in 1995 was 67.9 years.

Health care finance and expenditure

Health care expenditure in Uzbekistan at the start of the 1990s was higher than in the other central Asian republics, at 6 per cent of GDP in 1991, declining steadily until 1997, when it reached 3.3 per cent. Health care is, for the most part, funded from the state budget, but health care users increasingly are charged official fees, estimated in 1999 as 7 per cent of all health service revenues. Informal fees are widespread and have not been fully quantified. International agencies also provide substantial funds for the health care system, largely on a project basis. Voluntary health insurance is planned, but not yet in operation.

As well as the central direct funding for national institutions, local units are funded from regional and district budgets. Health care providers are reimbursed according to line item budgets, and input indices (such as the number of beds) are still important in determining budgets. Capital equipment expenditure is centralized. Health care professionals are paid salaries, although primary care fundholding is being piloted in the Fergana Valley region.

Organizational structure of the health care system

The Cabinet of Ministers, headed by the President, sets health policy and also determines overall health expenditure and medical research budgets. The Ministry of Health is seen as a division of the Cabinet of Ministers and oversees management and service delivery in the health sector. Most health facilities remain in public ownership, except for pharmacies and dental surgeries that mostly now are in the private sector. The Ministry of Finance approves overall budgets, both for the Ministry of Health and for the regional administrations, while the latter fund local health services. Voluntary-sector and public involvement is limited. The management skills needed since independence are being developed, but health care system management is largely by physicians who lack formal management training.

Health care delivery system

Primary health care is delivered (following the Soviet model) by feldsher/midwife posts (FAPs) in rural areas. These posts are generally the first point of contact and are staffed by feldshers, midwives and nurses. In rural population centres, rural physician ambulatory units (SVAs) are staffed with a number of physicians, typically a therapist, a paediatrician and an obstetrician/gynaecologist. In urban areas, primary care is delivered in polyclinics, which also provide ambulatory secondary care. Large industrial enterprises often provide occupational health services that double as parallel primary care providers.

There is considerable reliance on hospital services for basic care delivery. In 1991, a quarter of the population were hospitalized annually; since then the figure has decreased steadily and by 1998 it was at the low level of 12.9 per cent. There have been reductions also in the average length of stay and in the number of hospital beds per 1000 population. Utilization still is not optimal, with an average length of stay in 1998 of 12.8 days and low bed occupancy.

The Sanepid services still follow the Soviet model and are responsible for environmental health, food safety and communicable disease control. They are organized hierarchically, with peripheral units being accountable to the central units. The Sanepid services are organizationally distinct from clinical health care services, with vertical programmes in place for HIV/AIDS, family planning and immunization.

The number of physicians, although historically lower than in some of the other central Asian republics, has increased during the early 1990s, although it has fallen back slightly since. There has been relatively high attrition among physicians (5 per cent in 1995), partly due to emigration of ethnic Russians. A high proportion of physicians (80 per cent) work in the hospital sector.

Health care reforms

Health care reform has six key objectives in Uzbekistan: improving child and maternal health, promoting privatization, improving the quality of health services, cost containment, identification of additional resource streams and decentralization of health service management. Overall, there is a move towards increased private ownership and provision. Although the relaxation of central control is a stated objective, *ad hoc* decisions continue to be taken at the national level.

The long-term objective is to reduce the layers of health administration from six to three, by abolishing many categories of institutions and by transferring the feldsher/midwife posts (FAPs) to private primary health care. The intention is to move towards capitation-based financing of provider institutions, but this has yet to be realized. A system of parallel emergency care centres is being developed to provide all emergency health care. The first such centre is already in place in Samarkand and a further centre in Tashkent is nearing completion.

Source: Ilkhamov and Jakubowski (2000).

Note

1 DISCLAIMER: We would like to thank Lonely Planet Publications for granting permission to use their copyrighted web-based maps (www.lonelyplanet.com) of the

five central Asian countries: Kazakhstan, Kyrgyzstan, Tajikistan, Turkmenistan and Uzbekistan. The designations and presentation of material presented on these maps do not imply the expression of any opinion whatsoever on the part of the World Health Organization or Lonely Planet Publications concerning the legal status of any country, territory, city or area or of its authorities, or concerning the delimitation of its frontiers or boundaries, on which there may not be full agreement. Neither WHO nor the Lonely Planet accept any responsibility for any loss, injury or inconvenience sustained by any person resulting from information published in this book. We encourage you to verify any critical information with the relevant authorities before you travel. This includes information on visa requirements, health and safety, customs and transportation.

References

Ilkhamov, A. and Jakubowski, E. (2000) *Health Care Systems in Transition: Uzbekistan*. Copenhagen: European Observatory on Health Care Systems.

Kulzhanov, M. and Healy, J. (1999) *Health Care Systems in Transition: Kazakhstan*. Copenhagen: European Observatory on Health Care Systems.

Mamedkuliev, C., Shevkun, E. and Hajioff, S. (2000) *Health Care Systems in Transition: Turkmenistan*. Copenhagen: European Observatory on Health Care Systems.

Rahminov, R., Gedik, G. and Healy, J. (2000) *Health Care Systems in Transition: Tajikistan*. Copenhagen: European Observatory on Health Care Systems.

Sargaldakova, A., Healy, J., Kutzin, J. and Gedik, G. (2000) *Health Care Systems in Transition: Kyrgyzstan*. Copenhagen: European Observatory on Health Care Systems.

Index

Page number in *italics* indicate tables